Best Hikes Near
SAN FRANCISCO

HELP US KEEP THIS GUIDE UP TO DATE

Every effort has been made by the author and editors to make this guide as accurate and useful as possible. However, many things can change after a guide is published—trails are rerouted, regulations change, techniques evolve, facilities come under new management, and so on.

We would appreciate your comments concerning your experiences with this guide and how you feel it could be improved and kept up to date. While we may not be able to respond to all comments and suggestions, we'll take them to heart, and we'll also make certain to share them with the author. Please send your comments and suggestions to the following address:

The Globe Pequot Press
Reader Response/Editorial Department
P.O. Box 480
Guilford, CT 06437

Or you may e-mail us at: editorial@globepequot.com

Thanks for your input, and happy trails!

Best Hikes Near
SAN FRANCISCO

LINDA HAMILTON

GUILFORD, CONNECTICUT

HELENA, MONTANA

AN IMPRINT OF THE GLOBE PEQUOT PRESS

To buy books in quantity for corporate use
or incentives, call **(800) 962–0973**
or e-mail **premiums@GlobePequot.com.**

FALCONGUIDES®

Falcon and FalconGuides are registered trademarks of Morris Book Publishing, LLC

Interior photos by Linda Hamilton unless otherwise credited

Art page iii © Shutterstock

Text design by Sheryl P. Kober

Maps created by Ben Pease © Morris Book Publishing, LLC

ISBN 978-0-7627-4675-0

Library of Congress Cataloging-in-Publication Data is available on file.

Printed in China

10 9 8 7 6 5 4 3 2 1

The author and The Globe Pequot Press assume no liability for accidents happening to, or injuries sustained by, readers who engage in the activities described in this book.

Contents

Preface ix
Introduction 1
    Bay Area Weather 1
    Flora and Fauna. 2
    Wilderness Restrictions/Regulations 4
How to Use This Guide 4
    What You'll Find in This Guide 4
    How to Use the Maps 5
Getting around San Francisco 5
Map Legend 9
Trail Finder Chart. 10

Point Reyes and West Marin **12**
  1. Point Reyes National Seashore:
     Mount Wittenberg and Bear Valley Loop 14
  2. Point Reyes National Seashore: Tomales Point. 19
  3. Point Reyes National Seashore: Chimney Rock Trail. 24
  4. Point Reyes National Seashore:
     Palomarin Trailhead to Alamere Falls 29
  5. Tomales Bay State Park: Hearts Desire Beach to Shell Beach 34
  6. Samuel P. Taylor State Park: To the Top of Barnabe Peak. 39
Honorable Mentions
  A. Point Reyes National Seashore: Inverness Ridge. 44
  B. Point Reyes on Rainy Days 44

Mount Tamalpais and Its Foothills **46**
  7. Muir Woods: Bootjack Trail to Dipsea Trail Loop 48
  8. Phoenix Reservoir: Tucker and Bill Williams Trails 55
  9. Steep Ravine Loop to Stinson Beach. 60
  10. East Peak Loop 65
  11. Marin Headlands: Miwok Trail to Point Bonita 72
  12. Marin Municipal Water District: Kent Trail along Alpine Lake 80
  13. Mount Burdell Open Space Preserve. 86
  14. Ring Mountain. 91
Honorable Mentions
  C. Cataract Trail 96
  D. Camp Tamarancho. 96

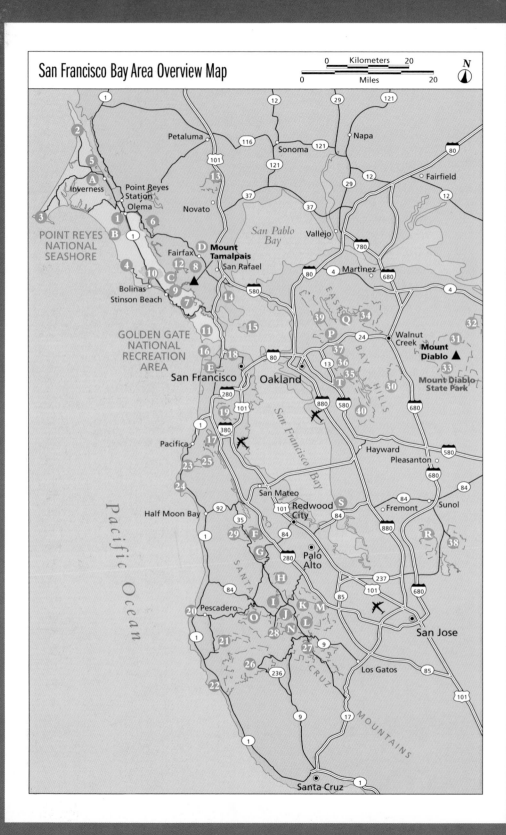

San Francisco Bay Area Overview Map

0 Kilometers 20
0 Miles 20

N

Petaluma

Napa

Sonoma

Fairfield

Inverness

Point Reyes
Station
Olema

Novato

San Pablo
Bay

Vallejo

POINT REYES
NATIONAL
SEASHORE

Fairfax

Mount
Tamalpais

San Rafael

Martinez

Walnut
Creek

Mount
Diablo

Bolinas

Stinson Beach

GOLDEN GATE
NATIONAL
RECREATION
AREA

San Francisco

Oakland

Mount Diablo
State Park

EAST BAY HILLS

Pacifica

Hayward

Pleasanton

Half Moon Bay

San Mateo

Redwood
City

Fremont

Sunol

Palo
Alto

Pescadero

San Jose

Los Gatos

SANTA CRUZ MOUNTAINS

Santa Cruz

Pacific Ocean

San Francisco and the Bay 98

15. Angel Island State Park 100
16. Cliff House Walk at Lands End 106
17. Sweeney Ridge: The Portolá Discovery Site 111
18. The Presidio: Lovers' Lane and the Ecology Trail 115
19. San Bruno State Park: Summit Loop Trail 121

Honorable Mention

E. Golden Gate Park 126

San Mateo County Coastline 128

20. Pescadero Marsh Trails 130
21. Butano State Park 136
22. Año Nuevo State Park and Reserve 142
23. McNee Ranch State Park and Montara State Beach 147
24. James V. Fitzgerald Marine Reserve: The Tide Pool Loop 152
25. San Pedro Valley Park 158

The Northern Santa Cruz Mountains 162

26. Big Basin Redwoods State Park: Berry Creek Falls Trail Loop 164
27. Castle Rock State Park 171
28. Portola Redwoods State Park 177
29. Purisima Creek Redwoods Open Space Preserve 182

Honorable Mentions

F. Huddart Park and Phleger Estate 188
G. Wunderlich Park 188
H. Windy Hill Open Space Preserve 189
I. Russian Ridge Open Space Preserve 189
J. Skyline Ridge Open Space Preserve 190
K. Monte Bello Open Space Preserve 190
L. Upper Stevens Creek County Park 191
M. Rancho San Antonio Open Space Preserve and County Park 191
N. Long Ridge Open Space Preserve 192
O. Pescadero Creek Park 192

Mount Diablo and Las Trampas Foothills 194

30. Las Trampas Regional Wilderness 196
31. Mount Diablo State Park: Rock City to the Summit 202
32. Mount Diablo State Park: Donner Canyon to the Falls Trail 211
33. Black Diamond Mines Regional Preserve 217

Three Ridges: San Pablo, Oakland/Berkeley Hills, Sunol **222**

34. Briones Regional Park 224
35. Redwood Regional Park: East to West Ridge Trails 229
36. Huckleberry Botanic Regional Preserve 234
37. Sibley Volcanic Regional Preserve 239
38. Sunol Regional Wilderness 245
39. Tilden Regional Park: Jewel Lake to Wildcat Peak 251
40. Anthony Chabot Regional Park 257

Honorable Mentions

P. Tilden Regional Park—Greater Tilden 263
Q. Briones Reservoir 263
R. Mission Peak Regional Preserve 264
S. Coyote Hills Regional Park 264
T. Joaquin Miller Park 265

Acknowledgments 267
Appendix: Hiking Clubs 269
Hike Index 275
About the Author 277

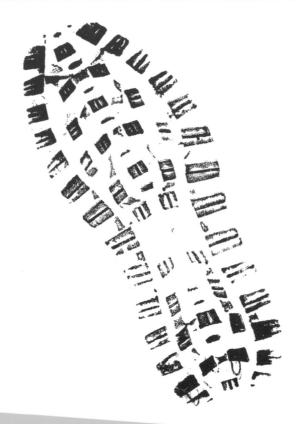

Preface

The two questions I hear most often as a hiking guide are: What makes your book different? Where can I hike in the Bay Area where no one else goes?

Two things make this book an essential addition to a Bay Area hiker's library. One, the information for each hike is comprehensive, with maps, directions, contact information, in-depth descriptions, and other important information. That's a FalconGuide!

The second thing that makes this book unique is the description of each hike, designed to bring the trails to life with stories of both their human and ecological history. I hope these stories enhance your sense of discovery and adventure on the trail.

To answer the second question, this guide contains more permit-only or permission-required hikes. The East Bay Municipal Utility District (EBMUD), Peninsula Open Space Trust (POST), the Marin Council of the Boy Scouts of America, and other agencies in the Bay Area offer hiking on access-restricted trails. Some require a fee, others just a phone call. This red tape definitely keeps the masses away. Other ways to avoid the crowds are hiking on weekdays, during off-season, or in poor (but not dangerous) weather conditions that may keep others from venturing out.

I feel lucky to have hiked in this area my whole life, since I became a hiker at the age of six. On that day, I was one mad six-year-old. Sitting cross-legged in a circle, I listened frustrated to the other first graders rattle off their religions. I didn't know what mine was. With hands on hips, I confronted my mother. To my surprise, our family had a religion, and she told me what it was. I couldn't wait to share this revelation at school.

The next day, when the topic came up again, I was ready. Pulling back my shoulders, I declared proudly, "I'm a pedestrian."

Ocean Beach, San Francisco, on a sunny day © Shutterstock

My mispronunciation has become the truth. Since I was six, walking has been my self-declared doctrine. I love the outdoors. So it is no wonder I wound up writing this book.

It seems an appropriate basis for a religion, if you think about it. Hiking feeds the spirit. Doctors write about its capacity to heal mind, body, and soul. Coexisting with the wilderness requires rules of behavior that translate well into positive ways of living. And I can't think of a prettier cathedral than a forest of 2,000-year-old redwood trees.

Born and raised in the East Bay, I watched the San Ramon Valley grow from scattered ranches and countryside to thriving cities and suburbs—and traffic jams. People sometimes don't believe me when I tell them that we didn't know what a traffic backup was when I was first driving in 1981.

Many people associate hiking with wilderness areas like the Sierras, and not a major metropolitan region like the Bay Area. But right here, just beyond our cities, sandwiched between our towns, is a wild, diverse, and beautiful landscape.

Taking a closer look at the hills and trails I adore, I found the history and spirit of the San Francisco Bay Area embodied in its open space. Still alive in our parklands are the stories of peaceful native life, of exploration, of survival and destruction, of staking claim and prospering in a new land, of the tough physical existence of western living and the genteel traditions of the San Francisco elite.

I am grateful for the experience of creating *Best Hikes Near San Francisco*. I hope that in sharing this book, I can guide you to places of magic and beauty you can only see by foot. You too may join me in saying, "I'm proud to be a pedestrian."

Happy hiking!

Golden Gate Bridge, the symbol of San Francisco © Shutterstock

Preface

Introduction

This book features the most diverse, exhilarating, and beautiful hikes around the bay.

Welcome to the wild variety of hiking in the San Francisco Bay Area. No other metropolitan area in the world offers so much open space so close to a major city. Whether you like it wet, dry, high, low, perfectly level, or mountain goat steep, there's something nearby for you.

Hiking is a wonderful way to discover the beauty of the Bay Area. Beyond the daily commute, beyond the sleepy suburbs, beyond the familiar tourist attractions, there are places where no roads go, where you can look out at nothing but hillsides or ocean, or take in the sights of the city from a lofty perch. Reach out and touch the trunk of a giant redwood or stick your hand into cool creek water, and you can almost feel the rich history of this place. The trails in this guide lead you to roaring waterfalls, silent glades, and wind-whipped mountaintops. They'll show you quiet meadows covered with wildflowers and swarming with butterflies, and deep, verdant forests where ferns grow lush and colossal trees stand like pillars holding up the sky. And they'll take you to places to breathe anew.

The purpose of this guide is to offer readers an opportunity to explore the San Francisco Bay Area's many facets. It was hard to create a perimeter for the hikes. The beauty of Northern California continues in all directions. Nonetheless, the epicenter, if you will, is the San Francisco Bay Bridge, and all the hikes, with only a couple exceptions, are within an hour and a half's weekend drive from there one way. Within this range, the book features the most diverse, exhilarating, and beautiful hikes around the bay, hikes that do justice to the region's history, natural diversity, and character. The hikes are geared for every level of experience, some with options for families and longer treks. Though all are day hikes, many chapters provide ideas for exciting overnight excursions.

Bay Area Weather

Possibly no other region in this country displays as many varieties of weather simultaneously as does the San Francisco Bay Area. The weather is every bit as varied as the landscapes. It can be sunny on the Las Trampas Ridge, raining on Mount Tamalpais, snowing on Mount Diablo, foggy on Sweeney Ridge, and windy on Montara Mountain all at the same time. On any one hike you can experience severe changes in temperature and humidity as trails take you abruptly from one ecosystem to the next. Atmospheric forces and geologic formations, including the area's unique combination of forest, river, ocean, bay, and elevations, come together to influence the weather, one of the most prominent phenomena being the jet stream that brings the famous summer fog pouring over the Golden Gate Bridge.

That thick summertime fog, along with mild winters, helps buffer large temperature swings and accounts for the milder climate in the coastal regions that sustains the temperate rain forest of coast redwoods. Hikers should remember that the chilly fog, which can occur in winter, too, often lies thick on the mountains in the morning and comes in fast in the afternoon. The average temperature in San Francisco ranges from 50° F to 60° F year-round. Averages are 5° to 10° higher as you head inland from the Golden Gate Bridge.

Flora and Fauna

With so many microclimates and diverse weather patterns, it's no wonder the Bay Area's vegetation and wildlife vary as much as they do. Of the 5,000-plus native plants in California, more than a third of them are endemic to the state, a high percentage of those occurring in the Bay Area.

The coast is famous for its redwood trees—the tallest living things on earth. Under the thick canopies of these giants, sword ferns carpet the forest floor, occasionally making room for clover-like redwood sorrel. Shady hills may feature a mixture of madrone, tan oak, bigleaf maple, and pungent California bay laurel. The coastal bluffs alternate between brushy chaparral, coastal scrub, and forested headlands, depending very much on the local microclimates. In Point Reyes National Seashore, over 700 plants have been identified. South-facing sunny slopes often host oak savanna with wildflower-filled, grassy meadows. Sagebrush, manzanita, and knobcone pines are characteristic of dry sandstone ridges, where plants must be able to tolerate meager precipitation and intense summer heat.

Golden Eagle © Shutterstock

Wildlife in the region is easily as impressive as the flora. Invertebrates, many endemic, are abundant in the muddy sediments of the San Francisco Bay estuary, an area rich in plant life and wildlife. The marbled murrelet and spotted owl, for example, are limited to old-growth forests. Wetlands, scattered along the coast and inland areas, provide important feeding and breeding grounds for migratory birds traveling the Pacific Flyway. Sandhill cranes, snow geese, and American coots all stop here. Ospreys nest in the tops of tall trees near the rivers they fish. Grassy

California sea lions © Shutterstock

hillsides all over the Bay Area support raptors like red-shouldered hawks and golden eagles, and the small mammals and birds upon which they feed.

Tule elk, once numbering in the tens of thousands, were hunted to near extinction before being protected. On the road to recovery, they now survive on Tomales Point in Point Reyes. Mountain lions, seldom seen, roam wherever deer are abundant. Bobcats, coyotes, ravens, raccoons, and skunks are also common. Exotic wild pigs, once released by hunters, are multiplying, causing a big problem in the area. They plow through land like rototillers, digging up roots for their supper.

Seals and sea lions are a common sight along the coast and in coastal estuaries. Harbor seals are the most visible, but California and northern sea lions are also abundant. The largest of the lot, northern elephant seals, hang out and breed on the beaches of Año Nuevo State Park and Reserve. Whale watchers can observe the yearly migrations of the gray whale from a high spot along the coast, like Point Reyes and Bodega Head.

While threatened by logging, agricultural runoff, dams, and overdevelopment, a few of the Bay Area's rivers still host seasonal trout and salmon runs. Coho salmon and steelhead trout make their way from the ocean up rivers and streams to spawn in the headwaters where they were born.

Among the area's endangered species are the San Francisco garter snake, the California clapper rail, the California least tern, the San Joaquin kit fox, the salt-marsh harvest mouse, and the red-legged frog.

Wilderness Restrictions/Regulations

The San Francisco Bay Area has a combination of county, state, and national parks, preserves and reserves, and open space. These lands have important bio-logical, cultural, economic, and recreational value. Permits, access quotas, and fees are part of the effort to allow human use without compromising the health and character of the wilderness.

Regulations vary, so it's important to check out rules about dogs, parking, fees, and trail use before departing. They are almost always posted at trailheads. Call ahead about backpacking rules and restrictions. Please heed this advice, follow regulations, and get required permits. It may seem like a pain, but with millions of people living in or visiting the Bay Area, wilderness is becoming an increasingly precious commodity. Help keep the wilderness wild.

As you take advantage of the spectacular scenery offered by the San Francisco Bay Area, remember that our planet is very dear, very special, and very fragile. All of us should do everything we can to keep it clean, beautiful, and healthy, including following the Green Tips you'll find throughout this book.

How to Use This Guide

Take a close look and you'll find that this guide contains just about everything you'll need to choose, plan for, enjoy, and survive a hike in the San Francisco area. Stuffed with useful information, *Best Hikes Near San Francisco* features forty mapped and detailed hikes and twenty honorable mentions.

Here's an outline of *Best Hikes Near San Francisco*'s major components.

What You'll Find in This Guide

Each region begins with an introduction, where you're given a sweeping look at the lay of the land. Each hike begins with an overview. These short summa-ries give you a taste of the hiking adventures to follow. You'll learn about the trail terrain and any surprises each route has to offer. Following the overview, you'll find the quick, nitty-gritty details of the hike: where the trailhead is located; hike length; approximate hiking time; difficulty rating; type of trail surface; other trail users; canine compatibility; land status; fees and permits; trail hours; map resources, trail contacts, and other information that will help you on your trek.

Finding the trailhead gives you dependable driving directions from a nearby city right to where you'll want to park and directions by public transportation where available. The hike description is the meat of each trail selection. Detailed and honest, it's a carefully researched impression of the trail.

In the **Miles and Directions** section, mileage cues identify all turns and trail name changes, as well as points of interest. The **Hike Information** (if it appears) section is a hodgepodge that might include trail hotlines (for updates on trail conditions), hike tours, and special events or attractions in the area. Each regional section ends with an **Honorable Mentions** section detailing some of the hikes that didn't make the cut, for whatever reason—in many cases it's not because they aren't great hikes, but because they're overcrowded or environmentally sensitive to heavy traffic. Be sure to read through these. Jewels lurk among them.

Don't feel restricted to the routes and trails mapped here. Be adventurous and use this guide as a platform to dive into San Francisco's backcountry and discover new routes for yourself. One of the simplest ways to begin is to turn the map upside down and hike the course in reverse. The change in perspective is often fantastic, and the hike should feel quite different. It's like getting two different hikes for one.

You may wish to copy the directions for the course onto a small sheet to help you while hiking, or photocopy the map and cue sheet to take with you. Otherwise, just slip the whole book in your backpack and take it all with you. Enjoy your time in the outdoors and remember to pack out what you pack in.

How to Use the Maps

Overview Map: This map (see page vi) shows the location of each hike in the area by hike number (or in the case of Honorable Mentions, by letter).

Route Map: This is your primary guide to each hike. It shows all of the accessible roads and trails, points of interest, water, towns, landmarks, and geographical features. It also distinguishes trails from roads. The selected route is highlighted, and directional arrows point the way.

Getting around San Francisco

Area Codes

The Bay Area is split into six area codes: 415 (San Francisco and North Bay), 510 (Oakland/Berkeley/Richmond), 925 (East Bay/San Ramon Valley), 408 (South Bay including San Jose and Silicon Valley), 831 (Santa Cruz), and 650 (San Mateo County). The North Coast (Sonoma and Napa) area code is 707.

Roads

In California, call CalTrans at (800) 427-ROAD (7623) or visit them at www.dot .ca.gov/hq/roadinfo for road conditions, closures, and construction status.

To connect to a live operator for Bay Area transit system information or for recorded traffic and incident information, call 511 Info at (510) 817-1717 or visit transitinfo.org. You can also dial 511 for local travel information.

By Air

Area airports include San Francisco International Airport (SFO), Oakland International Airport (OAK), and San Jose International Airport (SJO). SFO often has delays due to fog. Construction at the airport has not ceased since its conception in 1927, so plan time to navigate around the airport by foot and car. Oakland and San Jose are easier choices if your airline offers service to these smaller airports. Always leave time for airport security. Call your airlines for more details.

From the Airport

SFO Transportation Hotline (800-736-2008) provides information on transportation alternatives to and from SFO. You can find a list of operators at www.flysfo .com/transport/services/gt_tsv_search.asp. Bay Area Rapid Transit (BART) Rapid Rail operates service to northern San Mateo County, San Francisco, and the East Bay directly from SFO. BART also provides a direct connection to Caltrain at the Millbrae station. Caltrain provides rail service between San Francisco and San Jose. See www.caltrain.com for routes and schedules. For bus service to SFO from San Mateo County, call SamTrans at (800) 660-4287.

AirBART links BART's Coliseum station in Oakland to Oakland International Airport, running every ten to twenty minutes. Call (510) 465-BART (2278) or go to www.bart.gov for schedules. For other ground transportation to and from the Oakland airport, visit www.oaklandairport.com/ground_transportation.shtml.

For ground transportation to and from San Jose International Airport, go to www.sjc.org/travelers/ground_trans.html.

For complete travel information in the San Francisco Bay Area, including airport information, visit 511.org.

By Bus

Greyhound services most major towns and cities in California. Schedules and fares are available online at www.greyhound.com or by phone at (800) 231-2222. A few areas that are off the Greyhound routes are connected to the Greyhound network by local buses.

MUNI provides service within the city and county of San Francisco with diesel buses, trolley buses, Muni Metro streetcars, historic streetcars, and the world-famous cable cars. MUNI's eighty-one routes include sixteen express lines. Bicycle racks are available on some buses. Service operates twenty-four hours daily. Call (415) 701-2311 or its 311 info number or visit www.sfmta.com.

AC Transit covers Alameda and Contra Costa Counties. Call (510) 817-1717 or visit www2.actransit.org.

Golden Gate Transit provides regional bus service in San Francisco, Marin, and Sonoma Counties. Service is also available between Marin and Contra Costa Counties. Call (415) 455-2000 or 511 locally or visit www.goldengatetransit.org.

SamTrans covers the South Bay and the Peninsula. Call (800) 660-4BUS (4287) or go to www.samtrans.org.

For transit services in the Santa Clara Valley, including San Jose, contact the Santa Clara Valley Transportation Authority at (408) 321-2300 or visit www.vta.org.

By BART or Train

BART serves San Francisco, Alameda, Contra Costa, and northern San Mateo Counties with five interconnected rail lines and thirty-nine stations. There is bus service to all thirty-nine stations. Call (510) 465-2278 or visit www.bart.gov.

Regional rail services include Caltrain, a commuter line that runs down the San Mateo peninsula from San Francisco to San Jose and Gilroy. Call (800) 660-4287 or (650) 508-6448 or visit www.caltrain.org.

Altamont Commuter Express (www. acerail.com) operates rush hour service from Stockton to San Jose.

Amtrak's Capitol Corridor trains provide frequent service between San Jose, Oakland, and Sacramento; Amtrak Thruway buses connect these trains to many other destinations, including San Francisco, Napa Valley, Santa Cruz, and Lake Tahoe. There's a free shuttle for passengers between the Amtrak Emeryville station (the main station for the San Francisco Bay Area) and various San Francisco locations. Amtrak information and reservations are available online at www.amtrak.com or by phone at (800) 872-7245.

Amtrak's Coast Starlight train starts in Los Angeles and serves Oakland, Sacramento, Redding, and Dunsmuir on its way to Seattle. The California Zephyr is a long-distance train that starts in Chicago and ends in Oakland, stopping in Sacramento and Truckee. San Joaquin trains run from Oakland to the Central Valley, with bus connections to Yosemite National Park and Los Angeles.

By Ferry

Alameda/Oakland Ferry provides service to San Francisco (daily) and Angel Island (seasonal). Call (510) 522-3300 or visit www.transitinfo.org.

Harbor Bay Maritime provides weekday commuter ferry service between Harbor Bay Isle and San Francisco and seasonal service to Monster Park. Call (510) 769-5500 or visit www.alamedaharborbayferry.com.

Golden Gate Ferry provides round-trip service to the San Francisco Ferry Building from Larkspur and Sausalito in Marin County. Call (415) 455-2000 or visit www.goldengateferry.org.

Other services include the Angel Island–Tiburon Ferry Service (415-435-2131; www.angelislandferry.com); Blue and Gold Fleet ferries to Sausalito, Oakland, Angel Island, and Vallejo (415-705-8200; www.blueandgoldfleet.com); and Red and White Fleet ferries to Sausalito, Tiburon, and Angel Island (415-673-2900; www.redandwhite.com).

By Bicycle, Car Pool, or Shuttle

511 provides carpool, vanpool, bicycle, and other transit information and assistance. Call 511 or go to 511.org.

Emery Go-Round provides free shuttle service between Emeryville and the MacArthur BART station in Oakland. Visit www.transitinfo.org or www.emerygo round.com.

With Disabilities

The Bay Area has a range of public transportation options for people with disabilities. For information call 511 or visit www.transitinfo.org/disabled/index.asp.

Visitor Information

You can get information for the whole Bay Area at the San Francisco Visitor Information Center, which is located at Market and Powell Streets on the lower level of Hallidie Plaza, near the Powell Street BART station. Call (415) 391-2000 for information, (415) 391-2001 for recorded events information. The Web sites are www .onlyinsanfrancisco.com or www.sfgate.com/traveler/guide.

Other Bay Area visitor bureaus include:

Half Moon Bay Coastside Chamber of Commerce and Visitors' Bureau, 235 Main Street, Half Moon Bay; (650) 726-8380; www.halfmoonbaychamber.org.

Marin County Convention and Visitors Bureau, 1013 Larkspur Landing Circle, Larkspur; (866) 925-2060; www.visitmarin.org.

City of Oakland Convention and Visitors Bureau, 463 11th Street, Oakland; (510) 839-9000; www.oaklandcvb.com.

Santa Clara County Convention and Visitors Bureau, 1850 Warburton Avenue, Santa Clara; (800) 272-6822; www.santaclara.org.

Santa Cruz County Conference and Visitors Council, 1211 Ocean Street, Santa Cruz; (831) 425-1234 or (800) 833-3494; www.santacruzca.org.

San Mateo County Convention and Visitors Bureau, 111 Anza Boulevard, Suite 410, Burlingame; (650) 348-7600; www.smccvb.com.

Tri-Valley Convention and Visitors Bureau, 349 Main Street, Suite 203, Pleasanton; (925) 846-8910; www.trivalleycvb.com.

For California visitor information or a travel brochure, call the California Division of Tourism at (800) GOCALIF or visit the Web site at www.gocalif.ca.gov. The state's official site is www.ca.gov.

Legend

Roads

═══80═══	Freeway/Interstate Highway
═⟨101⟩═	U.S. Highway
─⟨1⟩─	State Highway
──────	Other Road

Trails

▬▬▬▬▬	Selected Route
------	Trail or Fire Road
──────	Paved Trail or Bike Path
▌▌▌▌▌	Steps
⟶	Direction of Travel

Water Features

⬭	Body of Water
∿	River or Creek
⋰⋰	Intermittent Stream
⋇ ⋇	Marsh or Wetland
∬	Waterfalls
⌒	Spring

Land Management

▢▢▢	Parks and Preserves
▭	National Seashore/Beaches
▭	Recreational Area
▢▢▢	Watersheds

Map Symbols

⑳	Trailhead
🛆	Picnic Area
❓	Visitor Center/Information
🅿	Parking
🚻	Restroom
📞	Telephone
🚰	Water
🛏	Lodging
▲	Campground
⚑	Ranger Station
⦿	Gate
≍	Bridge
)▬(	Tunnel
▲	Mountain/Peak
⌣	Pass/Gap
🐎	Stables
■	Building/Point of Interest
◧	Scenic View
✕	Major Airport
✦	Interpretive Panel
N ⬤	True North (Magnetic North is approximately 15.5° East)

Trail Finder

Hike No.	Hike Name	Hikes for Anglers	Hikes for Animal Lovers	Hikes for Backpackers	Hikes for Beach/ Coast Lovers	Hikes for Bird Lovers
1	Point Reyes: Mount Wittenberg and Bear Valley Loop				●	
2	Point Reyes National Seashore: Tomales Point (tule elk)		●			
3	Point Reyes: Chimney Rock Trail and Point Reyes Lighthouse (whale-watching)		●			
4	Point Reyes National Seashore: Palomarin Trailhead to Alamere Falls (Coast Trail)			●	●	●
5	Tomales Bay State Park: Hearts Desire Beach to Shell Beach				●	
8	Phoenix Reservoir: Tucker and Bill Williams Trail	●				
9	Steep Ravine Loop to Stinson Beach				●	
11	Marin Headlands: Miwok Trail to Point Bonita				●	●
12	Marin Municipal Water District: Kent Trail along Alpine Lake	●				

Trail Finder

Hike No.	Hike Name	Hikes for Anglers	Hikes for Animal Lovers	Hikes for Backpackers	Hikes for Beach/Coast Lovers	Hikes for Bird Lovers
20	Pescadero Marsh Trail				●	●
22	Año Nuevo State Park and Reserve		●		●	
24	James V. Fitzgerald Marine Reserve: The Tide Pool Loop		●		●	
27	Castle Rock State Park			●		
34	Briones Regional Park (San Pablo Reservoir)	●				
38	Sunol Regional Wilderness		●	●		
39	Tilden Regional Park: Jewel Lake to Wildcat Peak	●				
40	Anthony Chabot Regional Park (Lake Chabot)			●		
I.	Russian Ridge Open Space Preserve (raptors)					●
J.	Skyline Ridge Open Space Preserve					●
S.	Coyote Hills Regional Park					●

Point Reyes and West Marin

Drakes Bay out to Point Reyes from the Woodward Valley Trail (Hike 1)

Point Reyes National Seashore features unique elements of biological and historical interest in a spectacularly scenic panorama of thunderous ocean breakers, open grasslands, brushy hillsides, and forested ridges. The biological diversity stems from its favorable location in the middle of California and the natural occurrence of many distinct habitats. Nearly 20 percent of the state's flowering plant species are represented on the peninsula, and over 45 percent of the bird species in North America have been sighted here.

But Point Reyes is much more than this.

It's a dramatic tectonic zone where the North American Plate meets the Pacific Plate, epicenter of the 1906 San Francisco earthquake, a narrow peninsula that shifts northward a few inches each year. Ridges of damp redwood forests meet warm ocean beaches, with sandpipers scurrying along daintily over foamy sand, doubling their number in the reflection of the water. Rocks protect pools that at low tide reveal millions of creatures: starfish, anemones, and clams that cling to the watery stones and hide in crevices in this co-op home.

Point Reyes is home to one of the most spectacular wildflower displays on the West Coast, thousands of acres charred by fire that are now in determined and inspired rebirth, young pine forests in thick clumps stretching branches up toward the sky. The northern point protects a herd of tule elk, grazing freely as they once did all along the Northern California coast when the Miwok Indians lived here. Artisans gather in the historic towns of Point Reyes Station, Inverness, and Olema, towns that seem to have more bed-and-breakfasts than garages. Everywhere you look are living watercolors, photo-realistic at sunny noon, impressionistic at misty dawn, abstract in rain-drenched fading light. The lighthouse boasts that it protects the foggiest and windiest place on the Pacific, its light struggling to pierce the thick white mist, while across Tomales Bay, sunshine bathes a grassy path as equestrians sway upon their saddled horses.

This is Point Reyes.

> A spectacularly scenic panorama of thunderous ocean breakers, open grasslands, brushy hillsides, and forested ridges...

Mushrooms on Woodward Valley Trail (Hike 1)

Point Reyes National Seashore: Mount Wittenberg and Bear Valley Loop

From the meadows of Bear Valley, the hike enters a lush forest of Douglas fir and oak trees. Follow the ridgeline, enjoying views of Drakes Bay and the Pacific Ocean, then descend to the treeless, stark beauty of coastal bluffs. Have lunch on a tiny, idyllic beach, then walk through wind-manicured scrub, with ocean views, before heading inland through a fairy-tale woodland of chalk white alders along a meandering stream. End back at the Bear Valley Visitor Center.

Start: Bear Valley Trailhead at the end of the Bear Valley parking lot

Distance: 12.3-mile loop

Approximate hiking time: 6 hours

Difficulty: Strenuous

Trail surface: A steep dirt path climbs up and down through forest and meadow. A dirt trail through scrub follows a strip of the Pacific, then a flat, wide, double-track dirt-and-gravel trail follows the creek back to the trailhead.

Other trail users: Equestrians on weekdays; mountain bikers on most of Bear Valley Trail

Canine compatibility: Dogs not permitted

Land status: National seashore

Fees and permits: No fees or permits required

Schedule: Open year-round sunrise to sunset

Maps: USGS Inverness; Drakes Bay. A park map can be picked up at the Bear Valley Visitor Center and is available for download at www.nps.gov/pore/pphtml/maps.html.

Trail contacts: Point Reyes National Seashore/National Park Service; www.nps.gov/pore; Bear Valley Visitor Center, Point Reyes Station; (415) 464-5100

Finding the trailhead

By Car: From U.S. Highway 101 or Interstate 580 (Richmond/San Rafael Bridge), take Sir Francis Drake Boulevard west until it ends at Olema and Highway 1. Turn right (north) onto Highway 1, then immediately left (west) onto Bear Valley Road. Continue on Bear Valley Road for less than 0.5 mile. Turn left into the visitor center parking lot.

By Public Transportation: From the San Rafael Transit Center in downtown San Rafael, take the West Marin Stage North Route (Rte. 68). For times and more information, contact West Marin Stage at (415) 526-3239 or go to www.marintransit.org/stage.html.

THE HIKE

After taking off from the Bear Valley Visitor Center, a brief meadow jaunt brings you to the Mount Wittenberg Trail, the only uphill portion of the hike and a good 1,300-foot climb. At 1,407 feet, Mount Wittenberg is the highest point on the Point Reyes peninsula. It was named for a father and son who leased land here for a large—and hilly—dairy ranch in the 1860s.

Thick, lush Douglas fir and oak forest—with the occasional endangered Bishop pine—canopies a dirt trail textured with angular roots and surrounded by maidenhair, chain, and five-fingered ferns. It's a fairly popular weekend trail, but less so than the flat, wide, and easy Bear Valley Trail.

Sky Trail takes you along the ridge where, through the trees, you get your first glimpse of ocean to the northwest with Drakes Bay and the Estero de Limantour hugging the Limantour Spit. Tall Bishop pine trunks charred by the 1995 Mount Vision fire stand on hills to the west. But here and on Woodward Valley Trail, you can see young Douglas firs and Bishop pines reinvigorating the forest. Bishops, like Monterey and knobcone pines, are fire pines. It takes fire to "hatch" the seeds from their cones and start new growth. To identify them, note that Bishop pines have two long needles per cluster and large cones. Douglas firs have short needles that poke out from the branch like a bottlebrush and small, waxy-looking cones.

The Woodward Valley Trail takes you through hillside valleys bathed with afternoon sunlight and a woodland of mostly new-growth Douglas firs, then it opens up to a breathtaking view of the Pacific Ocean.

The Coast Trail offers the stark beauty of the bluffs, the contemplative view of the Pacific, the salty smell of the sea, and the mesmerizing sound of the waves. Yellow and blue-purple coast bush lupine adds color in the spring, along with golden yellow lizard-tail, coast fiddleneck, and gumplant. Pink bursts of sea thrift color the early summer.

A short detour to Sculptured Beach offers a great lunch spot if the wind is calm. Winter rains feed two creeks, which stream across the sand into the ocean, creating a wet barrier that isolates the little coarse-sand beach that takes its name from the jutting water-carved rocks exposed at low tide.

The Coast Trail section of the hike ends at Arch Rock. This arch is typical of Northern California's coastline, where in the past 10,000 years or so the ocean level has risen to inundate former valleys and has left behind sea stacks, sea caves, and arches like this.

The Bear Valley Trail heads inland, following Coast Creek, with its chalk white alder trees, to Divide Meadow. Here you will find picnic tables, log seats, and restrooms. In late August the far end of the meadow displays bright pink "naked ladies," old-world amaryllis lilies probably planted by owners of the hunting lodge that stood here long ago. In the early 1900s, Bear Valley Road

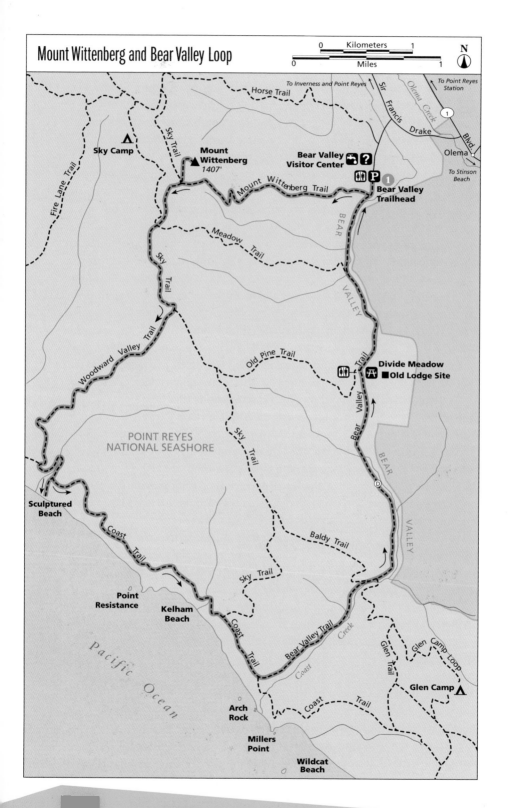

Mount Wittenberg and Bear Valley Loop

0 Kilometers 1

0 Miles 1

N

Sky Camp

Horse Trail

To Inverness and Point Reyes

To Point Reyes Station

Sir Francis Drake

Olema Creek

Olema

To Stinson Beach

Sky Trail

Mount Wittenberg
1407'

Bear Valley Visitor Center

Bear Valley Trailhead

Fire Lane Trail

Mount Wittenberg Trail

Meadow Trail

BEAR VALLEY

Sky Trail

Woodward Valley Trail

Old Pine Trail

Divide Meadow
■ **Old Lodge Site**

Bear Valley Trail

POINT REYES NATIONAL SEASHORE

Sky Trail

BEAR VALLEY

Sculptured Beach

Coast Trail

Baldy Trail

Point Resistance

Kelham Beach

Sky Trail

Bear Valley Trail

Coast Creek

Glen Trail

Glen Camp Loop

Glen Camp

Coast Trail

Pacific Ocean

Arch Rock

Coast Trail

Millers Point

Wildcat Beach

You can smell the salt air from Sky Trail.

brought travelers from Olema by horse-drawn carriage to hunt. Presidents William H. Taft and Theodore Roosevelt belonged to the hunting club, which disbanded when Point Reyes became a preserve in 1976.

Bear Valley beyond Divide Meadow is probably the single most traveled trail in Point Reyes, but near dusk, most tourists have already gone to town for cocktails and oysters. The path follows Bear Valley Creek, bordered with oak, bay, and Douglas fir, back to the visitor center.

MILES AND DIRECTIONS

0.0 Start from the parking lot at Bear Valley Visitor Center. Walk to the end of the lot, west toward the driveway to the old Morgan Ranch. The double-track Bear Valley Trail heads west across the meadow.

0.2 Turn right (west) onto Mount Wittenberg Trail.

2.0 To continue on the Mount Wittenberg Trail, turn left (west). It becomes Sky Trail toward Woodward Valley Trail.

2.4   Reach the trailhead for Sky Trail and Meadow Trail. Continue straight (south) on Sky Trail for 0.7 mile to Woodward Valley Trail.

3.1   Reach the Woodward Valley Trailhead. Turn right (southwest), heading 1.8 miles to Coast Trail. **Option:** For a shorter hike, continue straight on Sky Trail. Turn left onto Old Pine Trail, left onto Bear Valley Trail, and head back to the visitor center (a 6.7-mile loop).

4.9   Turn left (south) onto Coast Trail.

5.4   Detour to Sculptured Beach. Turn left (west) onto single-track trail that leads to the beach.

5.6   Reach Sculptured Beach. Return on the same path to the Coast Trail.

5.8   Turn right (south) onto the Coast Trail. After the second wooden bridge, watch for Arch Rock. Pass the trailhead for Sky Trail.

8.3   Reach the trailhead for the Bear Valley Trail. Turn left (east), heading inland along Coast Creek.

10.7 Reach Divide Meadow. Continue on Bear Valley Trail.

12.3 Reach the Bear Valley Visitor Center, parking lot, and starting point.

Option: Visit Kule Loklo, a re-created Coast Miwok village that is an easy 0.5-mile walk from the Bear Valley Visitor Center. For more information call the visitor center at (415) 464-5100.

HIKE INFORMATION

Local Information: Point Reyes National Seashore Association, Point Reyes Station; (415) 663-1200; www.ptreyes.org. Also visit www.pointreyes.net.

Point Reyes National Seashore: Tomales Point

Hiking Tomales Point is invigorating and mysterious. Though hikers are sometimes unsatisfied going back and forth on a single trail, the crashing of the Pacific against the shore and the majestic rocky sculptures and sea cliffs at the point offer a contemplative view that's worth revisiting. Add to that the stark beauty of the coastal bluffs, often appearing and disappearing in sheets of wispy fog, the whitewashed buildings of Pierce Point Ranch, isolated and haunting on the green hills, and springtime wildflowers, and you've got a trail worth visiting again and again.

Start: To the right of the historic Pierce Point Ranch at the end of Pierce Point Road
Distance: 9.2 miles round-trip
Approximate hiking time: 4.5 hours
Difficulty: Moderate
Trail surface: Double-track dirt trail that rises and falls moderately through grassland and scrub. A single-track dirt trail (1.6 miles) leads to the point.
Canine compatibility: Dogs not permitted
Land status: National seashore

Fees and permits: No fees or permits required
Schedule: Open year-round sunrise to sunset
Maps: USGS Tomales; Drakes Bay. A park map can be picked up at the Bear Valley Visitor Center and is available for download at www .nps.gov/pore/pphtml/maps.html.
Trail contacts: Point Reyes National Seashore/National Park Service, www.nps.gov/pore; Bear Valley Visitor Center, Point Reyes Station; (415) 464-5100

Finding the trailhead

By Car: From U.S. Highway 101 or Interstate 580 (Richmond/San Rafael Bridge), take Sir Francis Drake Boulevard west until it ends at Olema and Highway 1. Turn right (north) onto Highway 1 toward Point Reyes Station. Turn left (west) onto Sir Francis Drake Boulevard. Drive about 5 miles, past the town of Inverness. Bear right (north) on Pierce Point Road and follow it for 9 miles to the Pierce Point Ranch and parking lot.

By Public Transportation: From the San Rafael Transit Center at Third and Hetherton Streets in San Rafael, take the West Marin Stage North Route (Rte. 68). For schedules and more information, contact West Marin Stage at (415) 526-3239 or go to www.marintransit.org/stage.html. The park service runs a shuttle on weekends during winter. For shuttle information, contact the Bear Valley Visitor Center at (415) 464-5100.

A Pacific-side view from the trail—wow!

THE HIKE

Tomales Point's rich pasture caught the eye of a farmer named Solomon Pierce, who began a dairy here in 1858. Pierce and his son Abram produced fine butter, which was shipped to San Francisco from a wharf they built on Tomales Bay. In post–gold rush San Francisco, if a proprietor displayed the sign POINT REYES BUTTER, shoppers knew they were getting the best. For seven decades, the point remained in the Pierce family.

The walk begins at Upper Pierce Point Ranch at the Pierce family house, barn, and outbuildings, now maintained by the National Park Service. The path, the old ranch road, wanders over the green hills, which are seasonally sprinkled with yellow-orange poppies and tidy tips, orange fiddleneck, and purple iris.

Tomales Point, the northernmost boundary of Marin County and Point Reyes National Seashore, can make you feel as if you've reached the end of the world. The point is literally splitting away from the Bolinas Ridge, separated by Tomales Bay, which follows the San Andreas Fault line. The fault is where the Pacific and the North American tectonic plates move past each other in opposite directions.

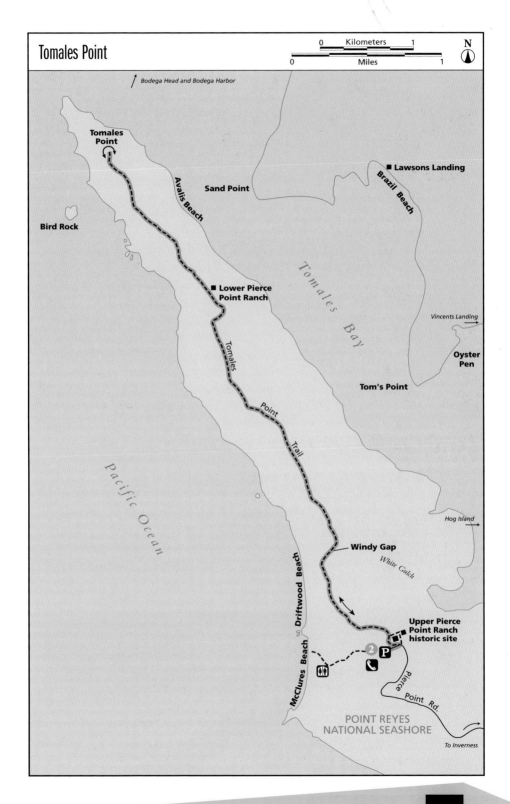

Tomales Point

Kilometers
0   1
0   1
Miles

N

Bodega Head and Bodega Harbor

Tomales Point

Sand Point

Avalis Beach

Lawsons Landing

Brazil Beach

Bird Rock

Lower Pierce Point Ranch

Tomales Bay

Vincents Landing

Oyster Pen

Tomales

Point

Trail

Tom's Point

Pacific Ocean

Hog Island

Windy Gap

White Gulch

Driftwood Beach

McClures Beach

Upper Pierce Point Ranch historic site

2

P

Pierce Point Rd.

POINT REYES NATIONAL SEASHORE

To Inverness

Views from this trail are superb, starting with the beach and surf to the west, with an occasional fishing vessel bobbing on the ocean. In February and March you can spot molting elephant seals on isolated beaches below the cliffs. As you crest the ridge, you can see little Hog Island to the east in the bay, and the village of Dillon Beach, oyster central. The old ranch road descends to the site of Lower Pierce Point Ranch, marked by a pond and a eucalyptus grove. This is where the "official" trail ends. But a well-worn social trail takes you out to a high vista point that looks down on Bird Rock, occupied by cormorants and white pelicans. From there, a faint path takes you to the very top of Tomales Point for stirring views of Bodega Head and Tomales Bay.

If you are trekking with children or are short on time, you can turn around at any point on the trail and still see the highlight of this trail: the tule elk. For thousands of years, as many as 500,000 tule elk thrived in California. The Miwok Indians lived peacefully with the herds on Tomales Point, but following the gold rush of 1849, the new settlers hunted the elk nearly to extinction and took over their habitat for agriculture and livestock grazing. By 1870, fewer than ten tule elk survived.

In 1874, ranch workers draining a marsh to create new agricultural fields near San Luis Obispo discovered a last remaining herd. Initially protected by a private landowner near San Luis Obispo, the state awarded the elk complete protection in 1971. In the spring of 1978, two bulls and eight cows were brought into Point Reyes from the San Luis Island Wildlife Refuge. They obviously liked their new coastal views; six of the cows bore calves that summer. By 1998, over 500 elk lived on the bluffs and more than 3,000 in different parts of California. The Point Reyes herd is one of the largest in the state.

The point is also home to an amazing number of hawks and falcons that rest on the scrub looking for moles and rabbits. Big black ravens sit in pairs on the blanched rock outcroppings that give the grassy ridgetop a sort of Stonehenge feel.

There are no facilities at the ranch, but a short drive will take you to restrooms and the trailhead to McClures Beach. A short, steep, downhill 0.6-mile walk brings you to this small cove with its intense surf.

> 🌿 **Green Tip:**
> *Observe wildlife from a distance. Don't interfere in their lives—both of you will be better for it.*

0.0   Start from the parking lot at Upper Pierce Point Ranch.

1.0   Reach Windy Gap (Driftwood Beach is below.

2.0   Climb to the highest point (535 feet). To the east is Tom's Point, jutting out into Tomales Bay; to the north, Brazil Beach.

3.0   Reach Lower Pierce Point Ranch. A sign points to a trail to Tomales Bay. To the east is Sand Point, with the town of Dillon Beach just north.

4.0   Arrive at the trail to the western edge of the point overlooking Bird Rock. Several faint trails heading northwest lead to Tomales Bluff, the tip of the point.

4.6   Reach Tomales Point (255 feet above sea level) and a view of Bodega Bay. Turn around and head back the way you came.

9.2   Return to Upper Pierce Point Ranch and parking lot.

HIKE INFORMATION

Local Information: Point Reyes National Seashore Association, Point Reyes Station; (415) 663-1200; www.ptreyes.org. Also see www.pointreyes.net.

Point Reyes National Seashore: Chimney Rock Trail

The Chimney Rock Trail is a short easy hike boasting one of the best wildflower displays on the coast and is the site of shipwrecks dating to 1585. The trail traces a bluff above 500-foot cliffs, providing spectacular coastline scenery. Add a visit to the Point Reyes Lighthouse, full of history, great whale watching, and 310 steep steps for additional exercise.

Start: At the end of Sir Francis Drake Boulevard in Point Reyes National Seashore
Distance: 1.8 miles out-and-back
Approximate hiking time: 1 hour
Difficulty: Easy
Trail surface: Single-track dirt pathway under cypress trees, overlooking cliffs; wind and fog likely
Canine compatibility: Dogs not permitted
Land status: National seashore
Fees and permits: None for parking or hiking; the shuttle bus is $3.50 per person on weekends from New Year's Eve to Easter when the weather is good.

Schedule: Open year-round sunrise to sunset
Maps: USGS Tomales; Drakes Bay; Inverness. A park map can be picked up at the Bear Valley Visitor Center and is available for download at www.nps.gov/pore/pphtml/maps.html.
Trail contacts: Point Reyes National Seashore/National Park Service; www.nps.gov/pore/; Bear Valley Visitor Center, Point Reyes Station; (415) 464-5100
Other: Wind and fog are likely both on the Chimney Rock Trail and at the lighthouse.

Finding the trailhead

By Car: From U.S. Highway 101 or Interstate 580 (Richmond/San Rafael Bridge), take Sir Francis Drake Boulevard west until it ends at Olema and Highway 1. Turn right (north) onto Highway 1 toward Point Reyes Station. Turn left (west) onto Sir Francis Drake Boulevard and follow it for about 20 miles. Turn left (east) onto Chimney Rock Road and take it to its end. The driving time from Highway 1 is about forty-five minutes.

On weekends from late December to mid-April, when the weather is good, the west end of Sir Francis Drake Boulevard is closed to vehicle traffic. Shuttle buses transport visitors to the Chimney Rock and lighthouse areas. For shuttle information contact the Bear Valley Visitor Center at (415) 464-5100.

By Public Transportation: Chimney Rock can only be reached by public transportation in the winter when weather is good. From the San Rafael Transit Center, take the West Marin Stage North Route (Rte. 68). For times and more information, contact West Marin Stage at (415) 526-3239 or go to www.marintransit.org/stage.html. The park service runs a shuttle on weekends from late December to mid-April. Shuttles are cancelled if weather is poor. For shuttle information contact the Bear Valley Visitor Center at (415) 464-5100.

THE HIKE

The forty-five-minute drive to Chimney Rock from Highway 1 (or the Bear Valley Visitor Center) reveals a beautiful landscape. The western end of Sir Francis Drake Boulevard takes you past Inverness and serene Tomales Bay, through rolling valleys, and beside ocean dunes. Historic dairy farms along the way post their dates of origin. The creameries still supply people around San Francisco with milk and cheese. You'll also pass several other trailheads and turnoffs to Point Reyes beaches, some with great tide pools.

On the bluffs along the trail, especially in spring, you will see a beautiful West Coast wildflower display. Yarrow, baby blue eyes, cobweb thistle, flowering flax, beautiful purple Douglas iris, yellow footsteps of spring, violet and yellow bush lupine, orange California poppy, red Indian paintbrush, large star linanthus, and seaside daisy grow in thick clumps on the hillsides sloping to the sea.

To your left as you face the Chimney Rock trailhead is Drakes Bay, named for sixteenth-century explorer Sir Francis Drake. An easy walk on the single-track trail to the end of the bluff brings you to Chimney Rock, a rock outcrop resembling a chimney stack that marks the meeting point of Drakes Bay, the headlands, and the sea. On isolated beaches below, you can observe elephant seals molting or mating.

This bluff and the nearby lighthouse platform are among the best places in Northern California to see migrating whales. When whale spotting, look for spouting (that's when a whale exhales air through its blowhole and the air rises 10 to 15 feet, condensing into a white vapor). Or if you're lucky, you may see a whale 30 to 50 feet in length breaching, hurling itself out of the water and landing smack on its back. Bring binoculars.

Along the Pacific side of the bluff, waves crash against the cliffs below you. You are at times only 5 feet from the edge. Hiking on the Overlook Trail on a clear day offers views of headland reserves and the Farallon Islands 20 miles off the point. The 948-nautical-mile area in between the point and the islands became the Gulf of the Farallones National Marine Sanctuary in 1981. It includes marshes, mudflats, a tidal zone, and deep ocean waters, and is home to numerous seabirds, diving birds, Steller and California sea lions, elephant seals, porpoises, dolphins, whales, harbor seals, flounder, halibut, Pacific herring, and invertebrate species.

These shores have also known many shipwrecks during the last few centuries, dating back to the first reported wreck, the *San Agustin* in 1595. Despite the dangers, a lot of trade and commerce used to take place here. Ships would motor or sail over the sandbar during high tide into Limantour and Drakes Bay to a little inlet called Scooter Bay. Area dairy workers would meet the ships on scooters, carrying butter, cheese, and dairy products that the vessels would take back to San Francisco. Even now, a year doesn't go by without a wreck of a personal vessel, fishing craft, or other boat here.

The Lifeboat House on the beach of Drakes Bay is available for touring and is worth visiting. The U.S. Life Saving Service built the first fully equipped station in Point Reyes in 1889. The station moved to its current site on Drakes Beach in 1912.

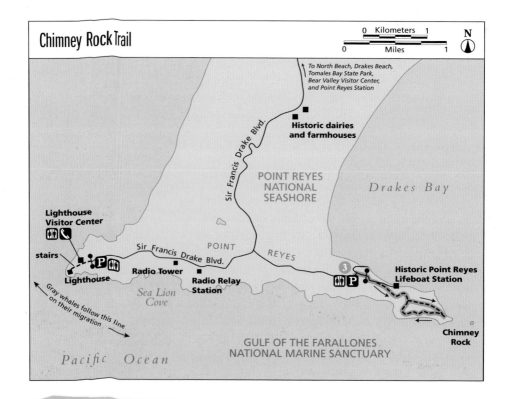

Chimney Rock Trail

Point Reyes Lighthouse

This hike may be short, but it is very satisfying and leaves you with energy to go to the historic Point Reyes Lighthouse fifteen minutes away (highly recommended!) or enjoy some tide pooling, walking on a beach, or loitering around Point Reyes Station.

MILES AND DIRECTIONS

0.0   Start at the Chimney Rock trailhead.

0.3   Reach the junction with Underhill Road. Continue straight on the Chimney Rock Trail. The U.S. Coast Guard Lifeboat Station is below.

0.9   Reach the end of the bluff, overlooking Chimney Rock. Head back on the Overlook Trail.

1.4   Arrive at the overlook area. Turn right onto the trail toward Drakes Bay.

1.5 Return to the junction with the Chimney Rock Trail. Turn left (west) and follow it back to your car, or continue down to tour the lifeboat station, then take the road back to the trailhead.

1.8 Arrive back at the parking lot.

Option: Drive to the parking lot on the west side of the peninsula to walk to the lighthouse. This 1.2-mile out-and-back hike has steep stairs. The lighthouse is open 10 a.m. to 4:30 p.m., Thursday to Monday, weather permitting. Take a few minutes at the Lighthouse Visitor Center, which has exhibits on human history, wildlife, and plant life of the area. Those cement domes across from the visitor center were built in 1870 for catching and storing rain for drinking water and steam for energy when lightkeepers staffed the lighthouse.

HIKE INFORMATION

Local Information: Point Reyes National Seashore Association, Point Reyes Station; (415) 663-1200; www.ptreyes.org. See also www.pointreyes.net.
Hike Tours: Bear Valley Visitor Center, Point Reyes Station; (415) 464-5100

Point Reyes National Seashore:
Palomarin Trailhead to Alamere Falls

The trail from Palomarin, on the southwestern edge of Point Reyes National Seashore, to Alamere Falls takes you through coastal bluffs with Pacific views and a Douglas fir forest filled with streams and quiet lily-covered ponds. You'll pass two lakes, four if you hike at low tide. The highlight is 50-foot Alamere Falls.

Start: Palomarin Trailhead for the Coast Trail at the end of Mesa Road
Length: 8.8 miles out-and-back
Approximate hiking time: 5 hours
Difficulty: Moderate, with a strenuous 0.1-mile climb down to the beach and back at the falls
Trail surface: Primarily double-track dirt trail, with a narrow, single-track trail to Alamere Falls. A rutted, steep shale and sandstone bluff heads to Wildcat Beach at the falls.
Other trail users: Equestrians
Canine compatibility: Dogs not permitted

Land status: National seashore
Fees and permits: No fees or permits required
Schedule: Open year-round sunrise to sunset
Maps: USGS Bolinas; Double Point; Inverness. A park map can be picked up at the Bear Valley Visitor Center and is available for download at www.nps.gov/pore/pphtml/maps.html.
Trail contacts: Point Reyes National Seashore/National Park Service; www.nps.gov/pore. Bear Valley Visitor Center, Point Reyes Station; (415) 464-5100

Finding the trailhead

By Car: Take Highway 1 north from Stinson Beach, passing the Bolinas Lagoon on your left (west). At the end of the lagoon, turn left (south) onto Olema-Bolinas Road. Turn right (west) onto Mesa Road at the stop sign and take it for 4 miles. It becomes a gravel road and passes the Point Reyes Bird Observatory. The gravel parking lot for the Palomarin Trailhead is at the end of the road.

By Public Transportation: From Marin City, begin at the Golden Gate Transit hub in the Gateway Shopping Center, located at Donahue and Terners Streets. Take the West Marin Stage South Route (Rte. 61) to Bolinas. For times and more information, contact West Marin Stage at (415) 526-3239 or go to www.marintransit.org/stage.html.

Hikers discussing Alamere Falls on the beach

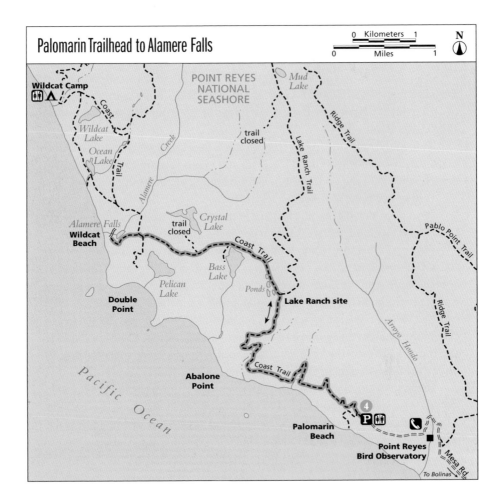

0   Kilometers   1

0   Miles   1

N

POINT REYES NATIONAL SEASHORE

Wildcat Camp

Mud Lake

Coast Trail

Ridge Trail

Wildcat Lake

Creek

Ocean Lake

trail closed

Lake Ranch Trail

Alamere Falls
Wildcat Beach

Alamere

trail closed

Crystal Lake

Coast Trail

Pablo Point Trail

Bass Lake

Double Point

Pelican Lake

Ponds

Ridge Trail

Lake Ranch site

Arroyo Hondo

Abalone Point

Coast Trail

Pacific Ocean

4

P

Palomarin Beach

Point Reyes Bird Observatory

Mesa Rd.

To Bolinas

THE HIKE

Your hike begins in 3-foot-high grassland between tall, soldier-like rows of eucalyptus. These Australian natives were probably planted as windbreaks for a ranch built on this spot, though there is a colorful but unlikely legend that people planted patches of eucalyptus around the Bay Area to create a habitat for imported koalas.

Past the turnoff for charcoal-shaded Palomarin Beach, you walk stark coastal bluffs through fields of yellow lupine, peach-orange monkeyflower, broom, coffeeberry, coyote brush, and California sagebrush. Rabbits streak across the trail in early morning and late afternoon. Binoculars help you see the sea lions and various seabirds. In March, those binoculars may even help you spot gray whales as they migrate north along the coast. If it's clear, the Farallon Islands seem only a long leap away. Farther south, you may see fishing vessels or freighters making their way into the San Francisco Bay.

The Coast Trail heads inland, passing over numerous finger creeks. You enter a forest of mature Douglas firs shadowing out most plants except moisture-loving ferns and grasses. Where sunlight gets through, you can see wild strawberries and manroot. Branches of Alamere Creek are on either side of the path. You'll come upon a series of still ponds to the left, with green lily pads growing on their surface. Then comes Bass Lake.

Among the romantic spots in the Bay Area, Bass Lake is also a popular swimming hole in summer and a good place to fish. It may be overrun on summer weekends, but in winter and on some weekdays, it is quiet and invites long gazing.

Farther along the trail, Pelican Lake is backed by two hillsides called Double Point that slope down in a V and kiss just at the lake's surface, revealing the Pacific backdrop. It looks like the lake is suspended just above the sea.

Alamere Falls is an amazing sight, especially in spring or winter. It is one of two coastal falls in California. (Its sister, McWay Falls, is a more accessible attraction at Big Sur.) Wide Alamere Creek tumbles over a terraced bluff, creating two smaller waterfalls on the hillside, then drops straight off the edge of a cliff 40 feet onto exposed rock and Wildcat Beach. At its heaviest flow, the falls are 25 feet across. During drier times, it may split into two narrower falls. As the tide rises, the salty surf comes up to meet the fresh water flowing in. A favorite lunch spot is on the cliff beside the falls. But getting there is an adventure.

To get to the bottom of the falls, you have to cross the cascading stream. Even in rainy winter, the crossing is not too wide, but it requires a jump. The trail also involves a climb down water-rutted canyons and slivering rock banks to view the upper and lower part of the 50-foot falls. But it is well worth the effort.

MILES AND DIRECTIONS

0.0   Start from the parking lot for the Palomarin Trail. The trailhead is on the east side of the parking lot next to the restrooms. Climb the stairs and turn left onto the Coast Trail.

0.1   Pass the trailhead for Palomarin Beach (0.6 mile to the beach). Continue on Coast Trail.

2.2   At the junction with Lake Ranch Trail, stay left (north) on the Coast Trail.

2.8   Reach Bass Lake. Admire it from the trail, or take the narrow trail on the north side of the lake.

3.1   Pass the Crystal Lake Trail. If it is accessible when you pass, you can reach the lake in less than 0.5 mile. (*Note:* Be careful; the trail is overgrown.) Otherwise, stay straight (northwest) on the Coast Trail.

3.6   Pass Pelican Lake and Double Point. Continue northwest on Coast Trail.

3.9 Arrive at the Alamere Falls Trailhead. Turn left (west) onto the Alamere Falls Trail to cliffs above beach. (*Note:* Watch for poison oak.)

4.3 Reach the top of Alamere Falls. Cross the stream below the second falls to reach the trail down to the beach. (Note: Be careful; loose rock.)

4.4 Enjoy the view of the falls from Wildcat Beach. Return by the same trail.

4.5 Return to the Coast Trail via Alamere Falls Trail.

4.9 Turn right (south) onto Coast Trail, and retrace your steps to Palomarin.

5.2 Pass Pelican Lake.

6.0 Pass Bass Lake.

6.6 Stay on Coast Trail past the junction with Lake Ranch Trail.

8.8 Return to the Palomarin Trailhead and parking lot.

Options: To reach Alamere Falls from Wildcat Camp, you can hike the beach the entire way within an hour of low tide. But this takes careful planning. Check tidal charts before you set out.

To make the lollipop loop from the Alamere Falls/Coast Trail junction, continue on the Coast Trail to Wildcat Camp, passing Ocean Lake and Wildcat Lake. Take the trail down to Wildcat Beach, then head south along the beach to the falls. Make sure you reach the trail junction just before low tide. Return to the Coast Trail via the falls trail, and retrace your steps to Palomarin.

HIKE INFORMATION

Local Information: West Marin Chamber of Commerce, P.O. Box 1045, Point Reyes Station, CA 94956; (415) 663-9232; www.pointreyes.org

Local Events/Attractions: Audubon Canyon Ranch, 4900 Highway 1, P.O. Box 577, Stinson Beach, CA 94970; (415) 868-9244; www.egret.org
Point Reyes Bird Observatory, on Mesa Road outside Bolinas; (415) 868-0655; www.prbo.org

Hike Tours: Bear Valley Visitor Center, Point Reyes Station; (415) 464-5100

🌱 **Green Tip:**
Recycle your old gear by giving it to someone or an organization that will reuse it.

y State Park: Hearts Desire Beach
ıch

...sses three of the Tomales park's four beaches; an extra mile gets you ... ...h as well. Between beaches, each more isolated than the last, the trail takes you through a thick woodland of oaks, bays, alders, willows, and Bishop pines. On the beaches, you can sort through shells and stones and watch California sea lions poke their torpedo-shaped noses above the water. Clam digging and fishing (with a license) are other options.

Start: Johnstone Trailhead at Hearts Desire Beach, beyond the main entrance of Tomales Bay State Park

Distance: 8 miles round-trip

Approximate hiking time: 4.5 hours

Difficulty: Moderate

Trail surface: Single-track dirt trail through woodland from beach to beach

Other trail users: Mountain bikers and equestrians

Canine compatibility: Dogs not permitted except in picnic areas on leash

Land status: State park

Fees and permits: $6 per car when the kiosk is attended

Schedule: Open year-round from 8:00 a.m. to sunset

Maps: USGS Inverness; Drakes Bay; Point Reyes NE; Tomales. A park map is available by writing Tomales Bay State Park, Star Route, Inverness, CA 94937; by calling the park at (415) 669-1140; or by visiting the Web site at www.parks .ca.gov.

Trail contact: Tomales Bay State Park, 1208 Pierce Point Rd, Inverness, CA 94937; (415) 669-1140; www.parks.ca.gov

Finding the trailhead

By Car: From U.S. Highway 101 or Interstate 580 (Richmond/San Rafael Bridge), take Sir Francis Drake Boulevard west until it ends at Olema and Highway 1. Turn right onto Highway 1 toward Point Reyes Station. Turn left onto Sir Francis Drake Boulevard. Pass the town of Inverness. Bear right (north) on Pierce Point Road (follow signs to Tomales Bay State Park). Turn right (north) at the main entrance to Tomales Bay State Park (follow the sign to Hearts Desire Beach). Beyond the kiosk, turn left into the Hearts Desire parking lot (there is additional parking down the road).

By Public Transportation: Getting to Tomales Bay State Park without a car is only possible if you bring a bicycle and are willing to ride the last few miles from Inverness to the trailhead. From the San Rafael Transit Center at Third and Hetherton Streets in San Rafael, take the West Marin Stage North Route (Rte. 68) to Inverness. For times and more information, contact West Marin Stage at (415) 526-3239 or go to www.marintransit.org/stage.html.

THE HIKE

The Coast Miwok people inhabited this region for 3,500 years, fishing, digging for clams and oysters, collecting edible and medicinal plants, and hunting game for food and clothing. The self-guided nature trail to Indian Beach tells some of the Miwok story, focusing on Native American uses of local plants. As you wander the beaches, you can picture the natives going about their daily routines. The Támal-ko ate Washington clams and used basket or heart cockles and bay mussels for tools and jewelry as well as food. They made other tools out of chert and formed sinker stones, probably for fishing nets, from obsidian. Archaeologists have also found leaf-shaped obsidian spearheads, fired clay balls, and clam disk beads, which may have been used as a kind of money.

Hearts Desire Beach

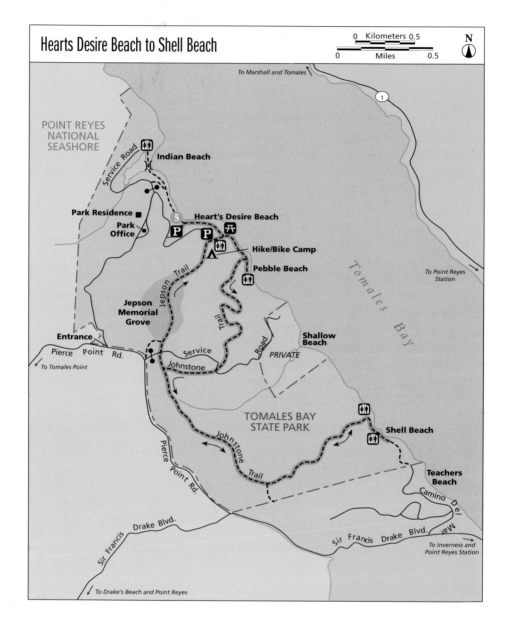

In 1579 Sir Francis Drake dropped anchor in Drakes Bay. To the Miwoks, Drake may have looked like a ghost. They believed that to the west, from which the Europeans had come, was úute-yómi, the "dead home," where the dead could be with Old Man Coyote, the creator. The Spanish arrived in 1595 but didn't settle in the area until the late 1700s. Russian and German scientists explored the area in the early 1800s, identifying many previously unknown plants. Most of the Indians died from disease brought by the settlers. Remaining descendants try to keep old stories and traditions alive, but they are very few.

Throughout the Point Reyes peninsula, you can see the influences of all these different cultures. From landmark names (for example, Olema comes from Miwok, Point Reyes from the Spanish, Drakes Bay from you-know-who) to ranching and dairy traditions and building styles, you can find adopted customs unique to this rich and isolated coastal community.

Today, the area offers hiking, fishing, boating (non-motorized boats may be launched at Hearts Desire Beach), swimming, ten camping sites with cold showers, and four beaches, all with restrooms and each with its own character. The trail to Indian Beach makes for a great family hike. Hearts Desire Beach, the most accessible, is a great swimming and picnic beach, but tends to get crowded on summer weekends. The romance that its name implies is definitely attainable on less busy weekdays and quieter cool winter afternoons.

Pebble Beach, 0.2 mile past the Vista Point picnic area, is a secluded swimming cove aptly named for the colorful stones decorating the sand. Shell Beach, the final destination of the hike, consists of two small beaches separated by rock outcrops covered with black-shelled mussels and white barnacles. Four miles from the main entrance, it is the quietest of the beaches. Clear mounds of jellyfish plant themselves on the beach in low tide. California sea lions frequent the bay waters, as do a variety of waterfowl; Brandt's cormorants can be spotted drying themselves on the rocks, and hikers also may spot puffins, great blue herons, and sandhill cranes.

The two adjoining trails that make up this hike are named for lovers and protectors of plants. Botanist and professor Willis Linn Jepson (1867–1946) founded the School of Forestry and funded the Jepson Herbarium at the University of California–Berkeley. One of the finest remaining virgin groves of Bishop pine in California is in the park's Jepson Memorial Grove. Conservationists Bruce Johnstone, a Marin County planner, and his wife, Elsie, worked long and hard to preserve Tomales Bay. The Johnstone Trail leads from Pebble Beach to Shell Beach. A trailside plaque pays them tribute. The beautiful path is shared with mountain bikers.

MILES AND DIRECTIONS

0.0   Start from the parking lot for Hearts Desire Beach. Walk to the left (north) end of the beach to Johnstone Trailhead.

0.1   Pass the picnic area for Hearts Desire Beach.

0.2   Pass the Vista Point group picnic area. Continue on the Johnstone Trail to Pebble Beach.

0.4 Bear left (east) to Pebble Beach. After you visit the beach, return to the single-track Johnstone Trail.

0.5 Turn left (west) onto Johnstone Trail, continuing to Shell Beach. A bridge crosses the creek. The trail heads uphill at a moderate grade. Lawsons Landing is to the east.

1.5 Reach a junction with a paved fire road. Cross the paved road, staying on the single-track dirt trail, now the Johnstone/Jepson Trail.

1.7 Reach the trailhead for Jepson Trail (which you will take on the way back). Take the left fork, continuing on Johnstone Trail to Shell Beach, which is 2.5 miles ahead. The flat trail starts to rise moderately. Viewing benches are set along the way.

4.2 Reach Shell Beach—your final destination. Wooden steps and a path lead to Shell Beach. (Beyond there is a 0.2-mile trail that leads south to Camino del Mar Drive.)

6.7 Return to the Jepson Trail. Turn left (north). In less than 0.1 mile, pass over a paved access road, and continue on the Jepson Trail to Jepson Memorial Grove.

7.7 Jepson Trail ends at the parking lot for Vista Point. Walk across the parking lot to the Vista Point picnic area.

7.8 In the Vista Point picnic area, turn left (north) onto single-track Johnstone Trail.

8.0 Arrive back at Hearts Desire Beach and the parking lot.

Option: Take the self-guided 0.9-mile nature trail loop on the other side of Hearts Desire Beach to Indian Beach.

HIKE INFORMATION

Local Information: Point Reyes National Seashore Association, Point Reyes Station; (415) 663-1200; www.ptreyes.org/index.shtml
Hike Tours: Tomales Bay State Park, 1208 Pierce Point Road, Inverness; (415) 669-1140
Tomales Bay State Park, 1208 Pierce Point Rd, Inverness; (415) 669-1140

Samuel P. Taylor State Park: To the Top of Barnabe Peak

Starting off by Devils Gulch Creek, Bill's Trail gently ascends to the top of Barnabe Peak and past a 30-foot waterfall. At the peak's lookout, the 360-degree view takes in Tomales Bay, the Pacific Ocean, the towns of San Geronimo and Lagunitas, and isolated Kent Lake and Peters Dam in the Marin County watershed. The fire roads on the way down allow you to enjoy those vistas a while longer.

Start: Devils Gulch Horse Camp sign on Sir Francis Drake Boulevard
Distance: 7.1-mile loop
Approximate hiking time: 3.5 hours
Difficulty: Moderate
Trail surface: Paved fire road for 0.1 mile to single-track dirt trail up the mountain at about a 5 percent grade. Return on dirt fire roads through grasslands.
Other trail users: Mountain bikers and equestrians on fire roads; hikers only on Bill's Trail
Canine compatibility: Dogs on leash on fire roads only
Land status: State park
Fees and permits: No fees are charged to hike the Barnabe Peak trail, but a $6 per car fee is charged at the park entrance to use the main picnic areas and campgrounds.
Schedule: Open year-round sunrise to sunset
Map: USGS San Geronimo
Trail contact: Samuel P. Taylor State Park, P.O. Box 251, Lagunitas, CA 94938; (415) 488-9897; www.parks.ca.gov/?page_id–469
Other: Wireless Internet service is available near the ranger station.

Finding the trailhead

By Car: From U.S. Highway 101 or Interstate 580 (Richmond/San Rafael Bridge), take Sir Francis Drake Boulevard west past the town of Lagunitas (about 15 miles from US 101). Continue past the main entrance to Samuel P. Taylor State Park for about 1 mile (also past the Madrone Camp) to Devils Gulch Horse Camp, and park in the gravel lot on the left (south) side of the road. Cross the street to the trailhead.

By Public Transportation: From the San Rafael Transit Center at Third and Hetherton Streets in San Rafael, take the West Marin Stage North Route (Rte. 68) to the main park entrance. Routes are subject to change. For times and more information, contact West Marin Stage at (415) 526-3239 or go to www.marintransit.org/stage.html.

THE HIKE

There are many firsts in this park's history. Samuel Penfield Taylor (1827–96), the park's namesake, was ahead of his time, one of the first to advocate responsible land use and recreation in this area. On this site he started the first paper mill on the West Coast and the first overnight camp for city dwellers. He established one of the first major towns on the Point Reyes peninsula (Taylorville, long gone), built the first fish ladder in the west, and developed the first "modern" grocery bag. He prospered, recycled . . . and rescued a mule. Now, that's California spirit.

View from bridge across Devils Gulch Creek

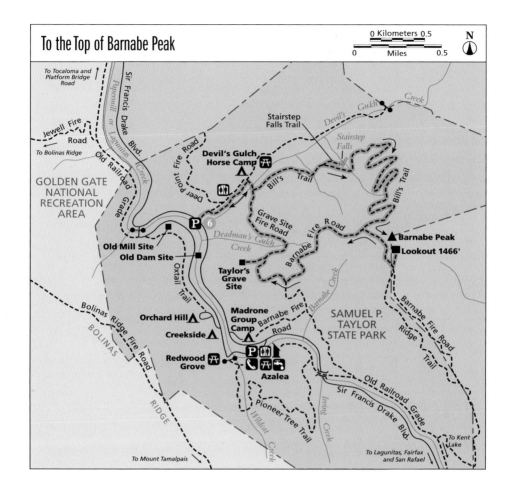

0 Kilometers 0.5

0 Miles 0.5

N

In 1874 Taylor built a rustic hotel in what is now the park's Redwood Grove picnic area to house friends and business associates. With the opening of a narrow-gauge railroad to serve the isolated Tomales Bay region, the general public started showing up. Taylor enlarged the hotel and added tent cabins and a dance pavilion big enough for a thirty-piece brass band. He and his wife called it Camp Taylor. It was the first campground for city children and their parents in the state of California. By 1888 over 3,000 people came to Camp Taylor each year. The state park service purchased the land in 1946. Samuel P. Taylor was one of the first parks in the United States to offer camping as part of its recreation program.

It's hard to believe all this bustle took place here as you walk through the quiet forests and picturesque picnic areas. There is a self-guided nature and history trail (2 miles plus) in the main part of the park that is a great option for a family hike. Enjoy a dip in the swimming hole—a favorite for over half a century—in warm weather.

Samuel P. Taylor is divided in two by Sir Francis Drake Boulevard. The featured hike is opposite the campground, passing the area where Taylor and his family lived and where his grave site is today, enclosed by a white picket fence.

The easy climb through serene forests takes you to the top of Barnabe Peak (1,466 feet), which is indeed named for a mule. He was a retired army mule who had crossed the plains with General John C. Fremont's troops. Taylor found the old, white burro at the San Francisco Presidio, named him Barnabe, and brought him back to Camp Taylor, where he became a favorite pet of the children and guests. A smart old ass, Barnabe often escaped his corral and trekked up to the top of the mountain to graze on the plentiful grasslands. And so the peak, which he claimed, took his name.

Today, the inhabitants of Barnabe Peak—except for the rangers who man the fire lookout station—are all wild. Red-tailed and red-shouldered hawks, kestrels, vultures, and ravens circle the skies. You may spot a fox, bobcat, or badger. Skunks, squirrels, mice, and snakes also make this home. Black-tailed deer are the most commonly seen big animals.

MILES AND DIRECTIONS

0.0   Start from the paved fire road past the gate signposted to Devils Gulch Horse Camp. Devils Gulch Creek is on the right (south).

0.1   Turn right (south) onto the unnamed, single-track dirt trail. To your left (east), up the hill, is the horse camp.

0.4   Turn right to cross the bridge over Devils Gulch Creek, then left (east and south) onto Bill's Trail (4 miles to the peak). The trail takes you over several numbered bridges that cross cascading creeks and springs that flow down the mountain and into Devils Gulch Creek.

1.2   Reach the trailhead to Stairstep Falls. Turn left (east) to the falls.

1.4   Arrive at Stairstep Falls. Head back the way you came to Bill's Trail.

1.6   Turn left (south), continuing up Bill's Trail to Barnabe Peak. A moderate grade, the path makes a series of hairpin turns. Watch for views of Tomales Bay to the west.

4.6   Reach the junction with the Barnabe Fire Road. Turn left (south) up the hill to reach the fire lookout tower.

4.8   Arrive at the fire lookout tower. Head back the way you came on the Barnabe Fire Road to Bill's Trail. Turn left (southwest).

5.0 Pass the trailhead to Bill's Trail, staying on the double-track dirt Barnabe Fire Road. The forest is on your right (north).

6.0 Reach a trail junction and turn right (north) onto Grave Site Fire Road.

6.1 Reach the trail to Taylor's grave site (0.1-mile round-trip). Turn left (west) to visit the site. Return to the Grave Site Fire Road.

6.2 Continue left (north) on Grave Site Fire Road toward the forest and Devils Gulch. *(Note:* The fire road may be muddy and washed out in places after winter storms.) You are passing through Deadmans Gulch (watch for narrow seasonal streams).

6.4 Reach a trailhead. A watershed access road to the right is closed to visitors. Take the double-track Deadmans Gulch Trail to the left. The trail meets up with Grave Site Fire Road heading down to Devils Gulch and the bridge.

6.9 Return to the bridge. Turn left (west) after the bridge onto the single-track trail you came in on.

7.0 The trail meets the paved fire road. Take this back out to Sir Francis Drake Boulevard.

7.1 Cross Sir Francis Drake Boulevard back to parking lot.

HIKE INFORMATION

Local Information: For camping reservations in the park, call (800) 444-7275 or visit www.parks.ca.gov.

Honorable Mentions

A. Point Reyes National Seashore: Inverness Ridge

A hike on Inverness Ridge takes you to a young forest, still in recovery from the 1995 Mount Vision fire. Everywhere, plants compete for precious sun and soil. Young Bishop pines grow in fast, healthy crowds on the hillsides around the charred remains of their ancestors who died in the flames. You look out across hillsides and valleys all the way to the sea. Now a green forest, imagine it after the firestorm finally died, everything ashen gray and smoldering. The surroundings on Drakes View and Bucklin Trails illustrate a story of devastation and renewal all around you.

The 7-mile loop starts off Limantour Road. Take Muddy Hollow Road to the Bayview Trail. Turn left (east) onto Drakes View Trail to the Inverness Ridge. Turn left (south) along the ridge for 0.5 mile, and go left (west) down Bucklin Trail, which affords great views of Drakes Bay and the ocean. Back on Muddy Hollow Road, turn left (southeast) again and follow it 1.4 miles back to the trailhead.

To get there from U.S. Highway 101 westbound, take the Sir Francis Drake Boulevard exit and head west. Where the road ends in Olema, turn right onto Highway 1. Take the first left onto Bear Valley Road. Take Bear Valley Road to Limantour Road. Turn left (west) onto Limantour Road. Turn right (northwest) onto Muddy Hollow Road, which ends shortly at the trailhead. For more information, check out the Point Reyes National Seashore/National Park Service Web site at www.nps.gov/pore/recreation/recreation.htm or www.nps.gov/pore, or call the Bear Valley Visitor Center, in Point Reyes Station, at (415) 464-5100.

B. Point Reyes on Rainy Days

It rains a lot here. And when it does, it's usually windy, too.

The last place you want to be on a stormy, wet day is the lighthouse. It sounds romantic, and it certainly would give you a taste of the life of the lonely, isolated, and weather-beaten lighthouse keepers of Point Reyes. But it's also one of the foggiest, windiest places in the world. Besides, on really socked in days, rangers will close this area to tourists.

In light rain or mist, most of the hiking trails are stunning. Light rain is great Point Reyes weather, darkening the hue of the forest, adding sparkle to leaves and crystal-hung spider webs. But the heavy stuff, gloomy sheets of rain and ice-chill winds, may require hiking on asphalt. Luckily, Point Reyes offers fascinating paved hikes.

Park at the Bear Valley Visitor Center, take in the slide show, then head across the parking lot to the Earthquake Trail. This 0.6-mile loop starts almost on the epicenter of the great San Francisco earthquake of 1906. Interpretive signs along the way show you how the right slip fault line actually works and illustrates how Point

Reyes is traveling north on the Pacific Plate, while the North American Plate moves west at the speedy rate of several feet per century. You can also walk 0.5 mile to Kule Loklo, a modern rendering of a Miwok village.

The surroundings offer a meandering creek, pretty wooden farm fences, scrub oaks, meadows, and grassy hills. Remember, it's bad luck to step on a banana slug. They'll be looking for pavement on rainy days, too.

The scenery at Point Reyes National Seashore is picture perfect! © Shutterstock

Mount Tamalpais and Its Foothills

Mount Tamalpais as a backdrop to a community in Sausalito © Shutterstock

The people of Marin County love their mountain. Mount Tamalpais, "The Sleeping Maiden" or "The Sleeping Lady," is an important part of the Bay Area's western skyline. Its foothills rise from the towns of Fairfax, Mill Valley, and San Anselmo to the east and end at the Pacific Ocean and the resort town of Stinson Beach to the west. Traveling up the mountain and down to the sea, a hiker can find a little bit of everything.

Fifty miles of trails within Mount Tamalpais State Park connect to a larger, 200-mile-long trail system managed by the Marin Municipal Water District. On the slopes are deep canyons with redwoods and Douglas firs, cascading creeks, grassland meadows, and ridges of manzanita and sandstone. An outdoor amphitheater hidden in trees hosts well-attended musicals every summer. You can also enjoy miles of trails in the friendly Mount Tam watershed, exploring pristine lakes. Also within the mountain's folds is Muir Woods National Monument, the nature lover's cathedral, with redwoods 500 years old covering 560 acres, filling the area with a rich aroma of citrusy needles and moist earth.

Out at the Marin Headlands, you'll find one of the best places in Northern California to watch raptors. Trails lead you through pretty countryside and into the rich history of the *vaqueros* (cowboys), Portuguese dairy farmers, military movements, and early seafarers. From Point Bonita Lighthouse, the San Francisco cityscape and Golden Gate Bridge prompt lots of picture taking.

> Up the mountain and down to the sea, a hiker can find a little bit of everything.

Mount Burdell, a distant cousin above Novato, gives the hiker a smaller mountain to climb, with meadows and a view into quarrying days. Nearby Olompali State Park is the site of a major Miwok Indian village that dates from A.D. 1100 to 1300.

While sacred to the Miwoks, Mount Tam also attracted foreign settlers, making their way up to the East Peak on the "world's crookedest railroad" to dance and drink or just admire the view. The rails gone, the route of the train is now a trail for hikers and mountain bikers, who climb the crest of the "Sleeping Maiden" as she emerges out of the fog in all her glory.

Muir Woods (Hike 7) © **Shutterstock**

Muir Woods: Bootjack Trail to Dipsea Trail Loop

On the first mile of your hike in Muir Woods, you'll contend with lots of camera-swinging tourists. Overwhelmed by the ancient trees and touched by the sheer tranquility of the place, many walk as if in a cathedral, whispering and respectful. Venturing past the milling masses, you are rewarded with solitude. There for your discovery are ridge trails lined with young pine trees dripping with grandfather's beard, bay and alder woodlands with flitting bushtits and hammering woodpeckers, sunny meadows, bridged streams with feathery ferns, hills full of huckleberries, and panoramic views of the Pacific.

Start: Muir Woods National Monument main entrance

Distance: 6.3-mile loop

Approximate hiking time: 3.5 hours

Difficulty: Moderately strenuous

Trail surface: 1 mile of paved pathway, then well-maintained, mostly single-track dirt trail

Other trail users: Equestrians

Canine compatibility: No pets

Land status: National monument

Fees and permits: Adults, $5; children 16 and under, free. National Park Annual Pass is $50; the Muir Woods Annual Pass is $20. There is no charge for parking.

Schedule: Open year-round from 8:00 a.m. to sunset unless otherwise posted

Maps: USGS San Rafael; Bolinas. A park map is available at Muir Woods National Monument, (415) 388-2595; or from the Web site at www.nps.gov/muwo.

Trail contacts: Muir Woods National Monument, Mill Valley, CA 94941; ranger's office, (415) 388-2595; Nature Hotline, (415) 388-2596; www.nps.gov/muwo. Muir Woods Visitor Center; (415) 388-7059; www.visitmuirwoods.com.

Other: Facilities are available only at the start of the hike. Dress in layers as the weather is changeable, especially in summer.

Finding the trailhead

By Car: From U.S. Highway 101 in Mill Valley, take Highway 1/Shoreline Highway toward Stinson Beach, following the signs. After 2.6 miles, turn right (north) onto the Panoramic Highway toward Muir Woods. After 0.8 mile, turn left (west) onto Muir Woods Road. After another 0.8 mile, turn right (north) to stay on Muir Woods Road. There is a large parking lot for the national monument. Roads to the park are steep and winding.

By Public Transportation: Free shuttle buses run during the peak summer season, on weekends and holidays only from Memorial Day weekend (end of May) through Labor Day weekend (first weekend in September). Shuttle buses operate as Golden Gate Transit Route 66 and run every half-hour between 9:30 a.m. and 3:30 p.m., with less frequent service after 3:30 p.m. The last bus departs Muir Woods at 7:05 p.m. Route 66 shuttle buses depart from two locations: the Marin City bus stop on Donahue Street at the Marin Gateway Shopping Center, and the Manzanita Park-and-Ride lot at the US 101/Shoreline Highway interchange. Signs direct visitors to shuttle parking areas and bus stops. For more information regarding the Muir Woods Shuttle, visit www.goldengate.org, or call 511 or Golden Gate Transit at (415) 455-2000.

THE HIKE

"This is the best tree lover's monument that could possibly be found in all the forests of the world."
—John Muir

In the early 1850s on Mount Tamalpais, hikers would have heard the sound of virgin redwoods and giant Douglas fir trees crashing to the ground. Lumber was in high demand for the booming new metropolises around San Francisco and Sacramento following the 1849 California gold rush. But because of inaccessibility caused by the steep slopes around it, the majestic old-growth forest in Redwood Canyon—now Muir Woods—survived. It is the only stand left in the Bay Area. Today's visitors mumble thanks as they wander down the path of giants.

In 1905, seeking to save the canyon from a dam and reservoir project, the wealthy Kent family bought 611 acres in the area and, in 1908, donated 295 acres, the heart of the canyon, to the American people. The Kents insisted the grove be named for their friend John Muir, champion of the nation's environmental movement. Agreeing, President Theodore Roosevelt proclaimed it a national monument.

Now, the monument attracts 1.8 million admirers every year. On summer weekends, the visitor center is packed, the roads are slow, and the parking lot is an obstacle course. (Try a weekday, or arrive before 10:00 a.m. for a day hike.) But even with the crowds, these giants, some more than 1,000 years old and over 200 feet tall, inspire and amaze. Traveling beyond the paved pathways, you may feel as if you know some great secret.

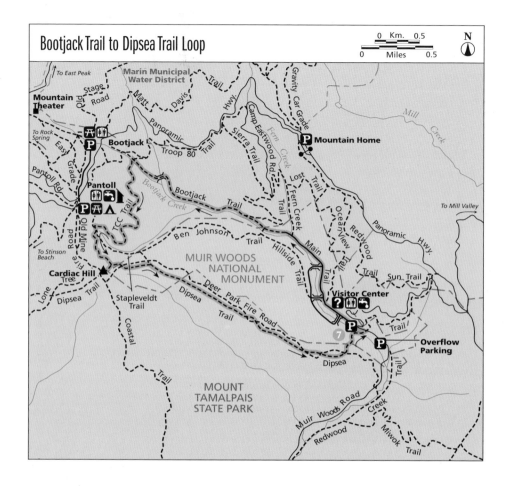

Bootjack Trail to Dipsea Trail Loop

Summer is the season of fog, azaleas, and aralias. With an abundance of nuts and flowering plants, gray squirrels scamper everywhere. Fall tends to be the warmest time of year, attracting ladybugs on the horsetail ferns and crayfish in Redwood Creek. Beautiful monarch butterflies pass through on their migration to the central coast of California and Mexico, where they winter. When rains start to fall, more than one hundred varieties of mushroom appear on the soaked forest floor, some popping up overnight and lasting only a few hours, others growing slowly and remaining for weeks. During winter, steelhead (migratory rainbow trout) and flashing silver or coho salmon migrate from the sea up Redwood Creek, their birthplace, to spawn.

Coming out of the canyon up Cardiac Hill, the open ocean view is startling. If clear, it is expansive. Rolling fog provides an equally dramatic sight. This is a great area to enjoy a picnic before the descent back into woodland.

Main Trail in Muir Woods—touristy for a good reason!

Muir Woods Seeds of Knowledge

- The widest tree in Muir Woods is 13.5 feet in diameter.
- Muir Woods was the seventh national monument, the first created from land donated by a private individual.
- Muir Woods is the only old-growth coastal redwood forest in the North Bay and one of the last on the planet.
- Nearly two million acres of forest once covered a narrow strip along the coasts of California and Oregon. Today, 97 percent of it has been destroyed or altered.
- An 800-year-old redwood tree toppled in Cathedral Grove on July 8, 1996. Fifty awestruck visitors watched as the 200-foot monarch fell with a roar that could be heard a half mile away. It caused no damage or injuries and was left where it fell to provide nutrients for the soil, nesting for birds, and bedding for plants.

Peering upward through a redwood

MILES AND DIRECTIONS

0.0 Start at the Muir Woods parking lot. Follow the main trail northwest along Redwood Creek. Bohemian Grove has some of the tallest trees in the park. Pass three bridges.

0.9 Take Bootjack Trail, continuing west along Redwood Creek. The path narrows and turns to dirt. The trail begins to climb; steps help with ascent.

2.3 Reach Van Wyck Meadow. Look for the large rock centerpiece and misspelled "population sign." Take the trail to the left of the meadow (posted STAPLEVELDT TRAIL), a Tamalpais Conservation Club (TCC) path. A bridge crosses the creek.

2.8 Reach a manzanita stand. To the left is a view of Mount Tam.

3.7 Go left (south) to stay on the TCC Trail. Shortly after this turn, you come to another trail marked TO STAPLEVELDT TRAIL, BEN JOHNSON AND DIPSEA. Stay to the right (west).

4.1 Reach the junction with the Dipsea Trail. Turn right (west) to climb uphill (about 200 feet) to Cardiac Hill.

4.5 Descend to the trail junction. Stay right to continue southeasterly on the Dipsea Trail, which crosses over Deer Park Fire Road several times.

4.7 Cross over a grassy hillside called the Hogsback.

5.9 The Dipsea Trail crosses Deer Park Fire Road, then bears left (east).

6.2 Reach the Dipsea Trail Bridge. Cross the creek. Turn left (north).

6.3 Return to the parking lot of Muir Woods.

Options: From Cardiac Hill, the Coast Trail heads down to Stinson Beach. You can also backtrack down Cardiac Hill and follow the Dipsea Trail to Muir Woods. This will take you to Deer Park Fire Road after 0.3 mile.

HIKE INFORMATION

Local Information: Mill Valley Chamber of Commerce, 85 Throckmorton Avenue, P.O. Box 5123, Mill Valley, CA 94941; (415) 388-9700; www.millvalley.org
Local Events/Attractions: Mountain Play Association, P.O. Box 2025, 177 East Blithedale Avenue, Mill Valley, CA 94942; (415) 383-1100; www.mountainplay.org
Hike Tours: Muir Woods National Monument ranger's office; (415) 388-2595; Nature Hotline, (415) 388-2596

In Addition: The Magic of Redwoods

The coastal redwoods (*Sequoia sempervirens*) are the tallest living things on earth (some over 360 feet tall) and grow only in the northwest United States, from Monterey County along the coast to Curry County in southwestern Oregon. But this was not always the case. In the age when dinosaurs roamed the earth, redwood forests covered the Northern Hemisphere. While the earth has shifted and reformed all around them, these trees have barely changed since the Jurassic period 170 million years ago.

Fog keeps redwood trees cool and moist in summer, and mild, wet winters keep the freeze away. The needles of the tree collect moisture and drop it onto its roots like rain. Redwoods have two ways of reproducing. One way is by seed from their small cones. But just as often, a new trunk begins as a sprout from the base of an old tree. These redwood sprouts create a burl ring, a dense mass of living shoots. The burl settles into the soil and grows wider with the new trunk, awaiting some sort of biological signal before shooting upwards to the sun. If the age of a redwood were measured by its roots, it could be 8,000 years old. Unidentified under the needle-carpeted floor in Muir Woods may be the oldest living woody plant on earth.

The rings of new trees are called family or fairy circles. Some people claim a spiritual connection standing in the middle of one. What we know for certain is that the trees in the circle are not separate individuals. All the trees make up one single living entity.

Repeated wind and fire do sometimes bring the trees crashing down, but not time. Unlike higher animals and other plants, redwoods do not seem to suffer physiological aging. They change as they get older, their growth slows down, but there is no inevitable deterioration like we experience as humans. They may be as close to immortal as anything on earth.

Phoenix Reservoir: Tucker and Bill Williams Trails

Beside a sparkling lake, admire a Victorian log cabin and watch anglers trying to land bass and trout. Below the branches of madrones, redwoods, bays, maples, and oaks, meander along a pleasant trail studded with wildflowers, including wild iris in spring. Under the shade of the redwoods in Bill Williams Ravine, discover a dam built in 1886.

Start: In the parking lot of Natalie Greene Park in Ross

Distance: 3.5 miles round-trip

Approximate hiking time: 2 hours

Difficulty: Moderate

Trail surface: A gravel road along the lake to a single-track dirt trail

Other trail users: Mountain bikers and equestrians around the lake

Canine compatibility: Leashed dogs permitted

Land status: Marin Municipal Water District

Fees and permits: No fees or permits required

Schedule: Open year-round sunrise to sunset unless otherwise posted

Maps: USGS San Rafael, CA. Mount Tamalpais Interpretive Association, P.O. Box 3318, San Rafael, CA 94901; (415) 258-2410; www.mttam.net

Trail contact: Marin Municipal Water District, 220 Nellen Avenue, Corte Madera, CA 94925; (415) 945-1455; www.marinwater.org

Finding the trailhead

By Car: From U.S. Highway 101 or Interstate 580 (Richmond/San Rafael Bridge), take Sir Francis Drake Boulevard west into the town of Ross. In Ross, take Lagunitas Road left (west) to Natalie Greene Park, past the tennis courts. The parking lot holds about twenty cars, and it fills up fast. Near the tennis club there is additional street parking. If you end up parking on the street, take the trail on the left (south) side of the street up to the hill. It will drop down to the main parking lot.

By Public Transportation: There is no direct route to the trailhead. For trip planning, visit www.goldengate.org or 511.org, or call 511 or Golden Gate Transit at (415) 455-2000.

🌿 Green Tip:
On the trail eat grains and veggies instead of meat, which has a higher energy cost.

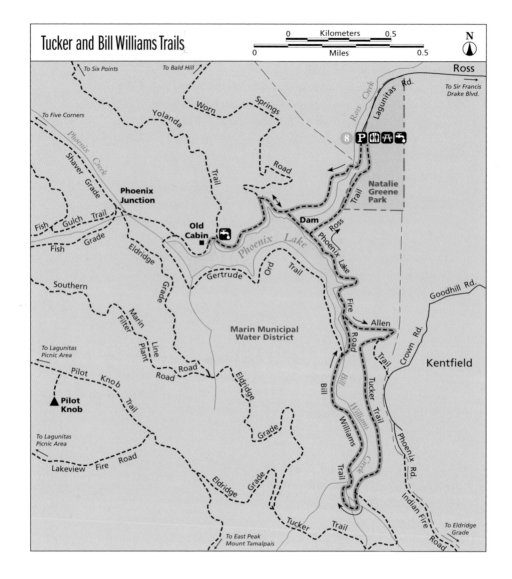

Tucker and Bill Williams Trails

THE HIKE

In 1905, dairy ranchers damned the Phoenix Dam that eventually created the reservoir. Built across the old Shaver stagecoach road, the dam was going to cut ranches off from Ross Station, which meant that milk had to be taken on the more tedious trip over the hill to Fairfax. Legend has it that, in resistance, one of the ranchers threatened the builders with a gun. In compromise, the Marin County Water Company built a road over the dam and up the canyon. This is the road that starts your hike on the right side of Phoenix Lake.

The Marin Municipal Water District (MMWD) now maintains the twenty-five-acre lake and its surrounding trails, a gem for local hikers, joggers, horseback riders, bicyclists, and anglers. It is equally beautiful wearing the oranges, yellows, and reds of autumn or the pastels of spring wildflowers; the dusted, green leaves and budding berry bushes of summer, or the artfully twisted branches of manzanita and buckeye trees against dewy ferns in winter.

You can create several pleasant routes here. This one features history and natural beauty. A walk on the gravel fire road by the reservoir takes you to a redwood log cabin erected in 1893 by estate owner Janet Porteous and her husband, James, for their coachman, Martin Grant. It predates the reservoir by twelve years. The Queen Anne–style turret over the front porch, the window frames made of an uncommon ribbon burl of wavy grain, and a pieced wood design on the front door seem out of place on a simple cabin. In the 1920s it was the only building spared in a fire that destroyed the rest of the Porteous estate. It was restored to its original condition in 1989.

Phoenix Lake from Phoenix Lake Fire Road, looking past a sycamore and a bay tree in autumn

Pied-billed grebes bob in the lake water and mallard ducks, wings spread for landing, break the glassy surface with a splash. Cormorants dive into the water after fish. Ospreys and hawks hunt from the trees. Anglers compete with the birds, shore fishing for black bass and trout. The Marin Rod and Gun Club's Fish Restoration Committee, in cooperation with the MMWD, has made the reservoir a self-sustaining bass fishery.

The single-track Allen Trail takes you into a small ravine with spring wildflowers and oak, bay, and buckeye trees. A wonderful cool, green smell of woodland gets even better on the Bill Williams Trail.

In the 1860s Bill Williams lived in a cabin upstream from the dam in the gulch that now bears his name. No one knows much about him, though some say he was a Confederate Army deserter. The biggest mystery, however, is where in the gulch he hid his buried treasure. The story goes that laborers building the Phoenix Dam spent more time looking for Bill Williams's gold than working. When the lake was drained in the mid-1980s, workers attempted another fruitless treasure hunt. The legend persists that Bill's hidden treasure remains buried here to this day.

But you can easily find this treasure of a trail, snaking into the canyon basin, following Bill Williams Creek into the seclusion of redwoods. Maidenhair and woodwardia ferns, trillium, huckleberry, creeping mint, and yerba buena make up the understory.

MILES AND DIRECTIONS

0.0 Start in the parking lot of Natalie Greene Park. Take the gravel road to the right (south).

0.2 The Phoenix Reservoir dam is on the left (south), the park residence to the right. Continue straight on the road to visit the old Queen Anne–style coachman's log cabin.

0.5 The coachman's log cabin is on the right (north). Turn around and head back to the dam.

0.8 Back at the park residence, bear right (south) to cross the Phoenix Reservoir dam. On the other side of the dam, continue along the road toward the Tucker Trail.

1.2 Reach the trailhead for the Allen Trail (which also connects to Crown Road). Turn left (east) onto Allen Trail. Harry S. Allen built the trail that bears his name as a shortcut from his summerhouse in Larkspur. The founder of Allen Newspaper Clipping Company, he was at one time president of the Tamalpais Conservation Club (TCC).

1.4 Reach a trailhead and fork in the road. Bear right (west) onto Tucker Trail toward Eldridge Grade. The trail passes over seasonal springs and through a small grove of redwoods. Tucker Trail runs south into Williams Gulch.

2.1 Reach the trailhead for Bill Williams Trail. Stay to your right (south, then north) on trail. Stairs help as you head downhill, still on a single-track dirt path. Around a hairpin turn at the end of the canyon, a bridge built by local Boy Scout Troop 101 in 2001 crosses the creek. This leads to the canyon floor, following Bill Williams Ravine, one of three feeder streams to Phoenix Lake.

2.2 Stay right on Bill Williams Trail past a small 1886 dam. (*Note:* A trail sign warns that path to the left is not a trail.) A trailhead in the middle of the trail leads to Phoenix Lake. Take this trail, which becomes double-track dirt. (*Note:* The trail can be muddy in winter.)

2.8 Return to the Phoenix Lake Fire Road. Continue by the lake until just before you reach the dam.

3.3 A trail sign on the right reads TO ROSS. Turn right (east) onto a single-track dirt trail. The parking lot is ahead and below; take one of two trails to the lot. The steeper trail comes out near pit toilets; the second trail is less steep and enters the lot 20 feet away.

3.5 Return to the parking lot.

Option: You can climb the Fish Gulch Trail from Phoenix Lake to Lake Lagunitas (1.9 miles) for a longer hike.

HIKE INFORMATION

Local Information: Town of Ross, P.O. Box 320, Ross, CA 94957; (415) 453-1453; www.townofross.org

Hike Tours: Mount Tamalpais Interpretive Association, P.O. Box 3318, San Rafael, CA 94901; (415) 258-2410; www.mttam.net

Steep Ravine Loop to Stinson Beach

*The Steep Ravine/Matt Davis/Dipsea Loop, with a stop at Stinson Beach, is consid-
ered by many the best hike in the North Bay. Start at Pantoll Station in Mount Tamalpais State Park. Heading downhill, you go through the dappled shade of mixed forest
and over grassy slopes soaking in the sunlight. Weaving down the trail past rock
outcroppings and trickling creeks with western views of sand and surf, you're suddenly in downtown Stinson Beach. Dipsea takes you through meadow and marsh to
Steep Ravine Trail, the pride of Mount Tamalpais State Park. In the deep-crested canyon, follow rushing Webb Creek under a canopy of tall redwoods. Up farther you are
rewarded with a 15-foot waterfall. Beside it is the 10-foot ladder, beloved by locals,
that you must clamber up to make your way back to the starting point.*

Start: From the Pantoll parking
lot, cross the main road to the
trailhead for Matt Davis Trail.
Distance: 7.2-mile loop
Approximate hiking time: 4 hours
Difficulty: Moderately strenuous
with a sturdy 10-foot ladder to
climb
Trail surface: Single-track dirt trail
with a short stint walking beside
the highway
Other trail users: Hikers only
except at Stinson Beach
Canine compatibility: No dogs
Land status: State park and
national recreation area
Fees and permits: $6 per car;
maps are free

Schedule: Open year-round from
7:00 a.m. to just after sunset unless
otherwise posted
Maps: USGS San Rafael; Bolinas.
A park map is available from the
Mount Tamalpais State Park's Pantoll Station, 801 Panoramic Highway, Mill Valley, CA 94941; (415)
388-2070; www.parks
.ca.gov/?page_id=471.
Trail contact: Mount Tamalpais
State Park Pantoll Station, 801
Panoramic Highway, Mill Valley, CA
94941; (415) 388-2070; www.parks
.ca.gov/?page_id=471
Other: There are full facilities at
Pantoll Station. Wireless Internet
service is available near the station.

Finding the trailhead
By Car: From U.S. Highway 101 in Mill Valley (between the Golden Gate Bridge
and the Interstate 580 interchange in San Rafael), exit onto Highway 1/Shore-
line Highway toward Stinson Beach. Follow the signs to continue on Highway
1 for about 4 miles to Panoramic Highway. Turn right (north) onto Panoramic
Highway and continue for about 4.5 miles to the junction with Pantoll Road.
Turn right (north) onto Pantoll Road and then left into the Pantoll parking lot.

By Public Transportation: From Marin City's Golden Gate Transit hub in the Gateway Shopping Center at Donahue and Terners Streets, take the West Marin Stage South Route (Rte. 61) to Pantoll Station or Stinson Beach. Seasonal Sunday service is offered from March 15 to November 15. For times and more information, contact West Marin Stage at (415) 526-3239 or go to www.marintransit.org/stage.html.

THE HIKE

Because this is a loop, you can start on either the Matt Davis or the Steep Ravine Trails from the Pantoll Station. Both ways are fantastic. Matt Davis and Dipsea Trails have the best views. Sunset at Table Rock on the Matt Davis Trail would definitely be memorable, and Steep Ravine Trail keeps you more entertained, but you want to see it for the first time in more than fading light.

The Matt Davis Trail takes you down through Douglas fir forest. Bridges take you over cascading creeks in the canyons. Then a blast of sunlight greets you in the grasslands that roll out, green in late winter and early spring, golden the rest of the year. The springtime hills host patchworks of yellow buttercups, orange poppies, and purple lupine. Raptors hover, hunting over the hillsides. You might see a bobcat run low to the ground for cover. Rabbits skitter by, especially at dusk and dawn. Open views to the northwest reveal Stinson Beach and the Bolinas mesa. To the southwest, Montara Mountain juts up beside the sea. Through every ravine is a reprieve in shaded woodland of firs, oaks, and California bay trees, perfuming the path with peppery spice. Table Rock presents a pleasant vista through trees that drip with grandfather's beard.

The Bischof Steps bring you to Belvedere Avenue and downtown Stinson Beach, along the Shoreline Highway. A short walk past boutiques, galleries, a deli, restaurants, and the local library takes you to the crescent-shaped beach.

🌿 Green Tip:
When hiking with your dog, stay in the center of the path and keep Fido close by. Dogs that run loose can harm fragile soils and spread pesky plants by carrying their seeds.

With light sand, level at the surf, Stinson Beach is good for wading and swimming. Lifeguards are on duty May through October. You can rent boogie boards, wet suits, surfboards, or kayaks from shops near the beach. With 3.5 miles of sand, it is a good running beach as well. Divided into three sections, the main part of the beach, by the parking lot, is run by the Golden Gate National Recreation Area (GGNRA). North of the parking lot, the county of Marin owns the land, and dogs are allowed. Farther north, the Seadrift subdivision, an upscale community of mostly weekend homes (some vacation rentals), owns the beach but allows public use. South of the Panoramic Highway, nestled in a cove, is clothing-optional Red Rock Beach.

Don't be alarmed if you hear the quick bleep of a siren while visiting. The Stinson Beach Siren is tested twice per day, at noon and 5:00 p.m. If you hear a fifteen-second continuous blast, you should evacuate to higher ground immediately (in the case of a tsunami or other disaster). Two short blasts indicate all clear.

Near where you came into town, a connector trail takes you to the Dipsea Trail, which ascends in oak woodland and descends gently into an open marshy meadow past a pond and an old military site, Hill 640. Up some stairs, the trail climbs moderately, parallel to the California shoreline, until it connects to Steep Ravine Trail. Dipsea is the oldest trail on Mount Tamalpais, dating back to dairy farm days. In 1905, it became the route of the famous 7.1-mile Dipsea footrace, the second oldest in the United States, from downtown Mill Valley to Stinson Beach. Each June 1,500 runners race down this trail. For more information visit dipsea.org.

In Steep Ravine, a lush, moist, cool canyon follows Webb Creek through redwoods and bay trees. Picturesque wood bridges crisscross the flowing stream. A popular 10-foot ladder takes you to the path above a rock face beside a plummeting waterfall. You will climb 1,000 feet in 2 miles. Near the top is the site of an old mining claim. Prospectors dug for gold and silver in 1863.

MILES AND DIRECTIONS

0.0 Start in Pantoll parking lot. Take wooden stairs up to the road and cross the Panoramic Highway carefully. You can see the trailhead for Matt Davis Trail.

0.4 Cross upper Webb Creek, continuing on the Matt Davis Trail, named for its builder, who worked on it for over fifty years.

1.2 The trail enters grassland open to sunlight and views. To the southwest is Montara Mountain.

1.7 At the junction with the Coast Trail, continue on Matt Davis Trail, the left (west) fork, to Stinson Beach. There are stairs around every switchback down wooded hillsides.

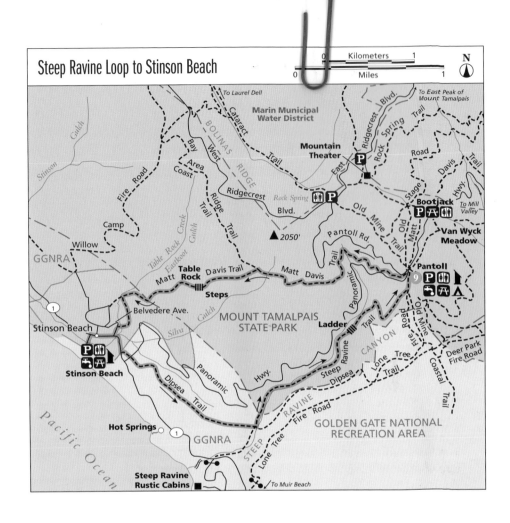

3.5 Stop at Table Rock (marked by a sign). Continue on the Matt Davis Trail. The Bischof Steps lead down 1,500 feet from Bolinas Ridge. (*Note:* Beware of rattlesnakes in this area. If you see one, leave it alone and walk away.)

3.9 At the trail junction, go left (south) and cross the bridge over Table Rock Creek. Where the trail splits ahead, go right. (The path to the left takes you to Panoramic Highway.) Table Rock Creek trickles down the Eastkoot Gulch by the trail.

4.1 Trail ends on Belvedere Avenue. Turn left, walking downslope past the community center to Shoreline Highway.

4.3 Turn right (north) and walk beside Highway 1 into downtown Stinson Beach.

4.5 Past most of the shops and restaurants on the coast side is the main entrance to Stinson Beach. Enjoy the beach, then return to Highway 1, heading south the way you came. Pass Belvedere Avenue. Look for Arenal Avenue, which goes west off Highway 1.

4.8 Across from Arenal Avenue, on the left (east) side of the street is the trailhead for Dipsea Trail. Turn onto double-track dirt trail.

5.0 The trail crosses the Panoramic Highway; cross carefully. Head toward Steep Ravine Trail.

5.3 Wooden platforms span a boggy area. Take stairs up to the fire road and cross the road to continue on Dipsea Trail.

5.8 At the trailhead for Steep Ravine, go left (northeast). Take Steep Ravine Trail back toward Pantoll through redwoods along the creek.

6.4 Climb up a 10-foot ladder beside a waterfall. There is no alternative route.

6.7 Steep Ravine Trail goes between two redwoods joined at the roots. Toward the top, go up stairs around switchbacks.

7.2 Come out onto the road at Pantoll. Walk up the road about 30 feet, and the parking lot is on your left.

HIKE INFORMATION

Local Information: Town of Stinson Beach; www.stinsonbeachonline.com
Tide Information: Tides Online; tidesonline.nos.noaa.gov
Hike Tours: Mount Tamalpais Interpretive Association, P.O. Box 3318, San Rafael, CA 94901; (415) 258-2410; www.mttam.net

East Peak Loop

This hike could be considered the "best of Mount Tamalpais," featuring the diverse habitat of the 6,300-acre state park and incredible views of the bay, cities, foothills, lakes, and ocean. Enjoy thick, quiet woodlands of coast redwood, Douglas fir, oak, bay, and madrone trees, as well as trickling waterfalls and cascading streams in moist ravines and canyons. Step out in wide, sloping, grass-covered meadows and along hillsides of gnarled manzanita and coyote brush. Pass by statuesque outcroppings of green serpentine and white chert and by tall banks of red, sunburnt soil and mossy green growth. The route also walks you through Mount Tam history, from popular East Peak down the Old Railroad Grade to the tavern at West Point Inn, and to an outdoor amphitheater with stone seats built in traditional Greek style.

Start: From the East Peak parking lot, walk down the parking area exit road (the paved road to the left is for hikers and bicyclists only), and turn left (south) through the gated Old Railroad Grade.
Distance: 7-mile loop
Approximate hiking time: 4 hours
Difficulty: Moderate; strenuous section on the International Trail
Trail surface: Some paved road, dirt fire road with an easy downhill grade, and single-track dirt trails through woods, chaparral, and grasslands. One trail has a short, steep, rocky incline.
Other trail users: Mountain bikers and equestrians on fire roads

Canine compatibility: Leashed dogs permitted
Land status: State park and municipal water district
Fees and permits: $6 day use fee
Schedule: Open year-round from 7:00 a.m. to just after sunset unless otherwise posted
Maps: USGS San Rafael. Muir Woods National Monument; (415) 388-2596; www.nps.gov/muwo
Trail contact: Mount Tamalpais Interpretive Association, P.O. Box 3318, San Rafael, CA 94912; (415) 258-2410; www.mttam.net
Other: Camps, picnic areas, and facilities are at several locations along the route, including at the trailhead

Finding the trailhead
By Car: From U.S. Highway 101 in Mill Valley (between the Golden Gate Bridge and the Interstate 580 interchange in San Rafael), exit onto Highway 1/Shoreline Highway toward Stinson Beach. Follow signs to continue on Highway

1 for about 4 miles to Panoramic Highway. Turn right (north) and continue for about 4.5 miles to the junction with Pantoll Road. Turn right (east) onto Pantoll toward the East Peak. Where the road splits again, go right toward the east ridgetop, traveling 4 miles to the East Peak parking lot. You will pass Air Force installation signs on the left (north).

By Public Transportation: The West Marin Stagecoach South Route (Rte. 61) provides four daily round-trips along the route of the Panoramic Highway through Mount Tamalpais State Park. There are marked stops in both the eastbound and westbound directions at the Mountain Home Inn, the Boot-jack Parking Lot, and the Pantoll Ranger Station. There is no service to the top of the mountain, but all of the aforementioned stops are close to trailheads that a hiker could take to get to and from East Peak. Schedules and service are subject to change, so check for the most current schedule before taking your trip by calling West Marin Stage at (415) 526-3239 or going to www.marintransit.org/stage.html.

THE HIKE

"Nevermore, however weary, should one faint by the way who gains the blessings of one mountain day."
—John Muir

At 2,571 feet, East Peak is the highest accessible point on the mountain. Before you've even begun hiking, the views are spectacular: On a clear day, you can see the Farallon Islands 25 miles out to sea, the Marin County hills, San Francisco and the bay, the hills and cities of the East Bay, and Mount Diablo. On rare occasions, you can even glimpse the snow-covered Sierra Nevada, 150 miles away. Most of this land belongs to the Marin Municipal Water District (MMWD). Mount Tamalpais State Park begins officially around the area of the Mountain Theater, although the park service also owns the parking lot and maintains the services on East Peak.

Weekdays or crisp winter days—some of the best on Tam—keep away the majority of the half-million people who drive to the top of the mountain each year. Unlike the weekend tourists, the native Miwok Indians rarely climbed the peak. The mountain was the place of "the poison people," or magic practitioners. Instead, they traveled into the foothills from their villages in Sausalito to hunt and gather grasses for ceremonies and seeds to eat. Hikers and outdoor enthusiasts began visiting the mountain as early as the 1800s. They came first by foot. Then, in the post–gold rush era, visitors rode partway up in stagecoaches. In 1896, Sidney Cushing and other

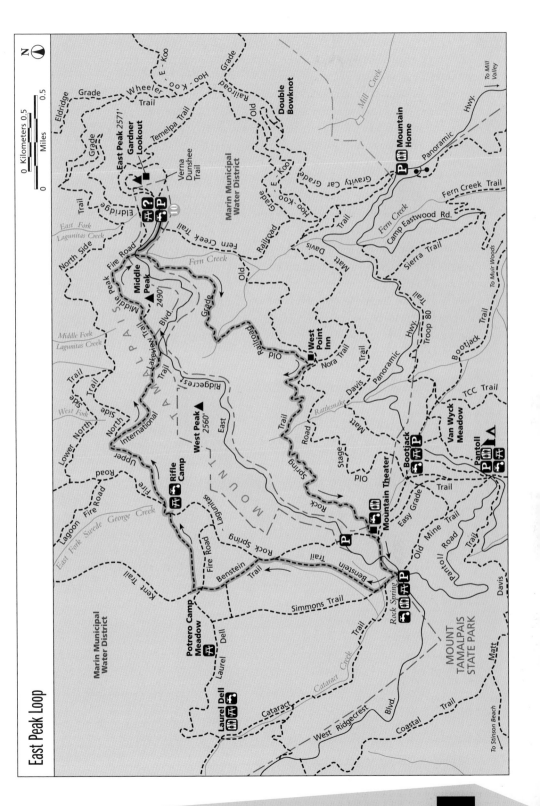

East Peak Loop

local businessmen bought rights to build a tourist railroad up to the East Peak. As you walk down the Old Railroad Grade, you follow its path.

The Tamalpais Conservation Club (TCC), a community group established in 1912 to be the "Guardian of the Mountain," raised $30,000 in 1928 to purchase the land to donate it to the state. In 1931 the park officially opened, encompassing over 6,000 acres covering the south slope, the ridgeline, and a portion of the west slope.

Of all the buildings once in operation on the mountain, only the Mountain Theater and West Point Inn are left. This hike visits both. Built in 1904, West Point Inn was a restaurant and stopover point for passengers taking the stage to Bolinas and Willow Camp (later renamed Stinson Beach). In the 1930s, the Civilian Conservation Corps (CCC) constructed the Mountain Theater, a natural-stone Greek amphitheater that seats 3,750 people. Other features include manzanita on Old Railroad Grade and banks of "blue goo," the thick clay holding hillsides together on Mount Tam. On the Rock Spring Trail, you'll pass numerous streams and small waterfalls. The Benstein Trail takes you through Douglas fir forest out into the wide Potrero Meadow. The Lakeview Trail gives you just that, with partial views of the watershed lakes through branches.

Serpentine rock field along Rock Spring Trail

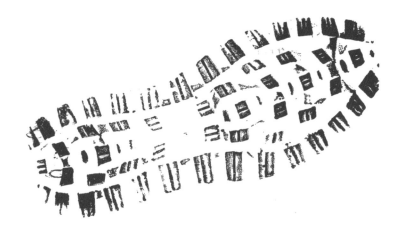

MILES AND DIRECTIONS

0.0 Start in the East Peak parking lot. Walk down the parking area exit road (the paved road to the left is for hikers and bicyclists only) to the Old Railroad Grade, a gated fire road.

0.1 Turn left (south) onto the Old Railroad Grade, passing an entrance gate (a sign reads TO WEST POINT AND MILL VALLEY). (*Note:* This is a popular trail for mountain bikers.)

1.6 Reach the West Point Inn. Pass the cabins on your left (south) and proceed to the main lodge. Across the driveway, to the west and slightly north of the inn, is the trailhead for the single-track Rock Spring Trail. Take the Rock Spring Trail west toward the Mountain Theater.

2.3 Enter the Mountain Theater. Continue along the upper tier straight onto the paved road that slopes down to Ridgecrest Boulevard.

2.4 Cross Ridgecrest Boulevard and turn right (north), walking about 40 feet. Turn left (west) onto the single-track dirt Simmons Trail.

2.5 Turn right (north) onto the Simmons Trail (Benstein reroute) to the Benstein Trail. Continue on the Benstein Trail through a meadow into the woods.

2.6 Turn right (north) onto the Benstein Trail. A series of hairpin turns leads uphill.

4.6 The Benstein Trail comes out on Lagunitas Fire Road. Turn left (north) and go about 20 yards to where the Benstein Trail continues to the left (north).

5.1 The Benstein Trail dead-ends on Laurel Dell Fire Road. Cross the fire road and continue straight (north) on a single-track dirt trail through a small grove of trees to Potrero Camp.

5.2 At Potrero Camp, turn right onto a single-track trail marked TO RIFLE CAMP. One of five ranches established on Mount Tam after the gold rush was located here.

5.5 The trail ends at Lagunitas Fire Road. Turn left (north) onto the fire road and walk 20 yards down the hill. Rifle Camp is on the right (east). Walk into Rifle Camp, down the stairs. On the other side of the camp is a trailhead; cross over the bridge and go straight (east on the trail to the left) on the North Side Trail (a sign reads TO ELDRIDGE GRADE). Follow the North Side Trail for about 0.5 mile. Pass a rock slide before reaching the International Trail.

6.0 Turn right (east) onto the International Trail.

6.5 The International Trail ends at Ridgecrest Boulevard. Do not cross the street. Turn left (east) and walk on the paved road 36 yards to the Lakeview Trailhead. Turn left (east) onto Lakeview Trail (to East Peak).

6.7 Turn left (northeast) onto Middle Peak Fire Road.

6.9 The fire road meets Ridgecrest Boulevard. Cross the road and turn left (east) onto the paved road marked for hikers and bicyclists only, heading up to the East Peak parking lot.

7.0 Return to the parking lot.

Option: To get to the true top of the mountain, take the ramped trail 0.3 mile to the observation area near the seasonal snack bar. The Verna Dunshee Trail is a twenty-minute loop around the peak itself, named for an avid hiker and protector of open space.

HIKE INFORMATION

Local Information: Mill Valley Chamber of Commerce, 85 Throckmorton Avenue, P.O. Box 5123, Mill Valley, CA 94941; (415) 388-9700; www.millvalley.org
Local Events/Attractions: Mountain Play Association, P.O. Box 2025, 177 East Blithedale Avenue, Mill Valley, CA 94941; (415) 383-1100; www.mountainplay.org
Hike Tours: Mount Tamalpais Interpretive Association, P.O. Box 3318, San Rafael, CA 94901; (415) 258-2410; www .mttam.net

The Crookedest Railroad in the World

To reach the peak in the early twentieth century, a 30-ton engine traversed a double bowknot, where the tracks paralleled themselves five times, the shortest radius of the curves at the turns being 75 feet. Locals and tourists alike riding the Mill Valley and Mount Tamalpais Scenic Railway delighted in jaw-dropping vistas at the summit, dinner at the Tavern of Tamalpais, and two-stepping in the dance pavilion on East Peak. At day's end, the daring would climb aboard the gravity car. The "gravity man" would "turn on the gravity," and down they would coast, around 281 turns on the mountain's 7 percent grade, to the Mill Valley depot or Muir Woods. The line became known as "the crookedest railroad in the world."

The $1.90 round-trip ticket from San Francisco to the summit attracted some 50,000 people each year. Sir Arthur Conan Doyle (of Sherlock Holmes fame) was among the passengers. "In all my wanderings, I have never had a more glorious experience," he said. Silent film actor and director Erich von Stroheim worked at the Tamalpais tavern starting in 1912 and met his first wife there.

In 1929, a great fire burned across the south face of the mountain, destroying 1,000 acres, primarily along the rail route. Already usurped in popularity and practicality by the automobile, the train was not resurrected, and soon thereafter the railway was torn up and the rails sold.

Few remnants of the historic buildings remain. The dance pavilion is now a parking lot. The tavern is the site of two geodesic domes that serve as radio towers. Near the end of the hike, look for a gravity car barn on East Peak, a permanent home for a re-created gravity car, and an interpretive display highlighting the railway's place in California and Mount Tamalpais history.

Green Tip:
If you're toting food, leave the packaging at home. Repack your provisions in ziplock bags that you can reuse and that can double as garbage bags on the way out of the woods.

Marin Headlands: Miwok Trail to Point Bonita

The Marin Headlands feature 15 square miles of beaches, marsh, lagoon, grass-covered valleys, and coastal hills with magnificent views. There is a large population of wild animals, including bobcats, mountain lions, and hunting raptors. You'll see about 150 years of military history, with batteries, bunkers, cannons, and missile launching sites all along the hike, adding an eerie contrast to the natural beauty. The walk also includes a tour of the Point Bonita Lighthouse that takes you through a hand-chiseled tunnel and across a suspension bridge to the dramatic site on a deteriorating cliff.

Start: Marin Headlands Visitor Information Center

Distance: 8.2-mile loop

Approximate hiking time: 4 hours

Difficulty: Moderate, with a few strenuous hills

Trail surface: Double-track and single-track dirt trails; a stretch of walking the beach and a sandy trail along the cliffs; a paved path to the lighthouse and some walking beside the road

Other trail users: Mountain bikers and equestrians; hikers only on Wolf Ridge, Rodeo Beach, and Point Bonita Trails

Canine compatibility: Leashed dogs permitted

Land status: National recreation area

Fees and permits: No fees or permits required

Schedule: The park is open 24 hours a day.

Maps: USGS Point Bonita. Muir Woods National Monument; (415) 388-2596; www.nps.gov/muwo

Trail contacts: Marin Headlands Visitor Information Center, Field Road, Marin Headlands, Sausalito, CA 94965; (415) 331-1540; www.nps.gov/goga. Golden Gate National Recreation Area; (415) 561-4700.

Other: The Marin Headlands Visitor Information Center is open daily from 9:30 a.m. to 4:30 p.m. Full facilities are available here. Point Bonita Lighthouse is open Saturday, Sunday, and Monday from 12:30 to 3:30 p.m. The Nike Missile Site and Nike Historical Society displays are open Wednesday to Friday and the first Sunday of each month from 12:30 to 3:30 p.m.

Finding the trailhead

By Car: The scenic route begins from U.S. Highway 101 just north of the Golden Gate Bridge. Take Alexander Avenue exit. If you are coming from the south, take an immediate left (west) turn, passing under the freeway. Turn right up the hill onto Conzelman Road toward the Marin Headlands. Be careful of bicyclists. Follow signs to the beach and Marin Headlands Visitor Information Center.

To leave the park, head out of the visitor center parking lot and turn left onto Field Road. At the yield sign, it becomes Bunker Road. Follow this out to the freeway. You go through a one-way tunnel with a five-minute traffic light. Follow signs to return to US 101 northbound and southbound.

By Public Transportation: Golden Gate Transit Route 2 provides service from San Francisco to the Marin Headlands Visitor Center on weekdays, except holidays. From downtown San Francisco, MUNI bus #76 stops at the Marin Headlands Visitor Center on Sundays and holidays only. Tickets are $1.25.

Other routes are available. For schedules, trip planning, and more information, contact Golden Gate Transit at (415) 455-2000, or visit www.transitinfo .org or 511.org. Other helpful contacts include Sausalito Taxi at (415) 332-2200; MUNI at (415) 673-6864; the Marin Airporter at (415) 461-4222; and Super Shuttle at (415) 558-8500.

THE HIKE

The experience of this hike actually starts on the drive in. The view of San Francisco and the Golden Gate and Bay Bridges from Hawk Hill (Battery 129) at the top of Conzelman Road is postcard perfect. After that point, Conzelman becomes a one-way street winding down to the headlands above death-defying cliffs. People afraid of heights should take the alternative route, using Bunker Road.

Where the hike starts, you have already stepped back in time, surrounded by whitewashed wooden buildings with red roofs. The visitor center was the old Fort Barry chapel; the youth hostel up the hill (two buildings) was the army hospital, dating back to 1907.

The Marin Headlands served as a military base until the late 1960s, designed, along with the Presidio, to protect San Francisco Bay from invasion from the Civil War through the Cold War. Sadly, each of the five installations constructed among the rolling hills was obsolete upon or before completion. Happily, none of them ever fired a gun.

The lagoon you pass—like Rodeo Beach—may have been named for the Rodier family, who settled nearby in the mid-1800s. Ducks, gulls, herons, and egrets are almost always present, resting in the reeds.

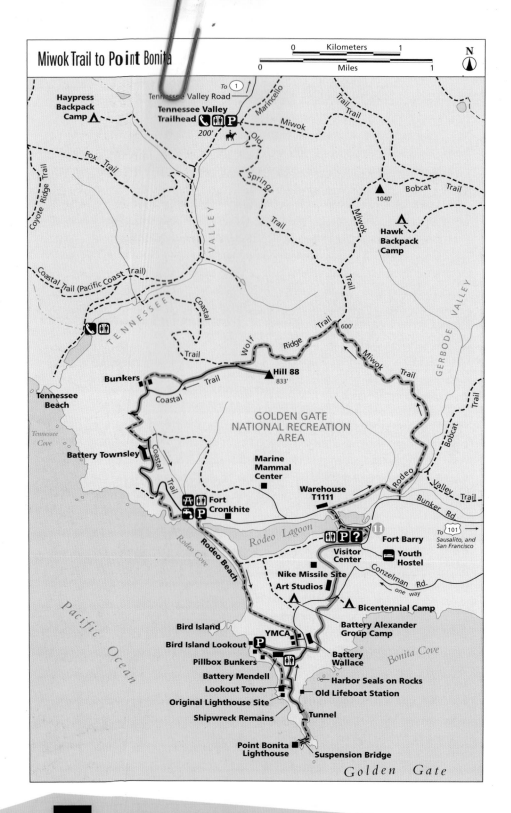

Miwok Trail to Point Bonita

Kilometers
0 — 1
Miles
0 — 1

N

To 1
Tennessee Valley Road

Haypress
Backpack
Camp ▲

Tennessee Valley
Trailhead
200'

Marincello
Trail

Miwok
Trail

Fox Trail

1040' ▲

Hawk
Backpack
Camp ▲

Coyote Ridge Trail

Springs
Trail

Miwok
Trail

Coastal Trail (Pacific Coast Trail)

TENNESSEE
VALLEY

Coastal
Trail

Coastal
Trail

600'

Wolf   Ridge   Trail

Miwok   Trail

GERBODE VALLEY

Bunkers

Hill 88
833'

Trail

Coastal

GOLDEN GATE
NATIONAL RECREATION
AREA

Bobcat
Trail

Tennessee
Beach

Tennessee
Cove

Battery Townsley

Coastal

Coastal Trail

Marine
Mammal
Center

Warehouse
T1111

Rodeo

Valley Trail

Bunker Rd.

Fort
Cronkhite

Rodeo Lagoon

Rodeo Cove

Rodeo Beach

Visitor
Center

Fort Barry

To 101
Sausalito, and
San Francisco

Youth
Hostel

Nike Missile Site
Art Studios

Conzelman   Rd.
one way

Bicentennial Camp

Bird Island

Bird Island Lookout

Pillbox Bunkers

Battery Mendell

Lookout Tower

Original Lighthouse Site

Shipwreck Remains

Point Bonita
Lighthouse

YMCA

Battery
Wallace

Battery Alexander
Group Camp

Bonita Cove

Harbor Seals on Rocks

Old Lifeboat Station

Tunnel

Suspension Bridge

Pacific Ocean

Golden   Gate

The Miwok Trail, starting at historic military warehouse building T1111, takes you above the Gerbode Valley into windswept hills. Alongside the trail are patches of tight-knit scrub, colorful rock outcrops, and marsh hidden in tall reeds and skinny trees. In late winter and spring, the valley and hills are covered with nearly fifty species of wildflowers. A pamphlet describing them is available at the visitor center. As the trail ascends into the hills, you are entertained by hunting raptors. The headlands are home to the Golden Gate Raptor Observatory's hawk watch site. Depending on the season, use your binoculars to spot ospreys, red-shouldered hawks, rough-legged hawks, ferruginous hawks, golden eagles, American kestrels, merlins, and peregrine falcons.

From Wolf Ridge Trail, you can look down at a farmhouse, barn, windbreak, and pond in the Tennessee Valley, a reminder of the area's ranching days. Up at the top of Wolf Ridge Trail is Hill 88, a former radar installation for guiding Nike missiles. Wander through the abandoned Cold War buildings and enjoy 360-degree views of Marin towns and foothills, the metropolis east and west of the bay, beautiful coastland, and the Pacific Ocean.

Down the Coastal Trail, you pass World War II–era bunkers and batteries to wander in and explore. The massive slabs of cement are slowly being taken over by nature. You can see where long-range cannons pointed out to the sea.

Rodeo Beach is popular with weekend sun worshipers and surfers. Because of its strong currents and deadly undertows, it is not recommended for swimming.

A highlight of the hike is a tour of Point Bonita Lighthouse. On the hike in, you can see the remains of a shipwreck, the bobbing black heads of sea lions in the water, and harbor seals lounging on rock islands. The lighthouse, built in 1855, was moved to its current location in 1877. It sits at the headlands' outermost tip. With the cliff slowly melting into the sea, someday the lighthouse will sit on an isolated sea stack. You will also pass the Nike Missile Site, with missiles on the premises. Even unarmed, they look spooky.

This route includes sections of road as well as trail to take in the many historic sites on the headlands, but there are plenty of trail-only hikes. Check a map at the visitor center for other options.

MILES AND DIRECTIONS

0.0 Start at the visitor center. A dirt fire road leads down the hill to Bunker Road.

0.1 Turn right onto Bunker Road and walk beside the paved road over the lagoon bridge to the old warehouse on the right (north) side of the road.

0.2 On the east side of the warehouse is the trailhead for Miwok Trail. Follow the Miwok Trail east (1.8 miles to Wolf Ridge Trail).

0.6 Stay on Miwok Trail, to the left (north) as it passes the trailhead for Bobcat Trail.

2.0 Reach the trail junction with the Wolf Ridge Trail. Turn left (west) onto the single-track, hikers-only trail. (*Note:* Stay on the trail to avoid poison oak.) To the northwest is one of the few remaining old ranch buildings in the Tennessee Valley. The valley and the cove were named for the 1853 wreck of the SS *Tennessee*.

2.7 At the junction with the paved Coastal Trail, turn left (east) to the top of Hill 88.

2.9 Reach the top of Hill 88. The buildings for the Nike Missile IFC (Fire Control) are still here, but are in a state of disrepair. At only 833 feet, the coastal view is amazing, north past Tennessee Point to the Point Reyes peninsula, south past Point Bonita to Ocean Beach, west to the Farallon Islands. Return to the trail junction and turn left (west), heading down on the Coastal Trail.

3.1 Continue down the paved Coastal Trail toward Rodeo Beach (2.3 miles). Notice remains of gun batteries. Below and ahead is Rodeo Beach and old military buildings.

4.1 Where the road has eroded away due to landslide, take the established dirt trail to the right (north) to an abandoned bunker. Continue on the dirt trail to the left of the bunker until you see the Pacific Coast Trail. You can take a quick detour west about 40 feet toward the cliff and trees where there's a great spot for contemplation. Take the single-track dirt Pacific Coast Trail down 106 steps.

4.2 Return to the paved Coastal Trail. Turn right (south). Listen for the foghorn of Point Bonita Lighthouse.

4.4 On the right side of the trail, look for a painted arrow on the pavement. It points to an otherwise unmarked dirt trail that veers left (south) down the hill. Take that trail. Where trail splits, stay left. You can see the paved Coast Trail below you.

4.6 Return to the paved Coastal Trail. Turn right (west) to Battery Townsley (a World War II defense station). Turn left (south) into the battery. On the ocean side of the gun station, follow the dirt trail to the left.

4.7 Pass another gun station of Battery Townsley. Head through the second tunnel of Battery Townsley to its entrance. Turn right (south) onto the paved Coastal Trail.

View from lighthouse station of the Golden Gate Bridge and San Francisco Bay

5.1 At a curve in the road—near an inviting grassy hillside—there is a double-track dirt trail right of the road toward Rodeo Beach. Take this trail to Rodeo Beach. When it splits, bear left toward the beach on the path with the wooden railing.

5.3 The trail again meets the paved Coastal Trail. Turn right (south) and walk the remaining short distance to the beach.

5.4 Arrive at Rodeo Beach. Walk along the beach, heading south, toward the bluffs on the other side. The sea stack beyond the point is Bird Island. Beyond it, to the west, is a shallow sandbar called the Potato Patch. (*Note:* Surf is dangerous here.)

5.7 Head up the bluff on the steep, single-track sand trail nearest the water. The unmarked path goes toward the Point Bonita Lighthouse. Bear right (southeast) on double-track dirt trail toward the YMCA Conference Center.

5.9 Enter the YMCA center area and walk toward the resident staff building. At the end of the building, turn right (west) onto a single-track dirt path that heads toward Battery Mendell.

6.1 Go right (west) on the paved road past Battery Mendell to the Bird Island overlook parking lot.

6.3 Take the dirt path left (south) along the cliff, passing two World War II–era pillboxes.

6.5 At the far end of Battery Mendell, continue along cliff.

6.6 The trail passes through the split trunks of a tree. Up ahead is an old Coast Guard radar tower. Continue along the cliff. The trail curves left. Take it out to the parking lot.

6.7 Turn right (south) onto the main paved trail to Point Bonita Lighthouse. Look down and to the right (west) to an isolated beach and the rusty remains of a wrecked ship. Watch to the left (east) for an old pier and the remains of the Life Saving Station, established in 1899.

6.9 On the right (west) side of the trail is a square cement foundation. This is where the fog signal was located before it was moved to its current location next to the lighthouse visitor center. The trail takes you through a tunnel when the lighthouse is open.

7.0 On the other side of the tunnel are interpretive signs and a view of San Francisco. After crossing the suspension bridge, look up at the bluff from the right side of the lighthouse building to see its original 1855 location. After touring the lighthouse, go back out the main path to the Point Bonita parking lot.

7.3 From the parking area, take the main road right (north).

7.4 On the left (west) side of the road, just beyond the stop sign, is a single-track dirt trail going up the hill to Battery Wallace. Take this trail.

7.7 Reach Battery Wallace (1942). Go through the battery tunnel to the main road. Turn left (north) and walk beside the road.

7.8 To the left is the last Nike missile site. Follow the signs TO BEACH, SAUSALITO, SAN FRANCISCO, turning right (north) at the stop sign. On the left (west) beside the missile site is the Marin Headlands Center for the Arts studio building.

8.2 Return to the visitor center and parking lot.

HIKE INFORMATION

Local Information: City of Sausalito; (415) 289-4100; www.ci.sausalito.ca.us

Local Events/Attractions: Bay Area Discovery Museum, 557 McReynolds Road, East Fort Baker, Sausalito, CA 94965; (415) 339-3900; www.baykidsmuseum.org

Golden Gate Raptor Observatory, Building 201, Fort Mason, San Francisco, CA 94123; (415) 331-0731; www.ggro.org

Headlands Center for the Arts, Building 944, Fort Barry, Sausalito, CA 94965 (415) 331-2787; www.headlands.org

Marine Mammal Center, Marin Headlands, 1065 Fort Cronkhite, Sausalito, CA 94965; (415) 289-7325; www.marinemammalcenter.org

Nike Historical Society, P.O. Box 602, Alameda, CA 94501; www.nikemissile.org

Hike Tours: Marin Headlands Visitor Information Center, Field Road, Marin Headlands, Sausalito, CA 94965; (415) 331-1540; www.nps.gov/goga/marin-headlands.htm

Golden Gate National Recreation Area; (415) 561-4700

Marin Municipal Water District: Kent Trail along Alpine Lake

A little bit of everything and a hike that takes you away from it all: This is an exhilarating walk along the conifer shores of Alpine Lake, up through a dark redwood forest onto a manzanita-covered ridge with good views. Along the way, you can pick huckleberries in the early fall, and admire many water-loving flowers among the ferns and mosses along the banks. This is treasured watershed land in Marin, for both its consumer and recreational value.

Start: Bon Tempe Dam near the Marin Municipal Water District's Sky Oaks watershed headquarters. Start at the parking area below the dam and head uphill to the spillway.

Distance: 5.2-mile lollipop loop

Approximate hiking time: 3 hours

Difficulty: Moderate

Trail surface: Gravel and dirt road followed by a narrow dirt path that climbs rather steeply for about 800 feet and is a bit rocky in places. A double-track fire road takes you back down to the dam.

Other trail users: Equestrians on all; mountain bikers on Rocky Ridge Road

Canine compatibility: Leashed dogs permitted

Land status: Municipal water district

Fees and permits: $7 per vehicle.

An annual pass is $50; for seniors the pass is $25.

Schedule: Open year-round from sunrise to sunset unless otherwise posted; gates close at 9:00 p.m.

Maps: USGS Bolinas; San Rafael. Mount Tamalpais Interpretive Association, P.O. Box 3318, San Rafael, CA 94912; (415) 258-2410; www.mttam.net. Maps are also available at the Sky Oaks kiosk when it is open.

Trail contacts: Sky Oaks Ranger Station, Fairfax-Bolinas Road, Fairfax, CA 94930; (415) 945-1182 on weekends. Marin Municipal Water District, 220 Nellen Avenue, Corte Madera, CA 94925; (415) 945-1455; www.marinwater.org.

Other: Restrooms are available at the Sky Oaks Ranger Station when it's open; drinking water is available there anytime (close to the source, too).

Finding the trailhead

By Car: From U.S. Highway 101 or Interstate 580 (Richmond/San Rafael Bridge), take Sir Francis Drake Boulevard west into Fairfax. Turn left onto Claus at the wooden Fairfax sign, right (west) onto Broadway, left (southwest)

onto Bolinas Road, then left (south) onto Sky Oaks Road. You will see a sign: LAKE LAGUNITAS, BON TEMPE AND WATER TREATMENT PLANT PARK GATE. Turn right (southwest) onto the road to Bon Tempe.

By Public Transportation: There is no direct route to the trailhead. For trip planning, call Golden Gate Transit at (415) 455-2000 or visit www.golden gatetransit.com. You can also call 511 or visit 511.org.

THE HIKE

Leaders of the ninety-year-old Marin Municipal Water District (MMWD) would tell you that managing the 24,000-acre watershed comes first, recreation is second. But both seem a passion and a pride.

Around the watershed's five reservoirs, and through the surrounding forests, the MMWD maintains 130 miles of trails. Kent Trail skirts Alpine Lake, which shimmers through mature Douglas firs and skinny, peeling madrones like a Sierra scene. Inlets near the trail expose hundreds of minnows squirming in the water, feeding on algae.

The MMWD has stocked Alpine and Bon Tempe Lakes with rainbow trout. Bass, bluegill, crappie, and catfish are also here. Anglers pick key spots along the shore; the Bon Tempe Dam seems to be a favorite. They report that the trout in Alpine tend to be larger—12 to 15 inches—but are harder to catch than in Bon Tempe. Catch and release is encouraged.

Along Kent Trail in spring, elegant white and lavender iris show off their blooms. Hound's tongue, pink shooting stars, and delicate white milkmaids decorate the forest floor. Farther along, there are patches of grassland with orange poppies and yellow buttercups. Deer like to graze on the wild oats and Spanish grass during morning and late afternoon hours. Jackrabbits are also numerous, but are more often heard than seen in the scrub. Butterflies flutter at the bases of oaks in summer.

Turning inland from the lake, the sunlight dims as you enter a grove of redwoods. Sword and maidenhair ferns fawn onto the moist earth.

On the sun-drenched Stocking Trail, the scenery takes a dramatic change, opening up into manzanita barrens, hillsides full of red snarled branches and green-penny leaves. The uphill trek to Rocky Ridge Fire Road rewards you with views.

In an area plagued by drought every ten years or so—California is, after all, mostly desert—the priority of the water district makes a lot of sense. In drought years, expect the lake levels to go down, like they did

during 1976–77, when MMWD gained recognition for its innovative conservation program that resulted in a 67 percent reduction in community water usage; or in 1986–89, when Marin County experienced the driest 32 months in 110 years and Lake Lagunitas, usually kept in reserve, had to be tapped as a water supply. The oldest water district in the state, it supplies 61 million gallons of water a day to 170,000 inhabitants in southern and central Marin County.

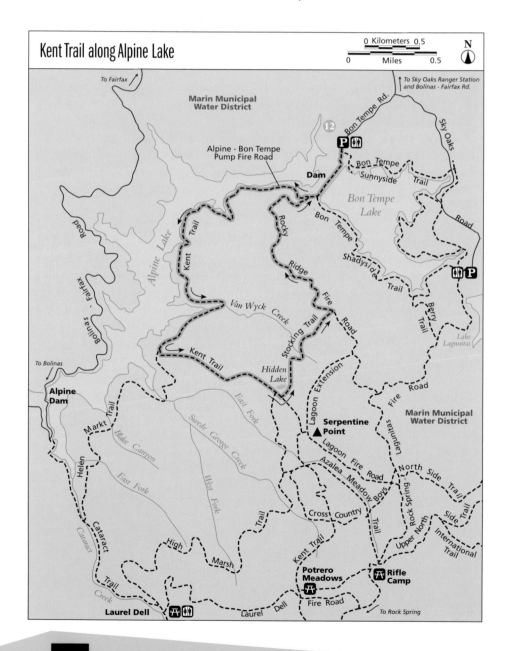

Kent Trail along Alpine Lake

Peaceful Alpine Lake from Bon Tempe Dam

The Mount Tamalpais area makes an ideal watershed. Storms from the coast climb up the steep ridge. The rapid lifting of clouds causes warming. They wring out over the mountain, and the rainwater "runoff" drains into Lagunitas, Ross, Redwood, and Old Mill Creeks and the seven reservoirs. Some 791 miles of pipelines, 134 storage tanks, 103 pump stations, and two treatment plants work to get the water to the people. Erosion control, whether through controlled burns, combating nonnative plant species, or limited road development, is very important. The quality of the water is directly related to the quality of the watershed, a good thing for us hikers.

MILES AND DIRECTIONS

0.0 Start at the parking lot below Bon Tempe Dam, then head uphill to the spillway. Cross the 94-foot-high dam overlooking Bon Tempe Lake, which is on your left (southeast).

0.3 Continue right (northwest) to Alpine Lake. The trail splits; take Kent Trail by turning right (northwest), heading downhill on the double-track trail above Alpine Lake. (The trail is also known as Alpine–Bon Tempe Pump Fire Road.)

0.8 The road ends at a pump house where water from Alpine is pumped to Bon Tempe Lake and on to a treatment plant. Kent Trail becomes single-track and follows curves of Alpine Lake.

1.8 Kent Trail continues through a conifer forest. Following the shoreline, the trail winds around the lake, then enters Van Wyck Canyon, with two small waterfalls and a bridge. The trail also passes into a silted canyon with a narrow streambed.

2.3 About 100 yards past the trailhead for Helen Markt Trail (to Cataract Gulch), take the Kent Trail left (southwest), away from the lake. After skirting Foul Pool on the right, the trail follows the east fork of Swede George Creek into a redwood grove.

3.1 Reach a junction with multiple trails. Go straight (south) on Stocking Trail to Hidden Lake. The trail heads downhill for about 200 yards, passing Hidden Lake. The trail then turns northeast and follows the ridge; to the left (northwest) is Van Wyck Creek.

3.5 Cross a bridge and continue on Stocking Trail away from the creek. The path leads to a heavily wooded area, then manzanita barrens and open prairies.

3.7 Stocking Trail dead-ends at Rocky Ridge Fire Road. Turn left (north). About 200 feet ahead is a great view of the bay: Angel Island, the Marin foothills and homes, and the Richmond refineries across the bay. The road then heads downhill. (*Note:* Watch for loose rock.)

4.9 Return to Bon Tempe Lake. Cross the spillway, and return the way you came.

5.2 Arrive back at the parking lot.

🌱 Green Tip:
Carry a reusable water container that you fill at the tap.
Bottled water is expensive; lots of petroleum is used to
make the plastic bottles; and they're a disposal nightmare.

HIKE INFORMATION

Local Information: Town of Fairfax, 142 Bolinas Road, Fairfax, CA 94930; (415) 453-1584; www.town-of-fairfax.org

Hike Tours: Mount Tamalpais Interpretive Association, P.O. Box 3318, San Rafael, CA 94930; (415) 258-2410; www.mttam.net

Marin Watershed Weather

- The greatest seasonal rainfall recorded is 112 inches in 1889–90.
- Maximum twenty-four-hour rainfall total is 10.45 inches on March 4, 1879.
- Twenty-five days of nonstop rainfall were recorded in December 1889, January 1916, and March 1983.
- The longest period of subnormal rainfall occurred from 1927 to 1934.
- The statistical relative improbability of two winters as dry as 1975–76 and 1976–77 is about 1 in 300.

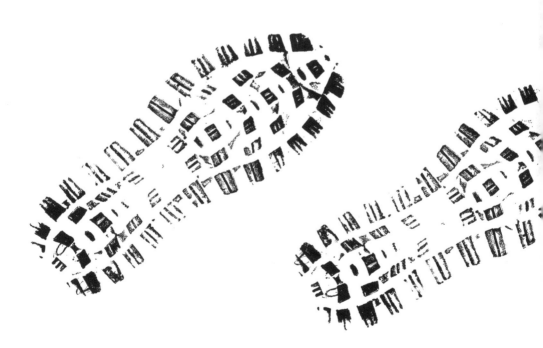

13

Mount Burdell Open Space Preserve

It's understandable why the Miwok Indians chose to keep a village at the base of Mount Burdell for 6,000 years. The rise they called Olompali had oaks shedding acorns, their main food source, and grasslands that supported plenty of animals to hunt for food. Starting in Novato's backyard, this hike ascends this once bountiful mountain, now passing quarry sites. It takes you over great expanses of golden grassland, sprinkled with a rainbow of wildflowers and butterflies in spring. It dips under the dappled shade of bay and oak trees, along gurgling seasonal creeks, then back onto open hillsides before you finally reach the ridge of this extinct volcano, Novato's highest hill. A low stone wall invites you to sit. Though hardly wilderness with a repeater station and satellite atop the crest, the views are still rewarding.

Start: At the open space preserve gate near the end of San Andreas Drive

Distance: 5-mile loop

Approximate hiking time: 2.5 hours

Difficulty: Strenuous because of elevation change

Trail surface: The dirt trail is rocky in places. It climbs through oak savanna and drops 1,400 feet in elevation. Much of the trail is in shade. The hike ends on a gravel fire road.

Other trail users: Mountain bikers and equestrians on fire roads

Canine compatibility: Leashed dogs permitted

Land status: Open space preserve

Fees and permits: No fees or permits required

Schedule: Sunrise to sunset unless otherwise posted

Maps: USGS Petaluma River; Novato. Marin County Open Space District, Marin County Civic Center, 3501 Civic Center Drive, Room 415, San Rafael, CA 94903; (415) 499-6387; www.co.marin.ca.us/depts/pk/main/index.cfm or www.marinopenspace.org

Trail contact: Marin County Open Space District, Marin County Civic Center, 3501 Civic Center Drive, Room 415, San Rafael, CA 94903; (415) 499-6387; www.co.marin.ca.us/depts/pk/main/index.cfm or www.marinopenspace.org

Other: No facilities in this preserve

Finding the trailhead

By Car: Take U.S. Highway 101 north past San Rafael. Take the Atherton/San Marin exit in Novato. At the light, turn left (west) onto San Marin Drive, passing through a neighborhood. Turn right (north) onto San Andreas Drive. Near the end of San Andreas Drive, look for the open space preserve gate on the right side of the road. Parking is on the street.

By Public Transportation: There is no direct route to the trailhead. However, Golden Gate Transit can get you within a half-mile walk via bus #70 or #113. For walking directions, schedules, fares, trip planning, and more information, visit 511.org or www.goldengatetransit.com or dial 511 or (415) 455-2000; within Marin go to marintransit.org.

THE HIKE

At Mount Burdell, signs of the past mix with views of the present. In the foreground are Spanish grasses, old quarry roads, and exposed patches of ancient rock. Views include distant suburban streets and a busy US 101 corridor. Mount Tamalpais rises high and quiet to the southwest, and the rivers of the Sacramento River delta snake through the valley to the northwest.

Around twelve million years ago, long after the ocean had receded and the coastline (15 miles farther out then) had sprouted life, molten rocks worked their way up through the jumbled oceanic rocks here, creating a rise of lava over the Franciscan sandstone and serpentine. This disturbance became Mount Burdell. Landslides over the years continued to shape the mountain, until bunchgrass, native scrub, and oak and bay trees took their place, growing in and over the rocky mixture.

When the Miwok Indians arrived, they called the mountain Olompali, "southern village" or "southern people." For hundreds of years, they lived in a village at its base, hunted successfully, and gathered acorns. Sir Francis Drake reported in his 1579 journals that the people were friendly and contented, blessed with an abundant food supply and an excellent climate.

And then Olompali was taken away. The Spanish, Mexican, and later American governments gave the land to settlers, encouraging them to ranch and farm the area. In some ways, it still feels like old ranch land, as you hike through meadows and canyons and up the side of the mountain, passing under oaks and bays. This oak savanna, so typical of the Bay Area, was once part of the 8,877-acre Olompali Rancho, a wedding gift to dentist Galen Burdell and his wife, Mary Black, from her father.

Now the park is bordered by houses and horse stables. The mountain has been returned to the birds, squirrels, and deer. But steep-cut hills and deep depressions in the earth that you see from the trails are reminders of the busy quarries that in 1888 produced the cobblestones to pave the streets of San Francisco. The southeast spur was quarried for asphalt as late as 1954.

Mount Burdell is now part of the Marin County Open Space District, which, since 1972, has preserved nearly 14,000 acres of land in thirty preserves. The Mount Burdell preserve totals 1,558 acres, most of it on the south-facing slopes above the city of Novato.

MILES AND DIRECTIONS

0.0   Go through the open space gate and turn right (southeast) onto the flat double-track dirt trail. After about 350 feet, turn right (southeast) onto San Marin Fire Road. It starts up the hill and passes San Andreas Fire Road.

0.2   Bear left (east) onto Big Tank Fire Road.

0.4   Turn right (east) onto the signed, hikers-only Michako Trail. Pass over a seasonal creek that has the potential of mud after rain. Pass through a cattle gate.

0.8   The Michako Trail bears right at the water trough.

0.9   Turn left (northeast) onto San Carlos Fire Road. It loops around a curve. Stay on San Carlos past the intersection with Salt Lick Fire Road.

A tree with acorns resembling Christmas tree ornaments in the meadow

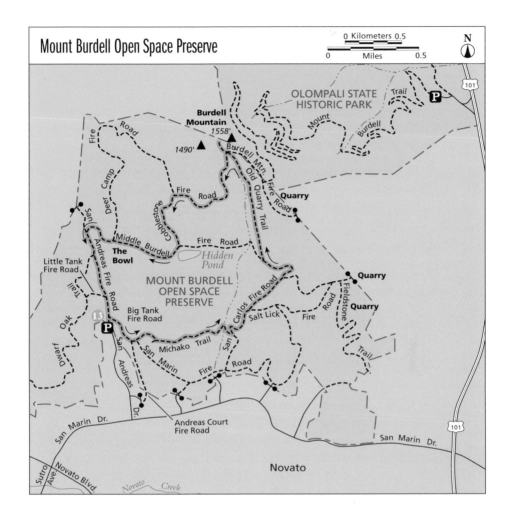

Mount Burdell Open Space Preserve

0 Kilometers 0.5

0 Miles 0.5

N

OLOMPALI STATE
HISTORIC PARK

Burdell
Mountain
1558'

1490'

Burdell Mtn. Fire Road

Quarry

Fire Road

Fire Road

Old Quarry Trail

Cobblestone

Deer Camp

Fire Road

San

Andreas Fire Road

Middle Burdell

The
Bowl

Little Tank
Fire Road

Hidden
Pond

MOUNT BURDELL
OPEN SPACE
PRESERVE

Quarry

Quarry

Fieldstone Road

Oak Trail

13

Big Tank
Fire Road

San Carlos Fire Road

Salt Lick

Fire

Trail

Dwarf

San Andreas Dr.

Michako Trail

San Marin Fire Road

San Marin Dr.

Andreas Court
Fire Road

San Marin Dr.

Novato

Sutro Ave.

Novato Blvd.

Novato Creek

101

101

1.3 Turn left (north) onto the Old Quarry Trail. Cross through a gate. The trail starts out flat, curves under a few trees with hillside views, and starts to ascend.

1.5 Take a short jog left onto Middle Burdell Fire Road and then turn right (north) onto the Old Quarry Trail where it resumes. For a while, this trail gets steep and rocky.

2.2 Old Quarry Trail ends at a junction with Cobblestone Fire Road and the paved and gravel Burdell Mountain Fire Road, which is also part of the Bay Area Ridge Trail. Go straight (north), crossing over the Burdell Mountain Fire Road and up the hill. A stone wall is ahead, built by Chinese laborers in the 1870s. At the fence, enjoy views to the north. Head back down to the trail junction on the fire road.

2.3 Take the double-track dirt Cobblestone Fire Road that heads at a 45-degree angle right (west) of the Old Quarry Trail. It is also part of the Bay Area Ridge Trail. Watch your footing in loose rocks on the trail. The trail moves into partial shade and becomes smooth and moderately sloped.

2.9 At the junction with Deer Camp Fire Road, continue straight (west) on the Cobblestone Fire Road, away from the summit. You can also go right on Deer Camp Fire Road, part of the Bay Area Ridge Trail, which is a loop.

3.3 Turn right (west) onto the Middle Burdell Fire Road. To your left (east) is Hidden Pond; beyond it lies The Bowl, a lovely meadow in fall and summer that is under restoration.

3.8 Stay left (west) on Middle Burdell Fire Road. Deer Camp Fire Road goes off to the right (north).

4.2 Turn left (south) onto the gravel San Andreas Fire Road, also part of the Bay Area Ridge Trail.

4.8 Stay on the San Andreas Fire Road past the Dwarf Oak trailhead and Little Tank Fire Road trailhead.

5.0 Return to the gate on San Andreas Drive.

Options: On another day, try hiking the north face of this mountain in Olompali State Historic Park (www.parks.ca.gov). Another choice, if you have two cars, is to park one in Olompali State Park. Take this hike to where Old Quarry Trail meets the Cobblestone Fire Road. Turn right (east) onto Burdell Mountain Fire Road. Turn left (northwest) onto Upper Mount Burdell Trail into Olompali to Lower Mount Burdell Trail to the park entrance.

HIKE INFORMATION

Local Information: Novato Chamber of Commerce, 807 DeLong Avenue, Novato, CA 94945; (415) 897-1164; www.novato.org

Local Events/Attractions: Miwok Park/Marin Museum of the American Indian, 2200 Novato Boulevard, Novato, CA 94945; (415) 897-4064; www.marinindian.com Novato History Museum, 815 DeLong Avenue, Novato, CA 94945; (415) 897-4320 Olompali State Historic Park, off US 101 in Novato; (415) 892-3383; http://parks .ca.gov/default.asp?page_id=465

Hike Tours: Marin County Open Space District, Marin County Civic Center, 3501 Civic Center Drive, Room 415, San Rafael, CA 94903; (415) 499-6387; www .co.marin.ca.us/depts/pk/main/index.cfm or www.marinopenspace.org

Ring Mountain

A small ridgetop between the towns of Tiburon and Corte Madera, Ring Mountain is enjoyable to hike and explore, although mountain is a misnomer. Still, the hike includes a moderate 600-foot climb that invigorates. On the way up, enjoy expanses of native grasslands, a compact bay, oak, and buckeye woodland, sculptural rock outcrops, trickling seasonal springs, and colorful wildflowers. Miwok Indians left signs of their habitation here 2,000 years ago, and environmentalists left traces of the strong spirit with which they fought to protect these precious 377 acres for hikers and nature lovers.

Start: On Paradise Drive in Corte Madera, just past Westward Drive

Distance: 2.3 miles round-trip

Approximate hiking time: 1.5 hours

Difficulty: Moderate

Trail surface: A mostly sunny dirt trail that climbs and descends 600 feet; some rocky and rutted areas, one short stretch in woodland

Other trail users: Mountain bikers and equestrians on fire roads

Canine compatibility: Leashed dogs permitted

Land status: County open space preserve

Fees and permits: No fees or permits required

Schedule: Open year-round from sunrise to sunset unless otherwise posted

Maps: USGS San Quentin; San Rafael. A map may also be obtained from the Marin County Department of Open Space, 3501 Civic Center Drive, Room 415, San Rafael, CA 94903; (415) 499-6387; www.co.marin.ca.us/depts/main/index.cfm or www.marinopenspace.org

Trail contact: Marin County Open Space District, 3501 Civic Center Drive, Room 415, San Rafael, CA 94903; (415) 499-6387; ranger's office, (415) 499-6405; www.co.marin.ca.us/depts/main/index.cfm or www.marinopenspace.org

Finding the trailhead

By Car: From U.S. Highway 101 in Corte Madera, take the Paradise Drive/Tamalpais Drive turnoff. Head east off the freeway and take the first right (south) turn onto San Clemente Drive, which becomes Paradise Drive. Park on Paradise Drive just past Westward Drive, and keep walking along the street toward the Marin Country Day School. Look for the nature preserve sign and gate on the right (south) side of Paradise Drive.

14

THE HIKE

At the start of the hike, the single-track Loop Trail crosses a bridge in Triangle Marsh, full of sticky gumplant, salt grass, salty pickleweed, and cordgrass. In the rainy season, the muddy fill is like solidified gelatin underfoot. In the fall, the ground is dry; the leaves on the scrub turn golden and orange behind clumps of toyon berries, and the grasses, thin and suntanned, sway in the slightest breeze.

Across the bridge, a plaque dedicates this preserve "in loving memory of Patricia Bucko-Stormer . . . at the Nature Conservancy." To a nature lover, this is a memorial worth noting. Before the international, nonprofit membership organization bought the land as part of their mission to "preserve plants, animals, and natural communities that represent the diversity of life on earth," Ring Mountain was threatened. Local groups, charged by the Marin Branch of the California Native Plant Society, battled to save it. And even on this small parcel there's a lot to save.

Of greatest pride is the Tiburon mariposa lily (*Calochortus tiburonensis*). Its long, shiny bronze leaves and yellow-green flowers can be seen nowhere but Ring Mountain. In 1973 Dr. Robert West, a physician and amateur photographer and botanist, identified the plant as a new species. Other rare plants include Marin dwarf flax, Tiburon buckwheat, Tiburon paintbrush, and Oakland star tulip.

The springs and watercourses in the rocks along the trail provide habitat for many resident animals and insects. The most unique is the rare and endangered blind harvestman spider, a type of daddy longlegs. While most of its kind are cave dwellers, this species resides under rocks on exposed hillsides, a true anomaly.

Though the spider may be blind, the three mice that commonly dwell here are not. Meadow mice move through tunnels in the valley to reach seed. Harvest mice, nocturnal omnivores, make birdlike nests in the marshes. Deer mice, a rather cuddly cinnamon brown with white underbellies, hide in burrows in the forest and feed at night on berries and insects.

Humans used to live here, too. Miwok Indians ground acorns in bedrock mortars along one of the seasonal streams. They left a midden site, basically a refuge heap, and a temporary occupation site on the mountain. They made petroglyphs, or rock carvings, in thirty sites on the mountain, the only ones recorded in Marin County.

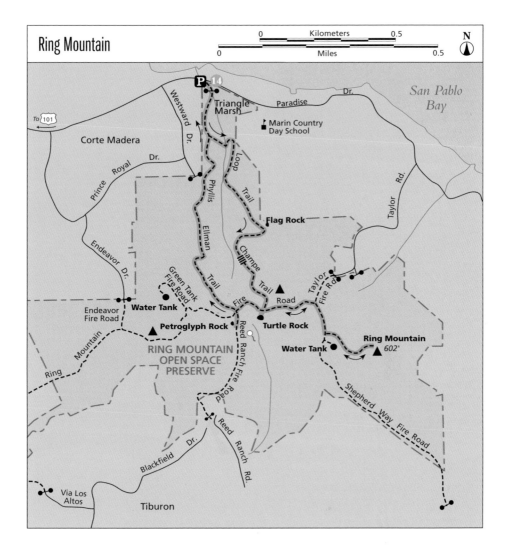

Ring Mountain is like a small island for nature and hiking, with Corte Madera, Sausalito, and the bay at its base. Climbing up, you see the ominous San Quentin Prison and ferries and freighters skidding through the bay. The serpentine soil that you walk on is a truly unique mixture, which includes a rare mineral called lawsonite. Looking closely, you may see miniscule garnets and watermelon tourmaline sparkling in the dirt.

Climbing through clumps of hobbit trees and up hills with grass rippling, you reach Turtle Rock. Only 602 feet above sea level, it still offers expansive views of bayside towns and the San Francisco skyline. To the west are the Marin Headlands, the towers of the Golden Gate Bridge, and shapely Mount Tamalpais. The loop brings you back to the bridge over the marsh.

The Statue of Man rock outcropping

MILES AND DIRECTIONS

0.0 Start at Paradise Drive in Corte Madera, just past Westward Drive. Look for the nature preserve sign and gate on the right (south). Go through the gate. The trail crosses a small bridge to an information display. Pick up a nature guide if it is available; you can also call the Open Space District Field Office to order one before your hike at (415) 499-6387.

0.2 Just past the information display, the trail splits. Take the trail to the left (east) through a stand of blackberry bushes and onto Loop Trail. There are sixteen numbered signposts on the self-guided nature trail. Turn right at marker #2 for the nature walk. The trail heads up moderately past some boulders.

0.3 At marker #4, there are several unofficial crossing trails. Continue right (south) on the main trail. It parallels a stand of oak and bay trees on the right.

0.4 At marker #5, turn left (east). Pass through grassland.

0.5 A rock maze is to the left (east) of marker #6. The biggest rock is named Flag Rock. Years ago, Marin Country Day School children used to play Capture the Flag near it.

0.7 Reach post #7. Look left (east) up the hill to see the Statue of Man rocks set in a clump of juniper trees. Cross two bridges; follow the trail straight up about 20 feet, then take the trail right (west) across the mountain and slightly downhill (parallel to the bay). The trail flattens out, curves, and heads toward the bay. Railroad ties protect trail edges. Stay to the left, going uphill. At marker #8 there's a shady little grove. On the railroad ties TRAIL and an arrow are carved into the wood to assure you that you are on the right trail.

0.8 At a trail post, with more railroad ties to mark your way, turn right into the grove of bay trees. Though not posted, this is the Champe Trail, named for the Nature Conservancy intern who laid out this part of the trail. The main trail takes you through the woods. Bear left to marker #10 where you can view Mount Tamalpais. The trail again splits, but you can see the next marker. The single-track trail opens up at marker #11.

0.9 Cross over the gravel and dirt ridge road to Turtle Rock. Walk east on the fire road along the hilltop.

1.1 The road becomes paved. Turn around and head back to Turtle Rock.

1.3 Back at Turtle Rock, head west on Ring Mountain Fire Road.

1.4 Reach the trailhead for the Phyllis Ellman Trail. At marker #13, to the left (east), is where the Tiburon mariposa lily grows. Turn around and proceed north on the Ellman Trail back toward the start.

2.3 Arrive back at the gate and Paradise Drive.

Options: To add another 2 miles to this hike, take the dirt road off the Ring Mountain Fire Road and head up the hill to the west, along the ridge and back.

HIKE INFORMATION

Local Information: Corte Madera Chamber of Commerce, 129 Corte Madera Town Center, Corte Madera, CA 94925; (415) 924-0441; www.cortemadera.org
Hike Tours: Marin County Open Space District naturalist-led interpretive walks; (415) 499-6405; www.marinopenspace.org

Honorable Mentions

C. Cataract Trail

One trail and a dozen waterfalls—that's the wonderful ratio on the Cataract Trail. Above Alpine Lake in the Mount Tamalpais watershed, the trail follows Cataract Creek uphill steeply. The first waterfall is less than a 100 yards up. And they get bigger and louder as you climb.

The trailhead is on Bolinas Road above Fairfax and beyond the Alpine Lake Dam (limited parking). About a mile up the trail, a wooden bridge crosses Cataract Creek. Take the fork to the right beyond it, following the creek until it levels out into a wide meadow and the Laurel Dell picnic area. The trail, though short, is of a fairly sharp grade. Give yourself plenty of time before dark, and stay on assigned trails.

From the Laurel Dell picnic area, you can connect to many trails on Mount Tamalpais. For a pleasant loop, take the Laurel Dell Fire Road to the Potrero Meadows picnic area. Cross the bridge and make a left (north) turn onto the Kent Trail. This connects to the Helen Markt Trail around the edge of Alpine Lake. You can take the Markt trail back to the Cataract Trail bridge. Or you can turn around at the top of the Cataract Trail and go back down the hill, admiring the falls from the top down for a round-trip of 2 miles. Either way, be sure to take a look at the Alpine dam before you go.

To get there, take U.S. Highway 101 to the Sir Francis Drake Boulevard exit. Follow the boulevard west to the town of Fairfax. Veer right (west) to Broadway, and turn left (south) onto the Bolinas-Fairfax Road. Go about 5 miles. Beyond the Alpine dam, the parking area is located near the hairpin turn and the trailhead. For more information, call the Sky Oaks Ranger Station at (415) 459-5267.

D. Camp Tamarancho

Camp Tamarancho allows hiking and mountain biking on its trails only with a permit. That makes the 480 acres of meadows, hillsides, lake, and redwood forests even more of an adventure. Managed by the Marin Council of the Boy Scouts of America, it houses a locally loved Boy Scout camp each summer. It is especially popular with mountain bikers, who thrill on the single-track trails. The trailhead is located off of Iron Springs Road in Fairfax. For a permit application, maps, and trail conditions, go to www.boyscouts-marin.org or call (415) 454-1081.

California poppies © Shutterstock

San Francisco and the Bay

View of Marin County from Mount Livermore—Tiburon, Belvedere, and Sausalito

San Francisco is one of the most visited cities in the world, with top-notch restaurants, museums, theaters, professional sports teams, music venues, and unique stores. But what many people don't know is that it also boasts the largest urban park system in the world, extending far north and south of the city. A short distance from this great metropolis, you could spend every weekend exploring some new trail or outdoor adventure. The coastal ranges and valleys support all kinds of plantlife and wildlife, both in water and on land. There's even great hiking right in the city.

A hike in Golden Gate Park goes through botanical gardens and memorial groves, past lakes, a rose garden, grazing bison, and Dutch windmills. At Lands End, 4 miles of Ocean Beach and Fort Funston offer scenic running or strolling. The Coast Trail can take you past China Beach and Baker Beach all the way to Fort Point and across the Golden Gate Bridge to Sausalito if you want. It also takes you to the

Presidio, the oldest continuously operated military post in the nation, which was transferred to parkland in 1994 and has been re-created as a live, work, and play space. Lovers' Lane, a forest of trees and military history, is there to explore. Crissy Field, once an airstrip, has lawns for picnicking near newly restored wetlands.

A ferry ride on the bay starts a memorable day of hiking on Angel Island. Past the infamous Alcatraz Island, its prison buildings still intact, the boat docks at Ayala Cove. Hiking or camping up on Mount Livermore, the island is yours for a day or a night. Trails take you through history that reaches from the Civil War to the island's use as an immigration station and later as a World War II army hospital.

To check out native plants more closely, consider the pleasant loop through chaparral to the peak of San Bruno Mountain. Fog may hamper the view, but that's the nature of the city by the bay.

The native coffeeberry on San Bruno Mountain

15

Angel Island State Park

You have to love a hike that you can only reach by ferry. But the Angel Island hike does not take you away from it all. Instead, you take in gobs of civilization from a lofty and isolated plateau. On a clear day from the top of Mount Livermore, you can see all four major bridges on the Bay. You can watch the fog roll over the city like a slow-moving avalanche. Even with limited visibility, you can admire landmarks of the unique San Francisco skyline, the street-faire towns of Sausalito and Tiburon, and a prison-to-prison view from San Quentin to Alcatraz, both with their fascinating histories. That's the keyword here: history. Angel Island, the largest island in San Francisco Bay, spans a microcosm of U.S. history, from its days as hunting ground for native Americans to serving as a Civil War post for the Union and a prisoner-of-war camp during World War II, and finally, as a public park.

Start: From Ayala Cove on Angel Island

Distance: 6.2-mile loop

Approximate hiking time: 3 hours

Difficulty: Moderate, with a climb and descent on Mount Livermore, then fairly flat the rest of the way

Trail surface: A single-track, well-maintained footpath leads to Mount Livermore. A less maintained path leads down to a double-track dirt road, then the paved road around the perimeter of the island.

Land status: State park

Other trail users: Mountain bikers on roads

Canine compatibility: No dogs permitted

Fees and permits: The round-trip ferry fare is $18 for adults; children

(5 to 11) are $10; juniors (12 to 18) are $14. Children 4 and under are free. If coming by private boat, slips are available from 8:00 a.m. to sunset for $10. Mooring buoys are $20 per night, first come, first served.

Schedule: Open year-round from 8:00 a.m. to sunset unless otherwise posted

Map: USGS San Francisco North

Trail contact: Angel Island Association, P.O. Box 866, Tiburon, CA 94920; (415) 435-3522; park information (415) 435-3972; www .angelisland.org. For group and docent tours, call (415) 435-3522.

Other: Bring a picnic lunch and carry water. Binoculars and a Bay Area map are recommended. To read more about Angel Island history, buy an Angel Island map brochure for $1.

THE HIKE

When you disembark from the Blue and Gold ferry at Ayala Cove on Angel Island, you are already steeped in history. For nearly 2,000 years, when the salmon were spawning through Raccoon Strait, the Miwok rowed across the bay from their Marin homeland in narrow canoes made of tule to camp, hunt, fish, and gather acorns.

In August 1775 Juan Manuel de Ayala, whose mission was to complete the first accurate survey of the area for future Spanish conquest, christened this little island Isla de Los Angeles. Over the years, the island served as a Spanish cattle ranch, a quarry during the war between Mexico and the United States, a Civil War installation, a quarantine station during the Spanish-American War, a detention camp during the Philippine Insurrection, an army discharge depot and processing center, a World War I immigration station, a World War II POW camp, and a Nike missile site.

In 1892 the quarantine station was opened at Ayala Cove (known as Hospital Cove). The forty buildings at the cove included a 400-bed detention barracks, a disinfection plant, and laboratories. The buildings are gone now, except for the bachelor officers' quarters (now the park museum) and the surgeons' homes, used as park offices.

Serpentine climbing leads up the steep Northridge Trail, where you pass native island trees and shrubs: oak, bay, and madrone, sagebrush, chamise, manzanita, toyon, elderberry, and coyote brush. Deer and raccoons live on the island, but you don't see them much anymore. In the 1970s, the deer overpopulated the island. They were so tame you could pet them, and they hovered over picnickers on Ayala Beach. After efforts to export the deer became too expensive, many were killed to protect the ecology of the island.

Mount Livermore (781 feet) is named for Marin County conservationist Caroline Livermore, who led the campaign to create Angel Island State Park in 1958. On a clear day, you have fabulous views of San Francisco, the Golden Gate Bridge, and the Marin Headlands. Look east to the Bay Bridge, Treasure Island, and on the East Bay hills, the campanile of the University of California–Berkeley and the castle-like Mormon Temple.

A bridge on Sunset Trail

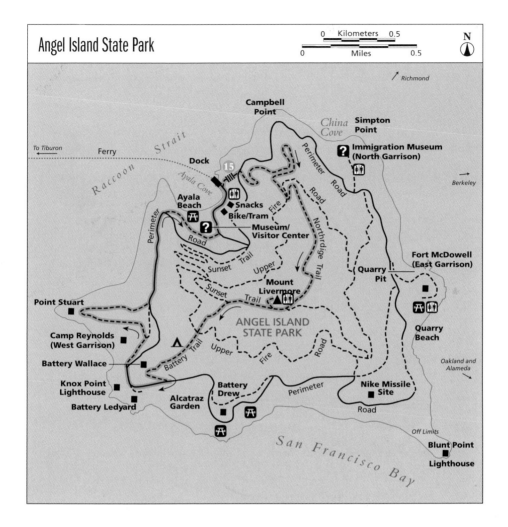

Angel Island State Park

Kilometers 0.5

Miles 0.5

N

Richmond

Campbell Point

China Cove

Simpton Point

Strait

To Tiburon

Ferry

Dock

15

Immigration Museum (North Garrison)

Raccoon

Ayala Cove

Berkeley

Ayala Beach

Snacks

Bike/Tram

Museum/ Visitor Center

Fire

Perimeter

Road

Northridge Trail

Fort McDowell (East Garrison)

Perimeter

Road

Sunset

Trail

Upper

Sunset

Trail

Mount Livermore

Quarry Pit

Point Stuart

ANGEL ISLAND STATE PARK

Quarry Beach

Camp Reynolds (West Garrison)

Battery

Trail

Upper

Fire

Road

Oakland and Alameda

Battery Wallace

Knox Point Lighthouse

Battery Ledyard

Alcatraz Garden

Battery Drew

Perimeter

Nike Missile Site

Road

Off Limits

Blunt Point Lighthouse

San Francisco Bay

Heading down the unmarked Battery Trail, you pass spectacular campsites. Suddenly, you'll see a massive block of cement. This is Battery Wallace. In 1886 a report critical of Pacific Coast harbor defenses led to the development of gun batteries facing the Golden Gate. You can't miss another massive slab, Battery Ledyard on the Perimeter Road. Five years after they were built, these artillery units became obsolete and were decommissioned.

In just a few minutes' walk on Perimeter Road, you come to Angel Island's Civil War site, Camp Reynolds. Fearing Confederate sympathizers might slip into the Bay and attack Union resources, the federal government established Camp Reynolds in 1863, among other installations. Rebel troops never did invade; accounts of soldiers stationed here reveal that their biggest challenge was fighting boredom.

After a pleasant loop to Point Stuart, it's about twenty-five minutes back to the Ayala Cove ferry terminal. On the ride back, you can plan your next visit to tour the other side of Angel Island, with Fort McDowell and the immigration station.

MILES AND DIRECTIONS

0.0 Start at the ferry dock in Ayala Cove. Facing inland, turn left (northeast). The Northridge Trailhead is clearly marked and starts with wooden steps.

0.1 Cross over Perimeter Road. Northridge Trail continues up across the road to the right (northeast).

1.2 Cross over the dirt Fire Road. Northridge Trail continues on the other side of the road.

2.4 Reach the Sunset Trail. Follow the trail north to the top of Mount Livermore.

2.7 Arrive on top of Mount Livermore. Return to Sunset Trail.

3.0 Turn right (west) onto Sunset Trail.

3.3 Reach a well-defined but unmarked trail to the left (southwest). Turn left onto unsigned Battery Trail. (*Note:* Watch for poison oak.)

3.5 Pass over Fire Road, continuing on the Battery Trail.

3.8 Battery Wallace is on the right (north).

3.9 Reach Perimeter Road. Turn right (north) to head toward Camp Reynolds.

4.1 Pass Battery Ledyard on the left (west).

4.3 Take the path that heads down to the left of Perimeter Road to the chapel.

4.5 Reach Camp Reynolds (West Garrison). At the top of the slope are the officers' quarters, gardens, and bake house. Walk the grassy parade yard down toward the bay to see the cannon fired. Facing the officers' quarters, go left on the small road that curves west toward Point Stuart.

4.7 Pass restrooms on the left.

4.9 Reach Point Stuart. Continue as the road turns to a hiker-only footpath going east toward Perimeter Road.

5.3 Back on Perimeter Road, turn left (north).

5.7   Take the footpath on the left (north) to Ayala Cove. The signs reads TO THE FERRY DOCK.

6.0   Arrive at the visitor center, picnic area, and Ayala Beach.

6.2   Reach the ferry dock.

HIKE INFORMATION

Local Information: Angel Island Tram Tours and Catered Events at (415) 897-0715; www.angelisland.com

San Francisco Convention and Visitors Bureau, Visitor Information Center, 900 Market Street, San Francisco, CA 94102; (415) 391-2000; www.onlyinsanfrancisco .com. You can also visit bayarea.citysearch.com.

Local Events/Attractions: Angel Island Immigration Station; (415) 435-3522

Fort McDowell, East Garrison, Angel Island; (415) 435-3972 or (415) 435-5390; www.angelisland.org

Hike Tours: Angel Island Association, P.O. Box 866, Tiburon, CA 94920; (415) 435-3522 or (415) 435-3972; www.angelisland.org

🌿 **Green Tip:**
Be courteous of others. Many people visit natural areas for quiet, peace, and solitude, so avoid making loud noises and intruding on others' privacy.

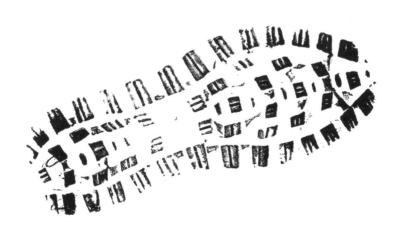

Cliff House Walk at Lands End

A popular family trail, this wide and pleasant dirt path follows the cliffs above the bay. It occasionally heads inland through scrub and eucalyptus trees, then works back to stunning views of the Golden Gate Bridge. A short stint on city sidewalks takes you past the mansions of upscale Sea Cliff. The hike heads to historic China Beach, where you can talk to surfers returning from a morning at Lands End, the popular surfing spot you can see from Eagle's Point.

Start: Trailhead at the end of the parking lot on Merrie Way off Point Lobos Avenue

Distance: 4.3+ miles round-trip

Approximate hiking time: 3 hours (including stops at Sutro Baths, Camera Obscura, and Ocean Beach)

Difficulty: Easy

Trail surface: A double-track dirt trail narrows to a single-track. One short stint is on city sidewalks.

Other trail users: Mountain bikers

Canine compatibility: Leashed dogs permitted on the Coast Trail; no dogs permitted on China Beach

Land status: Golden Gate National Recreation Area

Fees and permits: No fees or permits required

Schedule: Park grounds are open 24 hours a day.

Maps: USGS San Francisco North. Download a map from www.nps.gov/goga or pick one up at visitor centers.

Trail contact: Golden Gate National Recreation Area, (415) 561-4700; www.nps.gov/goga

Other: If you're making a day of it, check out the California Palace of the Legion of Honor museum, just off the trail and across from the Lincoln Park Golf Course.

Finding the trailhead

By Car: In San Francisco, follow Geary Boulevard west. Geary turns into Point Lobos Avenue. Turn right (north) onto Merrie Way and the parking lot. Two other large parking areas are available across the street on Point Lobos Avenue and just up the hill on Seal Rock Drive.

By Public Transportation: Take an outbound Route 38L: Richmond District or 38 Geary or 31 Balboa bus, and ride to the end. Call Golden Gate Transit at (415) 923-2000 or MUNI at (415) 673-MUNI (6864); www.transitinfo.org.

Looking down at Sutro Baths ruins from Merrie Way parking lot, with Seal Rocks beyond

THE HIKE

Lands End is a tourist destination and as such can be crowded on weekends, so this is not a getaway trail. But it's well worth visiting for the views and fits the bill if you want a short, scenic hike.

The walk along the cliffs immediately offers you breathtaking views of the Marin Headlands across the Golden Gate, with Point Bonita Lighthouse on the westernmost tip and, of course, the copper-stained Golden Gate Bridge.

You will also pass the manicured lawns of the Lincoln Park Golf Course, which hosts the San Francisco City Golf Championship, the oldest and largest continuous event in U.S. golf history. (A monument on the cart path northwest of the clubhouse remembers it as a site of an old Chinese cemetery.) The California Palace of the Legion of Honor, next to the golf course, hosts an impressive collection of mostly European art, featuring an early cast of *The Thinker* by Rodin.

The only way to China Beach, if you don't have a boat, is on city sidewalks, but the short walk through the prestigious Sea Cliff neighborhood takes you past beautifully designed, multimillion-dollar homes, many built soon after the 1906 earthquake. China Beach was once a small camp, a shrimping and abalone gathering spot, and by the 1880s a safe anchorage for Chinese fishermen, who made up 50 percent of all fishing crews in the Bay Area. In 1979, the National Park Service took over protection of the historic location.

At the trailhead, you can visit the ruins of the grand old Sutro Baths. Erected by philanthropist Adolph Sutro in 1886, the six baths, large amphitheater, and three restaurants sprawled across three acres. Photos in the Cliff House show the grand public park and statuary that San Franciscans visited here in the 1880s and 1890s. In 1966, land developers bought the Sutro Baths site to build high-rise apartments and began demolition. A fire destroyed what was left. In 1980, the remains became part of the Golden Gate National Recreation Area.

The historic Cliff House was originally built in 1858; the current structure in 1909. (The mansion had survived the 1906 earthquake, only to burn to the ground in a fire the next year.) The fifth Cliff House opened in 1950. From the Sequoia Lounge or the observation deck, you can watch the hundreds of sea lions, pelicans, gulls, and cormorants that gather on Seal Rocks, beyond the Sutro ruins.

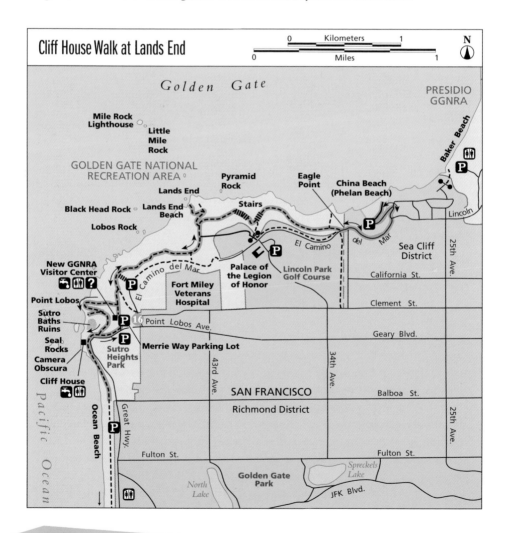

Cliff House Walk at Lands End

The Camera Obscura, a tourist attraction dating from 1948, is on the National Register of Historic Places. Inside, you stand in a darkened room and watch as a rotating lens and mirror (based on a design by Leonardo da Vinci) project a panoramic view of the area.

Looking south from the Cliff House, you see the greenbelt of Golden Gate Park, ending with its windmills. Surfers and dog walkers claim Ocean Beach, the longest beach in the San Francisco area, which offers a wonderful extension of your hike if you enjoy a sandy stroll. It is known for its cold, windy conditions and ferocious waves (not for swimming), though you can sometimes find fantastic sunbathing days in the fall. For a fine picnic spot or to extend your stroll, cross Point Lobos Avenue from the trailhead to Sutro Heights Park. These were once the gardens and grounds surrounding Sutro's mansion.

MILES AND DIRECTIONS

0.0 Start at the trailhead at the northeast end of the parking lot on Merrie Way. Once on the double-track dirt trail, follow it to the right, going toward the north and east. Look for an orange-and-white caisson beyond Lands End. This is Mile Rock Lighthouse, the modern version.

1.2 The trail goes up wooden stairs and slightly inland, where it narrows.

1.7 Reach Eagle Point and the Lincoln Park Golf Course. From the observation platform at Eagle Point, descend stairs and look west to the tip of Lands End. Return to observation platform, then continue on the trail to its end and on to the sidewalk beside El Camino del Mar.

2.0 Follow city streets to China Beach. After your visit, head back the way you came to the Coast Trail.

4.0 Arrive back at the Merrie Way parking lot. Walk on the western sidewalk, then turn right down the paved path to the Sutro Bath ruins.

4.1 From the rise above the baths on the northwestern corner, enjoy a view of Seal Rocks. Continue on the paved path up to Point Lobos Avenue and the Cliff House.

4.2 Arrive at the Cliff House. Follow signs that lead right, down stairs, to the observation deck. Exit back up to the sidewalk, and you can go right (downhill) past the Cliff House to Ocean Beach. Otherwise, turn around and take the sidewalk back to Merrie Way.

4.3 Arrive back at the parking lot at Merrie Way.

Option: From China Beach, continue to Baker Beach and catch the Coast Trail on the north side of the beach, following it all the way to the Presidio and Golden Gate Bridge, about 4 miles.

HIKE INFORMATION

Local Information: San Francisco Convention and Visitor Center, 900 Market Street, Lower Level, Hallidie Plaza, San Francisco, CA 94102; (415) 391-2000; www .onlyinsanfrancisco.com

Local Events/Attractions: California Palace of the Legion of Honor, 100 34th Avenue, San Francisco, CA 94121; (415) 750-3600; www.famsf.org. Closed Monday; admission charged

Camera Obscura, 1090 Point Lobos Avenue, San Francisco, CA 94121; (415) 750-0415; admission $1

Lincoln Park Golf Course, 34th Avenue and Clement Street, San Francisco; (415) 221-9911; www.lincolnparkgc.com

Cliff House, 1090 Point Lobos Avenue, San Francisco, CA 94121; (415) 386-3330; www.cliffhouse.com

Hike Tours: Golden Gate National Recreation Area; (415) 561-4700; www.nps .gov/goga. City Guides; (415) 557-4266

Mile Rock Lighthouse

In 1904 it was one of the great lighthouse engineering feats of all time. Now, Mile Rock and Little Mile Rock are just a pair of stones about a half mile north of Point Lobos outside the San Francisco Bay. The larger of the two rocks is 40 feet by 30 feet, and rises about 20 feet above sea level. Mariners considered the rocks a serious hazard due to fog and strong currents. In 1901, when the *Rio de Janeiro* was wrecked near Fort Point and 140 lives were lost, engineers went to work to protect ships from the dangerous rocks. The first construction crew refused to work on the isolated, sea-swept rock, so the contractor hired deep-water sailors to do the work. They had only a few hours each day at low tide, and workers were constantly being knocked into the cold water. But they managed to erect a steel tower of three tiers and a lantern room. They painted the lighthouse tower white, the caisson below it black. Keepers had to commute by boat during low tide and climb a ladder to the lighthouse to do their isolated job. They had to wear earplugs for the loud fog signal. In powerful waves and high winds, a keeper could literally be blown from one of the tower's catwalks. Despite these hazards, some keepers enjoyed the assignment. Keeper Lyman Woodruff served on Mile Rock for eighteen years. In the 1960s, despite protests from the general public, the tower of Mile Rock was dismantled; the U.S. Coast Guard had deemed the station best suited to automation.

Sweeney Ridge: The Portolá Discovery Site

This small open space area on scrub-covered moors is for locals an oasis in an urban desert that includes the San Francisco International Airport and the busy freeway corridors. Protected as part of the Golden Gate National Recreation Area in 1984, the ridge (at about 1,250 feet) offers 360-degree views of up to 30 miles on clear days. Bring a jacket if the weather is cold, as daytime temperatures can range from the upper 20s in January to 100 degrees in September. The north ridge is home to an abandoned Nike missile site. The south ridge offers short, single-track trails that leave civilization behind for a time.

Start: At the gate at the end of Sneath Lane
Distance: 5.8 miles round-trip
Approximate hiking time: 3 hours
Difficulty: Moderate, due to elevation gain
Trail surface: A paved path takes you up to the ridge. A double-track dirt trail goes the length of the ridge, with very narrow single-track dirt trails creating a loop on the south end.
Other trail users: Equestrians and mountain bikers

Canine compatibility: Leashed dogs permitted
Land status: Golden Gate National Recreation Area
Fees and permits: No fees or permits required
Schedule: Open daily from 8:00 a.m. to dusk
Maps: USGS San Francisco South. Download a map from www.nps.gov/goga or pick one up at visitor centers.
Trail contact: Golden Gate National Recreation Area; (415) 561-4700; www.nps.gov/goga
Other: There are no facilities.

Finding the trailhead
By Car: Take U.S. Highway 101 south to Interstate 280 south. Take the Pacifica/Highway 1 exit. Get off at Skyline Boulevard south, Highway 35. Go about 4 miles, past the Skyline College entrance, and turn right (west) onto Sneath Lane. Follow Sneath to its end. The parking area is on the right past the entrance gate.
By Public Transportation: SamTrans offers multiple routes to the site. Call (800) 660-4287 or (510) 817-1717 or visit www.samtrans.com.

THE HIKE

In 1769 a Spanish expedition led by Don Gaspar de Portolá was ordered to find a land route from colonial Mexico to Monterey Bay, a "fine harbor, sheltered from winds." Leaving from the tip of Baja California in July of that year with sixty-four men and 200 horses, Portolá was guided by only vague descriptions of the place as seen from the sea, and a mariner's navigation handbook of the California coastline. When Portolá and his men saw the mouth of the Salinas River, they were greeted by stinging winds and rough seas. Concluding this could not possibly be the place, they continued north.

Food and supplies were running short when they reached the peaceful San Pedro Valley. One of Portolá's scouts, Jose Francisco Ortega, climbed a nearby ridge. To his surprise, there to the east was, in his own words, "an enormous area of the sea or estuary, which shot inland as far as the eye could see." He became the first European reported to see the San Francisco Bay. On November 4, 1769, Captain Portolá and the entire party followed Ortega up to the ridge to see for themselves. Portolá named the body of water San Francisco Bay and claimed it as part of New Spain.

You can stand in the spot where Ortega took in this vista for the first time. A monument on the site is dedicated to Carl McCarthy, who was among those that ensured public ownership of this open space. It illustrates the peaks you see: Mount Diablo, Mount Hamilton (the highest peak in the region), Montara Mountain, Point San Pedro, Mount Tamalpais, and San Bruno Mountain.

A paved path and hearty cardiovascular climb take you up the hill to the ridge, with pretty San Andreas Lake to your left (east). The active San Andreas Fault runs beneath it and Crystal Springs Reservoir to the southeast.

A short stint north brings you to the decaying structures of the U.S. Army Nike Missile Radar Station, which was in operation here between 1957 and 1974. It was rendered obsolete by the Anti-Ballistic Missile Treaty that year.

The loop going south offers a peaceful stroll on narrow paths—muddy after rains—showing off the vegetation and wildlife on the ridge in quiet detail. Someday, you will hopefully be able to continue your hike south past the reservoir on the Bay Area Ridge Trail. A group of volunteers called Friends of Sweeney Ridge, in cooperation with the Pacifica Land Trust, is doing what it can to preserve the space that is open and accessible to the public.

If you end up hiking in the fog, you won't see much beyond white-tailed rabbits and wildflowers. Sometimes it gets so thick you can barely see 20 feet ahead. It is isolating and disorienting, so stay on the trails. The yellow line down Sneath Lane is a fog line painted to keep bikers and hikers from going off the edge. When you actually see it in fog, you totally understand.

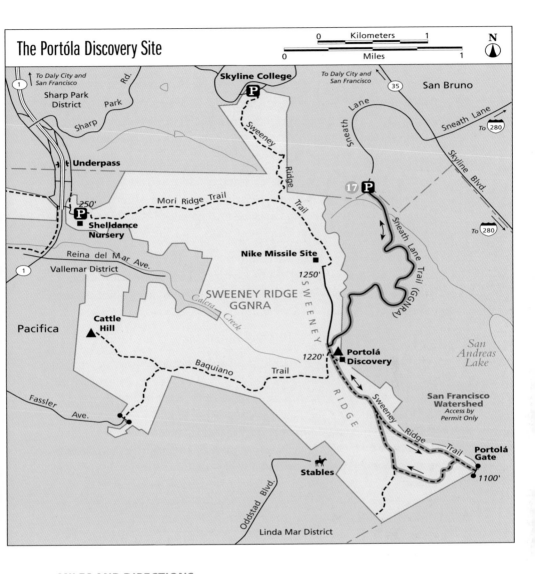

The Portóla Discovery Site

To Daly City and San Francisco

Sharp Park District

Rd.

Park

Sharp

Skyline College

P

To Daly City and San Francisco

35

San Bruno

Sneath Lane

Sneath Lane

To 280

Skyline Blvd.

Underpass

250'

P

Sweeney

Ridge

Trail

Mori Ridge Trail

Shelldance Nursery

17 P

Sneath Lane Trail (GGNRA)

To 280

Reina del Mar Ave.

Vallemar District

1

Nike Missile Site

1250'

S W E E N E Y

SWEENEY RIDGE GGNRA

Calera Creek

Pacifica

Cattle Hill

Baquiano Trail

1220'

Portolá Discovery

San Andreas Lake

R I D G E

Sweeney Ridge

Fassler Ave.

Trail

San Francisco Watershed
Access by Permit Only

Oddstad Blvd.

Stables

Sweeney Ridge Trail

Portolá Gate

1100'

Linda Mar District

MILES AND DIRECTIONS

0.0   Start at the gate at the main entrance to Sweeney Ridge. Go to the double-track, paved Sneath Lane. To the south is San Andreas Lake.

1.0   The fog line begins on trail; road gets steeper. A stand of eucalyptus grows near top of trail to the south.

1.7   Reach the top of the ridge, with ocean views to the west on clear days. The double-track dirt Sweeney Ridge Trail heads south; to the north, it goes to Skyline College. The whole circuit is part of Bay Area Ridge Trail. Turning south (left as you face the ocean), walk a short way to the Portolá Discovery

Site on the left (east) side of the trail. Return to the main trail and continue south on Sweeney Ridge Trail. Pass the Baquiano trailhead on the right (west).

2.3 Reach a Bay Area Ridge Trail sign. Stay on Sweeney Ridge Trail past this single-track dirt trail, which goes to horse stables at the end of Linda Mar Valley; you will be returning on this trail on the southwestern loop.

2.8 At the junction with another unmarked dirt trail, turn right (west). Ahead, south on Sweeney Ridge, is a gate barring entrance into the San Francisco Watershed area, warning no trespassing. The trail narrows and rises and falls in the scrub. (*Note:* Long pants are recommended. Also, the trail gets muddy after rains.)

3.2 Reach a trail junction. Take the fork to the right (northeast), which heads back to the Sweeney Ridge Trail (the left trail leads to the horse stables). (*Note:* Watch out for horse droppings. More equestrians than hikers use this trail.)

3.6 Back on the Sweeney Ridge Trail, turn left (north).

4.1 Turn right (east) onto Sneath Lane, heading back down the hill.

5.8 Arrive back at the trailhead and parking lot.

Option: To extend this round-trip hike to 7.4 miles, go straight past the junction with Sneath Lane on the Sweeney Ridge Trail, heading north to Skyline College and past the abandoned Nike missile radar site, which is less than a mile from the trail junction.

HIKE INFORMATION

Local Information: Pacifica Visitor Center, 225 Rockaway Beach #1, Pacifica, CA 94044; (650) 355-4122; www.cityofpacifica.org
Hike Tours: Golden Gate National Recreation Area, Ocean District; (415) 561-4700; www.nps.gov/goga
Friends of Sweeney Ridge and Pacifica Land Trust, P.O. Box 988, Pacifica, CA 94045; (650) 359-7191; www.pacificalandtrust.org/sweeneyridge/sweeneyridge.html

The Presidio: Lovers' Lane and the Ecology Trail

With the closing of military bases all over the West Coast in the 1990s, San Francisco's Presidio, one of the oldest, dating back to 1776, became yours to wander. This hike takes you through military and social history, through scenic forests and across green lawns, and along the path of lovers. Besides some interesting history and ecology, the trail covers most stages of a relationship: strolling down Lovers' Lane, passing a "proven" well of fertility, reaching Inspiration Point, cruising by the chapel, and walking by the old officers' family homes, ending with the post hospital, where babes were born and loved ones said good-bye. As a bonus, there's a bowling alley near the start of the hike, where you can play a game with your date after your hike.

Start: William Penn Mott Jr. Visitor Center

Distance: 2.7-mile loop

Approximate hiking time: 2 hours

Difficulty: Easy

Trail surface: Single- and double-track dirt trail and paved pathways

Other trail users: Bicyclists on paved pathways

Canine compatibility: Leashed dogs permitted

Land status: Golden Gate National Recreation Area

Fees and permits: No fees or permits required

Schedule: Open year-round from sunrise to sunset. The visitor center is open from 9:00 a.m. to 5:00 p.m.

Maps: USGS Point Bonita; San Francisco North. Download a map from www.nps.gov/goga or pick one up at visitor centers.

Trail contacts: William Penn Mott Jr. Visitor Center, Building 102, Montgomery Street, San Francisco, CA 94123; (415) 561-4323; www.nps.gov/prsf. The visitor center is temporarily located in the Presidio Officers' Club, Building 50, on Moraga Avenue. Golden Gate National Recreation Area—Presidio, Fort Mason, Building 201, San Francisco, CA 94123; (415) 561-4700, www.nps.gov/prsf

Finding the trailhead

By Car: In the Presidio, from Lincoln Boulevard, turn left (south) onto Montgomery Street and park near the clearly marked William Penn Mott Jr. Visitor Center, a red brick building on the right-hand (west) side of Pershing Square.

Public Transportation: San Francisco Municipal Railway (MUNI) buses serve the Presidio via the 28, 29, 43, and 82X lines. Bus service from the North Bay to the Golden Gate Bridge toll plaza is available through Golden Gate Transit. Commercial cable car buses are available from Fisherman's Wharf. For more information, call (415) 673-6864 or visit www.transitinfo.org.

In the Presidio woods, the ground is sand.

THE HIKE

At Pershing Square, where the hike begins, you can lay your hands on two of the oldest known cannons in North America. The bronze "San Francisco" (1679) and the "Virgin of Barbaneda" (1693) once guarded the Spanish fort built here in the eighteenth century.

Past the chapel (built in 1864, but greatly modified in the 1950s) you walk down Lovers' Lane. This paved, lamp-lit pathway is absolutely straight and leads directly to the Presidio Boulevard Gate (1896), a main entrance for the Presidio grounds. By foot, this is still the quickest way out of the fort and into town. Probably the oldest travel corridor in San Francisco, this trail has witnessed the passing of the Spanish, Mexican, and American soldiers who served here during the last two centuries.

From Lovers' Lane, turn west to wander in the woods. When the Spanish arrived, this area was low dunes and wind-swept bunchgrass. Along the shore, extensive marshes hosted seagulls, pelicans, a few deer, and sometimes a hungry mountain lion or grizzly bear. In 1848, the U.S. government decided to tame the wind and sand. In a beautifying effort starting in 1883, Major William A. Jones and his crew planted 400,000 seedlings of 200 tree species on the slopes around the Presidio, most of them in orderly rows like soldiers in formation. It was the most ambitious landscaping effort the U.S. Army had ever undertaken. Eucalyptus, cypress, and pine trees thrived the best, altering the landscape forever.

Just when you thought it was safe to drink the water, beware El Polin. Now a cement fixture surrounded by paved pathways and lawn, it's not much to look at, but legend says if a woman drinks the water of the well on a full moon, she will be very fertile and likely to have many children. Although the Spanish wrote of the legend, it is possible that it goes back to the native Ohlone people. The wives of the first Spanish officers at the Presidio drank regularly from this spring and proceeded to have twelve, fifteen, and twenty children.

To the left of the fountain on the hillside is an example of the abundant serpentine grasslands of the past, one of the most threatened natural ecosystems in North America. The Presidio *Clarkia franciscana* and the Marin dwarf flax are coming back on these few acres. Thirteen plants found at the Presidio have been designated as rare, threatened, or endangered.

Inspiration Point is mostly a parking lot now, but still worth the detour for the memorable vista and interpretive signs about the area. The name Inspiration Point dates back to the mid-1800s, when the trees did not block part of the view.

The Ecology Trail brings you back to Funston Avenue and Officers' Row. For more than 140 years, this street was home to commissioned officers and their families. Despite the military setting, life here in the 1800s was typical of middle-class America. Pick up a free brochure, "Main Post Walk: 200 Years of History and Architecture," which covers the fascinating architectural mile of this hike, at the visitor center.

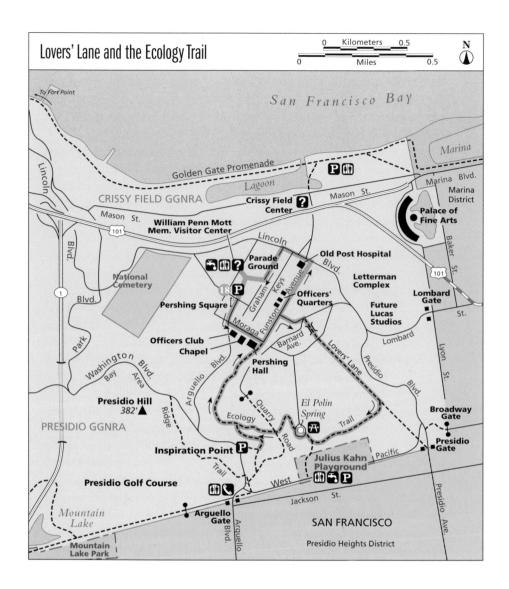

Turning the corner onto Lincoln, you come to the post hospital, built in 1863, rounding out the Lovers' hike "in sickness and in health." Go around back to check out the 1906 fire and earthquake refugee camp exhibit and an example of two of the tent cottages the U.S. Army provided for quake survivors.

MILES AND DIRECTIONS

0.0 Start from the parking lot on Montgomery Street in front of the visitor center. Walk southwest (away from the bay) toward white flagpole in Pershing Square.

0.1 Walk up the sidewalk between cannons and cross Moraga Avenue.

0.2 Pass the Officers' Club and continue left (east) on Moraga Avenue, past the chapel to Funston Avenue.

0.3 Cross Moraga Avenue and walk downhill to the Alameda. The trail behind Pershing Hall is the return route on this loop. Pass the site of the Funston Avenue Archeological Research Project and officers' family housing (1862). Halfway down Funston Avenue, the Alameda (Spanish for *avenue*) served as the post's official entrance from the 1860s until 1895.

0.5 Turn right (east) onto the Alameda. You will complete the rest of the Main Post Historic Walk at the end of this loop trail.

0.6 Where Presidio Boulevard meets Barnard Avenue, you'll see a footpath. (Leashed pets are welcome.) Turn right (southeast) onto the paved pathway with wild blackberries on either side of the trail (ready to eat in fall months). Cross over the brick footbridge dating to 1885 and proceed onto Lovers' Lane.

1.0 Five hundred feet before West Pacific Boulevard, turn right (west) onto an unmarked but well-worn dirt and sand trail that leads to the Presidio woods. This is the Ecology Trail.

1.3 Bear right to the Paul Goode baseball and recreation field. Head around left of the field; take the path left of the white houses. (*Note:* If you need a restroom, you can detour up the hill to the left to the Julius Khan Playground.)

1.4 Walk down the stairs to El Polin and the lawn area. Walk to the left (west) of the fountain to view the native plant restoration on the hillside.

1.5 Cross over the trail leading to Quarry Road; continue straight (west).

1.7 Take the single-track dirt trail up the hill to the left (south) to take in the vista at Inspiration Point. Head back down to the Ecology Trail, turning left (west) to continue.

2.0 The trail runs along Barnard Avenue. Follow the path to Pershing Hall.

2.1 Walk beside Pershing Hall back onto Funston Avenue. Continue the Main Post Historic Walk, heading down Funston Avenue past Victorian-era houses toward the corner of Lincoln Boulevard.

2.4 Turn left (west) at Lincoln Boulevard; look for the fire station. Cottages that date back to 1906 are around the back. Continue west on Lincoln to Graham Street. Barracks (1886) are on the left (east).

2.5 Cross to the other side of Graham Street, turn left (west), and begin to walk on the street. Enlisted barracks (1862) are on the right. Continue uphill to Owen Street.

2.6 Take Owen Street back to the parking lot (parade ground) and Montgomery Street.

2.7 Arrive back at the visitor center.

HIKE INFORMATION

Local Information: The California Welcome Center/San Francisco, Pier 39, Building "P," Second Level, Unit Q5, (Beach Street and Embarcadero), San Francisco, CA 94133; (415) 981-1280; www.visitcwc.com/destinations/sanfrancisco/index.php

Local Events/Attractions: Exploratorium, 3601 Lyon Street, San Francisco, CA 94123; (415) 563-7337; www.exploratorium.edu

Fort Point National Historic Site, Long Avenue, San Francisco; (415) 561-4395 or (415) 556-1693, www.nps.gov/fopo

Presidio Bowl (corner of Moraga Avenue and Montgomery Street), the Presidio, San Francisco; (415) 561-BOWL (2695); www.presidiobowl.com

Hike Tours: William Penn Mott Jr. Visitor Center, Building 102, Montgomery Street, San Francisco, CA 94129; (415) 561-4323

Golden Gate National Recreation Area—Presidio, Fort Mason, Building 201, San Francisco, CA 94123; www.nps.gov/prsf

San Bruno State Park: Summit Loop Trail

Though the sounds of the freeway and urban white noise are unavoidable on the lower trails of San Bruno Mountain, a hike up the mountain makes for an enjoyable visit with local flora and stunning vistas. The mountain's ridgeline runs in an east–west configuration, with considerable slopes and elevations ranging from 250 feet to 1,314 feet at the summit. A protected zone in Golden Gate National Recreation Area since 1983, the 2,326 acres serve as a model plan for conserving natural habitats in an ever-spreading metropolis.

Start: At the picnic area parking lot near the park entrance

Distance: 3.8-mile loop

Approximate hiking time: 2 hours

Difficulty: Moderate, due to elevation gain

Trail surface: A short stint on a paved path to single-track dirt trails. Cross a paved service road before descending on dirt paths.

Other trail users: Equestrians

Canine compatibility: Dogs not permitted

Land status: State and county park

Fees and permits: $3 per car

Schedule: Open daily from 8:00 a.m. to dusk

Map: USGS San Francisco South

Trail contact: San Bruno Mountain State and County Park, 555 Guadalupe Canyon Parkway, Brisbane, CA 94005; (650) 992-6770 or (415) 587-7511 (gatehouse); www.co.sanmateo.ca.us/portal/site/SMC# and click on Departments: Park Departments

Other: There are full facilities at the start. Dress in layers. Bird and wildflower lists are available at the park kiosk.

Finding the trailhead

By Car: From U.S. Highway 101, take the Bayshore/Brisbane exit (for the Cow Palace). Take Bayshore Boulevard to Guadalupe Canyon Parkway. Turn right (west) onto Guadalupe Canyon Parkway and drive uphill about 2 miles to the park entrance on the right (north) side of the road.

By Public Transportation: No public transit goes directly to the park. Take BART to the Daly City terminal. At Location 7, catch bus 130 and disembark at the corner of Orange Street and East Market Street. You have to walk or bike the remaining 2.2 miles. Contact SamTrans at (800) 660-4287 or (510) 817-1717 for more information. The Web site is www.samtrans.com.

View from Summit Loop Trail looking west

THE HIKE

When you look around San Bruno Mountain, you are seeing a slice of an ancient Bay Area, long before European settlement. In the Cretaceous period, 130 million years ago, this was all under water. The earth's crust buckled in the region, creating fault blocks. One of the fault blocks was elevated, becoming San Bruno Mountain. For perhaps a thousand years, until the 1800s, Costanoan Indian tribes camped here seasonally, gathering seeds and plants for food, collecting materials for basketry, and hunting small game in the scrub. Tule elk and antelope fed on the grasses. Every few years, the Indians set fire to the mountain in controlled burns to encourage new growth of grasses and to keep the scrub under control. A lot of the scrub you see today has replaced grasslands in the last twenty or so years.

Captain Bruno Heceta explored the western shore of the San Francisco Bay in 1775 for Spain. He named the largest landmass on that side of the peninsula Mount San Bruno after his patron saint. By 1869, civilization surrounded the mountain, but no people lived on it. This was a saving factor for the native coyote brush, yarrow, and snowberries.

In the 1870s, railroad baron and banker Charles Crocker acquired the property. After his death, the Crocker Land Company leased or sold parcels of land for light industrial uses and mineral resources recovery. During the Cold War in the 1950s, the summit became home to a Nike missile early warning radar site. Ruins mark the site.

In the 1960s, the urban tide threatened the mountain. Housing developers and industrialists started slugging it out with conservation groups, individual citizens, and government agencies for the land. It wasn't until 1982 that the fight was settled with the creation of the San Bruno Mountain Habitat Conservation Plan.

Some areas around the mountain are designated for housing, but according to the conservation plan, construction and grading must occur at a time and in a way that protects endangered butterfly habitats, including those of the rare Mission blue butterfly, the San Bruno elfin butterfly, the Callippe silverspot butterfly, and the Bay checkerspot. Also, fourteen endangered plants survive here, including San Bruno Mountain manzanita, coast rock cress, Pacifica manzanita, and Franciscan wallflower. Along with the more sensitive species, the common raven and red-winged hawk, deer, and bush rabbits are pretty happy to have a home, too.

A grassroots group called Friends of San Bruno Mountain maintains a native plant nursery here; a meander through the gardens helps you identify the flora on the way to the peak (1,314 feet). While listening to the song of sparrows and meadowlarks along the way, you can differentiate the coffeeberry, with its round, little fruits in shades of maroon, from red elderberries, some growing into trees, with bunches of bright red berries. Enjoy the wonderful wildflower display in spring that includes wild coastal iris, orange California poppies, clumps of blue, cream, and lavender lupines, and pink checkerbloom. From February to April, start looking for those very special moths and butterflies.

At the top of the mountain, the magnificent vistas distract you from the unsightly antennae, satellite dishes, and service vehicles. For a family hike, try the 0.8-mile Bog Trail (starting from the picnic area).

MILES AND DIRECTIONS

0.0 Start at the picnic area parking lot near the park entrance. Facing the restrooms, turn right onto the paved path and right (south) again at its end, following signs to the Summit Loop Trail. Pass under the overpass of the parkway onto a gravel path toward the native plant nursery to the main trailhead.

0.2 Reach the native plant garden and trailhead. Facing the sign, turn right (west) to start the Summit Loop Trail. At the Summit Loop Trailhead, start the loop by taking the trail to the right (northwest). This will take you past coffeeberry and red elderberry before heading into a eucalyptus grove.

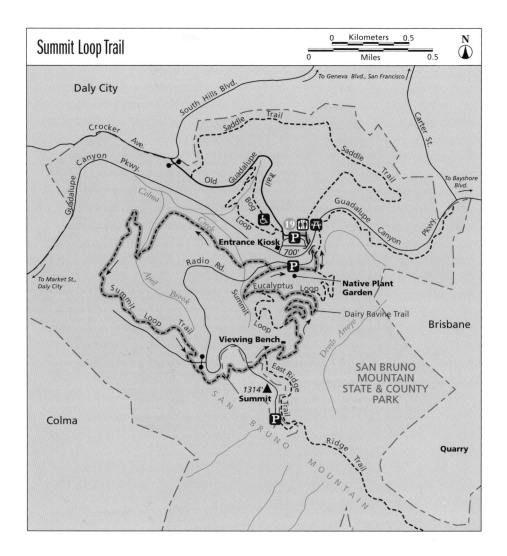

0.5 The trail heads away from the street and begins a moderate climb on the northeast side of the mountain.

2.1 Cross over Radio Road again, continuing on the dirt Summit Loop Trail. To the southwest you can see Montara and San Pedro Mountains; to the northwest, Ocean Beach. Beyond this is Rodeo Beach and Tennessee Point in the Marin Headlands, and Mount Tamalpais. Nearby are San Bruno, Daly City, Colma, and South San Francisco.

2.4 Pass a green building and cross the service road once more to continue on Summit Loop Trail. At the junction with East Ridge Trail, continue straight (east) on the Summit Loop Trail.

2.5 Take the short trail to your right for a great viewing point. Continue on Summit Loop Trail.

2.8 At the junction with the Dairy Ravine Trail, turn right (east) onto Dairy Ravine Trail.

3.2 At the intersection with the Eucalyptus Trail, take the leg to the left (west), to pass through eucalyptus grove.

3.5 Reach the Summit Loop Trailhead. Stay right (east), heading back to the native plant garden.

3.6 Return to the garden and the upper parking lot. Go back the way you came on the sidewalk and paved trail under the Guadalupe Canyon Parkway.

3.8 Arrive back at the parking lot and picnic area.

Option: The 2.43-mile Ridge Trail is a dead-end path that leads to the eastern end of San Bruno Mountain. This will extend your hike by up to 4.9 miles. From the trail you will enjoy views of Mount Hamilton, Mount Diablo, and the Oakland Hills, as well as the cities of Alameda, Oakland, and Berkeley. Also, you can see Candlestick Park (home of the San Francisco 49ers). An abandoned gravel quarry is on the north base of the main ridge.

HIKE INFORMATION

Local Information: Daly City–Colma Chamber of Commerce; 355 Gellert Boulevard, Suite 138, Daly City, CA 94015; www.dalycity-colmachamber.org
Hike Tours: San Bruno Mountain State and County Park, 555 Guadalupe Canyon Parkway, Brisbane, CA 94005; (650) 992-6770 or (415) 587-7511 (gatehouse)
Friends of San Bruno Mountain, 824 Templeton Avenue, Daly City, CA 94015; (415) 584-5114

Honorable Mention

E. Golden Gate Park

Golden Gate Park is green, lush, varied, and utterly man-made. In fact, it is one of the largest man-made parks in the world. The 3.5-mile-long park runs from the Haight-Ashbury area to Ocean Beach, through the Sunset District. It covers 1,013 acres with over one million trees and nine lakes, as well as museums, casting pools, playgrounds, playing fields, a carousel, and much more.

Near Kezar Stadium is the AIDS Memorial Grove, a short walk of remembrance for those in San Francisco who have died in the continuing epidemic. Just west of the California Academy of Sciences are the Shakespeare Gardens, with flora chosen from lines in the bard's plays. Nearby are well-tended rose gardens. Across Martin Luther King Jr. Drive from the Shakespeare Gardens is the Strybing Arboretum. Some paved and some dirt trails take you through displays of native plant life from around the world.

You can stroll around Stow Lake, while people paddle across on rented boats, and even cross a bridge onto Strawberry Island. West of the Highway 1 crossover are numerous small lakes. At Spreckels you can watch model yachts sailing, and at Lloyd Lake you can walk through the "Portals of the Past." Elk Glen Lake and North Lake have trails leading to them, too. Ocean Beach makes a great destination for a walk, run, or rollerblade through the park. In the spring, visit the Queen Wilhelmina Tulip Garden, famous for its 10,000 tulips and windmill.

Fountain by the M. H. DeYoung Memorial Museum © Shutterstock

Golden Gate Park is most easily accessed off 19th Avenue, which runs through the middle of it. You can also enter from any of the major streets that bound it. There is street parking in much of the park and lot parking between the DeYoung Museum and the California Academy of Sciences, scheduled to reopen after renovations in the fall of 2008. Free shuttles run through the Golden Gate Park on summer weekends and holidays, about every fifteen minutes.

For information and maps, call the City of San Francisco Parks and Recreation at (415) 831-2700; for guided tours e-mail lnelson@ineTours.com, call (415) 447-8442, or go to www.inetours.com/Pages/SFNbrhds/Golden_Gate_Park.html.

Golden Gate Park © Shutterstock

San Mateo County Coastline

Knobcone pine (Hike 21)

California boasts one of the most accessible coastlines in the world, and San Mateo County has a lot of it to explore. You can walk the dunes, coastal bluffs full of lemon yellow lupine, and trails under windblown cypress trees.

In Pacifica, San Pedro Valley County Park offers rolling coastal hills and wildflowers, a seasonal waterfall, and mellow picnicking in an area that was once the winter camp for Coast Miwok Indians. Above, Montara Mountain invites a climb. Walking on a wide path of Montara granite through manzanita and Monterey pines, you enjoy almost continuous ocean views.

The James V. Fitzgerald Marine Reserve at Moss Beach has the longest intertidal reef in California. Hundreds of marine animals hang out in the tide pools, and you can see them all. Combined with a walk on the bluffs, where rum was smuggled during Prohibition, it forms a great loop hike. Along the Coast Trail through Half Moon Beach, hikers can access more than five separate beaches and swim on hot summer days.

San Mateo County has a lot of coastline to explore.

The little town of Pescadero, aside from its artichoke and strawberry fields, has several great hikes nearby. Pescadero Marsh is host to migrating seabirds on the Pacific Flyway. Egrets, geese, ducks, and loons rest in the lagoon among the rushes and feast on fish and insects, readying to continue their journey. Across from the wetlands, harbor seals lounge on rocks by Pescadero Beach. Just inland, Butano State Park, the coast's best-kept secret, has creeks and alder trees, redwoods and oaks, wildflowers in spring, and mushrooms in winter. A little farther down the coast at Año Nuevo State Park, visitors gawk at the hundreds of snorting elephant seals gathered to give birth, mate, and molt on the beach. In March and September, gray whales cruise by the coast on their semiannual migration. It is quite a sight to see one breach.

After hiking, little coastal towns beckon you with friendly bed-and-breakfasts and great fresh fish restaurants with Pacific views. Can't beat that.

Be aware of poison oak, especially in Hikes 20 and 21

Pescadero Marsh Trails

Pescadero Marsh, 360 acres of protected wetlands on the San Mateo Coast south of Half Moon Bay and north of Año Nuevo State Park, offers hikers a memorable opportunity to witness a rich natural habitat. The trails are short but full of life. Add a walk on the dunes of Pescadero State Beach, and you have a nice circuit of shoreline and wetland to explore. This is not a hike for stretching out the legs and working up a sweat, but a worthwhile meandering tour of nature. Of the three short trails, the flat Sequoia Audubon Trail is best for a family hike and the one to take if you are short on time. Dress in layers with long pants; there's a lot of poison oak, and the lack of funds has reduced trail maintenance. Bring water and binoculars. With 250 species of birds out here, a bird identification book would also come in handy. A short drive is required to reach the third trail.

Start: In the parking lot for Pescadero State Beach, just north of the Highway 1 bridge over the lagoon

Distance: 5.3 miles for all three trails, with a 0.2 mile drive to the last trailhead

Approximate hiking time: 3 hours

Difficulty: Moderate because of invading scrub on the paths

Trail surface: Sand, dirt, bridges and undoubtedly some mud (it is marshland, after all); flat narrow trails bordered with scrub and blackberry bushes

Other trail users: Hikers only

Canine compatibility: Dogs not permitted

Land status: Natural preserve and state beach

Fees and permits: $6 per car

Schedule: Open daily from 8:00 a.m. to dusk

Map: USGS Franklin Point

Trail contact: Pescadero State Beach and Pescadero Marsh Natural Preserve, P.O. Box 370, Pescadero, CA 94060; (650) 879-2170; www.parks.ca.gov

Other: A pit toilet is available in the parking lot.

Finding the trailhead

By Car: Pescadero State Beach is 14.5 miles south of Half Moon Bay on Highway 1. Turn left (west) into the first parking lot. If you miss it, you can turn around at one of the two other parking areas for the beach or at Pescadero Road.

By Public Transportation: From the Hillsdale CalTrain, take bus 294 to Half Moon Bay. Route 15 takes you from Half Moon Bay to Pescadero. If the driver won't stop at the beach, you can disembark at the corner of Pescadero Road and Highway 1 and do the hikes in reverse order. For SamTrans information call (800) 660-4BUS (4287) or visit www.transitinfo.org or www.samtrans.com.

North Pond and dunes

THE HIKE

Historically, wetlands like this have been viewed as wastelands. According to the old adage, being sold a piece of old swampland meant you were robbed. Agriculturally minded humans looked upon marshes like this, with their dry coarse plants, muddy unmanageable earth, and strong smell of methane, as nothing but acres of wasting decay. But consider that it was in mud and slime like this that life was born. And those microscopic one-celled organisms, our evolutionary ancestors, are still here, coexisting with complex creatures that have evolved over hundreds of millions of years.

The marsh is home to 250 species of birds, more than fifty species of mammals, thirteen kinds of reptiles and amphibians, and 300 varieties of plant life. Many of them can survive nowhere else but in wetland areas, and those areas have been rapidly shrinking for over a century.

Currently, California has 450,000 acres of wetlands. There used to be four million. Of the coastal wetlands surviving, 90 percent are around the San Francisco Bay and estuary. But 90 to 95 percent of the salt marshes around the San Francisco Bay have been filled in. Here in California, organizations like the Trust for Public Land have been buying up and preserving as much prime habitat along the

Pacific Flyway as they can. It's a battle. Yet the wetlands provide even more than vital nesting and feeding areas for wildlife. They act as giant sponges that help regulate winter floodwaters, refill underwater aquifers, filter pollutants from runoff, and improve water quality.

Pescadero Marsh includes not just marsh but sand dunes, tidal flats, and rolling hills. The freshwater streams—Pescadero Creek and Butano Creek—meet in the lagoon and flow into the sea. As you hike, you go from salt to freshwater and back again, a bit like the steelhead trout that spawn here.

Walk on the nearly 40-foot-high Pescadero sand dunes, formed from 5,000 to 3,000 years ago by drifting sand. Plants here have grown tough, impervious to the strong sun and salty air. Low to the ground, they avoid the harsh winds and keep the hillsides together. On the beach, surf scoters crush bottom-dwelling shellfish with their thick beaks. Sanderlings scurry after the waves, searching the wet sand for small bits of food. The endangered snowy plover also nests on this beach, laying its eggs in low depressions in the sand. Just offshore, parallel to the bridge, a crowd of lazy harbor seals lie against the contours of rocks, basking in the sun.

Walking inland under the bridge, you come to the marsh, lagoon, and the divide in the creeks. In geologic terms, the brackish marsh is a baby (the word brackish refers to a blend of fresh and salt waters). Fifteen thousand years ago, neither it nor the beach was here. The ocean was 300 feet lower, the coastline 15 miles farther west. Glacial melting later caused the sea level to rise, flooding the depression at Pescadero Valley and forming a marsh about 6,500 years ago. In or near the marsh are several other endangered animals, including the red-legged frog, salt-marsh harvest mouse, and San Francisco garter snake. The western aquatic garter snake and the elusive western pond turtle keep the many migrating and local waterfowl company.

MILES AND DIRECTIONS

0.0   Start from the northernmost parking lot for Pescadero State Beach. Cross the highway to single-track dirt North Marsh Trail. The trail ascends a ridge.

0.1   Pass an interpretive sign with pictures of some of the animals in the area.

0.8   Reach the observation platform. Head back the way you came.

1.5   Cross the highway back to the parking lot and take the trail out toward the beach, turning left (south) onto the roped, wooden walkway that goes over dunes.

1.9   Pass an interpretive sign and trail marker for Pescadero Marsh Natural Preserve. Follow the trail, turning left (east/inland) under the bridge. Continue to the sign with the international hiker icon (about 0.2 mile east).

2.1 Reach the Sequoia Audubon Trail. Follow the single-track sandy path.

2.3 At the bridge, continue straight on the Sequoia Audubon Trail. (*Note:* Some of the trail on the narrow levee between the creek and marsh is eroding but still passable.)

2.8 Stop at the sign that warns about poison oak. (*Note:* The trail is overgrown beyond this point, and a bridge over the creek is down. These conditions may change.) Turn around and head back the way you came, stopping at the bridge.

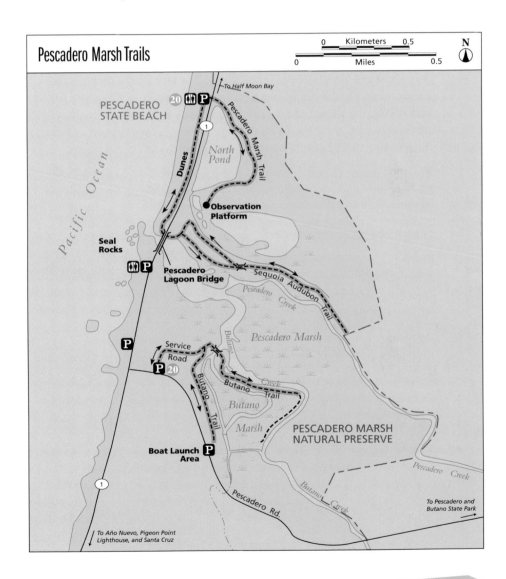

Pescadero Marsh Trails

3.3 Go back over the bridge and turn right (northwest).

3.5 Bear left back onto the double-track Sequoia Audubon Trail. After joining Sequoia Audubon Trail, take the first fork to the left and loop toward North Marsh. A right turn, as you near the marsh, will allow you to loop back to the Sequoia Audubon Trail.

3.6 Reach the sandbank beside the stream. Turn right (west) and head back under the bridge. Walk to the southwesternmost corner next to the creek to view harbor seals. If you can cross the water safely, the view from the bluffs is great.

3.7 Reach the viewing point of seal rocks. Turn right, heading north either along the beach or back along the dunes.

4.1 Back at the car, drive south on Highway 1 to Pescadero Road, then turn left (east) and park in the gravel area beside the road (you can also park at the southernmost parking area for Pescadero Beach and cross the highway). Just east is a dirt service road. To start the third hike, turn left (north) onto the service road. Your destination is a bridge with a view of the marsh.

4.3 The service road ends; a single-track dirt trail begins at the end of the road and heads through the grassland. Continue on the Butano Trail along the levee.

4.4 The trail splits. Turn left (east).

4.5 Reach the bridge for a view of the marsh. Continue on the Butano Trail along the levee. (*Note:* The trail is overgrown with prickly blackberries. Wear long pants and stay on the trail.) Cross the bridge to the narrow levee between creeks.

4.8 The prickly berry plants start to overtake the trail here; turn around and head back the way you came.

5.5 Arrive back at the car.

HIKE INFORMATION

Local Information: Half Moon Bay Coastside Chamber of Commerce and Visitors' Bureau, 235 Main Street, Half Moon Bay, CA 94019; (650) 726-8380; www .halfmoonbaychamber.org

Local Events/Attractions: Phipps Ranch (petting zoo/pick-your-own farm), 2700 Pescadero Road, Pescadero, CA 94060; (650) 879-0787; www.phipps country.com

Hike Tours: Pescadero State Beach and Pescadero Marsh Natural Preserve; (650) 879-2170; www.parks.ca.gov

What Is a Wetland?

A wetland is an area saturated or covered by water at least part of the year. There are five major types: marine, estuarine, lacustrine, riverine, and palustrine. Marine and estuarine wetlands are connected to the ocean and include coastal wetlands, such as tidal marshes. Lacustrine wetlands are found around lakes. Riverine wetlands are associated with rivers and streams. Palustrine wetlands include marshes, swamps, and bogs, and may be isolated or connected to wet areas.

Butano State Park

In the secluded wilderness of 3,560-acre Butano State Park, you have the opportunity to walk miles under pillared groves of coastal redwoods. As a matter of fact, most of this hike is under the shade of trees that insulate you from the outside world. Stop on numerous wooden bridges to admire cascading and gurgling creeks. Take in views from the contrasting high ridges among dry manzanita and knobcone pines. From the ridges you see an unforgettable picture of the densely wooded Santa Cruz Mountains and the sweeping Pacific Ocean. The camping here is great, the crowds minimal.

Start: Six Bridges Trailhead
Distance: 8.3-mile loop
Approximate hiking time: 4.5 hours
Difficulty: Moderate
Trail surface: Single- and double-track dirt trails featuring many wooden bridges crossing creeks
Other trail users: Equestrians and mountain bikers on Butano Fire Road only

Canine compatibility: Dogs on leash allowed only on fire roads and in developed areas
Land status: State park
Fees and permits: $6 per car
Schedule: Open daily from dawn to dusk
Map: USGS Franklin Point
Trail contact: Butano State Park, 1500 Cloverdale Road, Pescadero, CA 94060; (650) 879-2040; www.parks.ca.gov

Finding the trailhead

By Car: Take Highway 1 south from Half Moon Bay for about 16 miles to Pescadero Road and turn left (east). About 5 miles past the town of Pescadero, turn right (south) onto Cloverdale Road. Watch for a sign for Butano, and take a left (east) turn into the main entrance. Park past the kiosk in the lot on the right (south).

By Public Transportation: There is no direct route to the park. From the Hillsdale CalTrain, take bus 294 to Half Moon Bay. Bus route 15 takes you from Half Moon Bay to Pescadero. You will have to bike, walk, or catch a ride from there to the park entrance (5 miles). SamTrans information is at (800) 660-4BUS (4287); you can visit www.transitinfo.org or www.samtrans.com.

🌱 **Green Tip:**
Hiking is a great carbon-free winter activity!

Jackson Flats Trail

THE HIKE

B utano, according to Native American lore, means "drinking cup" or "a gathering place for friendly visits." The park lends itself to just that, fantastic for day hikes or overnight camping.

Butano's second-generation redwoods and mature Douglas fir trees survived because of the canyons that made them hard to remove. The mother redwoods, some 500 or even 1,000 years old, were not so lucky. They provided good revenue for families during the post–gold rush growth spurt of Northern California.

The natives (their tribal names were lost when Spain colonized the area; they are called the Butanoans) who lived in the valley rarely ventured into the forest of giants. They had spiritual and practical reasons to avoid it. They felt a "presence" among the trees, concluding that the redwoods hosted powerful spirits and were not to be disturbed. Some hikers say those spirits are alive and well. The canopy's shadow does not allow for the growth of many edible and usable plants, so they had little motivation to go into the woods anyway.

In the 1860s, when this became American territory, several families settled in what is now Butano State Park. The Jackson family occupied the north side of the canyon, known as Jackson Flats. An abandoned landing field sits on top of the Butano Fire Road. The county used it for fire suppression. Descendants of the European settlers continued to live in the canyon until the State of California purchased the land and dedicated the park in 1961.

Forged by nature and the presence of man, Butano contains a diverse range of habitats, each with its own community of plant life and wildlife. This loop hike, recommended by frequent Butano hiker and retired physician John Salzer, gives you a taste of all the different environments and a great introduction to the park.

Starting on Six Bridges Trail from the picnic area, you'll crisscross a feeder creek lined with chalky-barked alder trees. Beneath are stinging nettles, dogwood, willow, and lots of different berry bushes providing shelter for insects, reptiles, and small mammals.

Around the ranger station is open grassland, dominated by coyote brush and bush lupine, with purple flowers in spring. Blue-eyed grass and yellow coastal suncups grow among them. This is where you are most likely to spot the larger mammals in the park: black-tailed deer, bobcats, coyotes, and rabbits. This area and the chaparral on the upper slopes are the most popular hunting grounds for peregrine falcons. (During summer and off-season weekends, the nature center offers insight on what you see along the trail.)

The Jackson Flats Trail takes you into redwood groves. Some of the trees damaged by fire over the last 150 years have caves in their wide bases, providing homes for bats. Huckleberries top the wide stumps of fallen trees. You share the trail with slow-moving banana slugs and California newts. Blooming from February to April is the park's star attraction, the purple calypso orchid. The Little Butano Creek Trail shows off the redwoods the best, with ferns and clover around the pretty cascading creek.

The top of Jackson Flats and Butano Fire Road are bathed in sunlight; the path is sandstone. The chaparral consists of long-needled knobcone pines, scrub oaks, and manzanita. Indian paintbrush provides dabs of red-orange in the springtime landscape.

On Goat Hill, you'll go through a section of tanbark oak woodland. Stay on the path to avoid poison oak. Enjoy the sight of bright orange chanterelles—thick fluted gourmet mushrooms—and honeysuckle among the berry bushes where chickadees and warblers whistle spring tunes.

MILES AND DIRECTIONS

0.0 Start at the Six Bridges Trailhead in the picnic area, about 20 yards east of the restrooms. The single-track dirt trail leads back to the park entrance, crossing over one of the six bridges on the trail. (*Note:* Be careful of poison oak.) The trail splits. Take the fork to the right (north).

0.1 Reach the bat habitat and turn left for a quick detour to see it. Return to Six Bridges Trail.

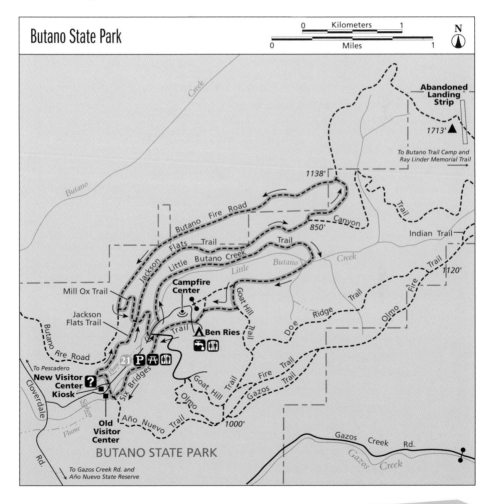

0.2 Turn left (west), continuing on Six Bridges Trail. Cross the next two bridges.

0.3 At the trailhead for Año Nuevo Trail, turn right (north) and cross the creek to stay on Six Bridges Trail. When the creek is really flowing, a wooden board helps you across, but be careful—it's a little slippery.

0.4 Arrive at the park entrance, kiosk, and nature center. Even when unattended, help yourself to a map in the wooden box on the side of the kiosk building. Cross the road to the Jackson Flats Trail through redwood groves. Narrow, single-track trail serpentines moderately uphill.

1.2 At the trailhead for Mill Ox Trail, stay northeast on the Jackson Flats Trail.

1.4 Pass the marsh on the left. Watch out for newts in this area, especially in February and March. The trail goes over and under fallen trees (trail volunteers have cut gaps in more obtrusive logs).

2.7 At the junction with Canyon Trail, stay on Jackson Flats Trail, bearing left (northeast). There's one steep grade toward the top.

3.0 Reach the top of the ridge. Views open up to the Pacific Ocean beyond densely wooded Santa Cruz foothills.

3.2 Reach the trailhead for the double-track, multiuse Butano Fire Road. Turn left (west) onto Butano Fire Road.

3.7 Pass the ruins of an old cabin on the right (north). Land to the north along Big Butano Creek is still privately owned.

4.7 Reach the trailhead for Mill Ox Trail. Turn left (southeast) onto the single-track dirt trail going downhill. (*Note:* The trail is steep in some sections.) The route follows an old logging skid trail.

4.9 Cross over the Jackson Flats Trail, staying on Mill Ox Trail, still heading downhill. You are back in the redwoods, passing by dedicated groves.

5.2 Reach Little Butano Creek and a picnic table. Take a bridge across the creek to the paved main park road. Stay on the same side of the street, turning left (northeast), and walk about 150 yards to the trailhead for Little Butano Creek Trail. Turn left (north) onto the hikers-only, single-track dirt trail. The creek is on the left (south). Cross a bridge again; the trail widens to double-track. Cross several more bridges, including an arched one, following the creek.

6.0 A short social trail to the left follows a feeder creek with a 5-foot cascade during the wet season. Continue on Little Butano Creek Trail. The trail soon starts to climb to the pump house, above the creek to the left.

6.7 Little Butano Creek Trail merges into the dirt Pump House Road, which intersects with the main park road (gravel and dirt). Go uphill on Pump House Road.

7.0 Turn left (south) onto the single-track Goat Hill Trail.

7.2 Turn right onto the trail to Ben Reis Campground.

7.4 When the trail splits, continue left to the campground. Pass the walk-in campsites. Take steps up to the campground loop road. Turn left, past campsites 16, 15, and others and continue downhill on the paved campground road.

7.6 Pass the sign for campground host; watch for the sign to the campfire center. Turn left onto that trail.

7.7 Reach the Campfire Center. Before the campfire stage, look for the Six Bridges Trail. The double-track dirt trail passes through mixed woodland. Watch for a seasonal pond. After one bridge, cross a gravel and dirt fire road and continue on the now single-track Six Bridges Trail. Cross two more bridges. The creek separates you from the paved main park road on the right. Pass the employee residence, continuing on Six Bridges Trail.

8.3 The trail splits. Go right to the picnic area and parking lot.

Option: To turn the hike into a backpacking trip, from the intersection of the Jackson Flats and Canyon Trails, take the Canyon Trail to Indian Trail.

HIKE INFORMATION

Local Information: Half Moon Bay Coastside Chamber of Commerce and Visitors' Bureau, 235 Main Street, Half Moon Bay, CA 94019; (650) 726-8380; www.halfmoonbaychamber.org

Local Events/Attractions: Phipps Ranch (petting zoo/pick-your-own farm), 2700 Pescadero Road, Pescadero, CA 94060; (650) 879-0787; www.phippscountry.com

Hike Tours: Butano State Park, 1500 Cloverdale Road, Pescadero, CA 94060; (650) 879-2040; www.parks.ca.gov

Año Nuevo State Park and Reserve

Come here to watch the elephant seals in their yearly rituals. From April through November, you can hike the trail yourself, but you must obtain a hiking permit to enter the Wildlife Protection Area at Año Nuevo Point. Molting elephant seals bask on beaches that are visible from viewpoints along the designated path. During the December 15 to March 31 breeding season, you can see the reserve only by joining one of the regularly scheduled guided walks. These highly informative walks have been designed to minimize disturbance to the animals and their natural habitat. Advance reservations are recommended and can be made as early as October. Beyond the seals, you'll find another 4,500 acres in the park to explore.

Start: The parking lot of Año Nuevo State Park

Distance: 3-mile lollipop loop

Approximate hiking time: 2.5 hours

Difficulty: Easy

Trail surface: Loose sand and some rocks

Other trail users: Hikers only

Canine compatibility: Dogs not permitted (dogs cannot be left inside parked vehicles in the parking lot either)

Land status: State park and reserve

Fees and permits: Parking fee is $6 per car. Visitors must obtain a hiking permit (free) to enter Wildlife Protection Area at Año Nuevo Point (from 8:30 a.m. to 3:30 p.m. only). Docent-led tours are $5 per person. Check the Web site at www.parks.ca.gov for the latest information. To make reservations for a guided walk, call (800) 444-4445 starting in October.

Schedule: Open year-round from 8:00 a.m. to sunset. Check the Web site at www.parks.ca.gov for the latest information about special viewing hours.

Maps: USGS Año Nuevo; Franklin Point. Año Nuevo State Reserve; www.parks.ca.gov. You also can pick up a park map in the visitor center.

Trail contact: Año Nuevo State Park and Reserve; (650) 879-2025; (650) 879-0227 for recorded information; www.parks.ca.gov

Finding the trailhead

By Car: Año Nuevo State Reserve is located about 27 miles south of Half Moon Bay and 20 miles north of Santa Cruz on Highway 1. Reserve signs are located on the highway in both directions. (Some people miss the brown signs. Be alert.)

By Public Transportation: On weekends in January and February, you can take the special Seal Line bus that departs from the Hillsdale Shopping Center in San Mateo and the Albertson's Shopping Center in Half Moon Bay. Price ($12 per person) includes round-trip fare and the guided walk. The 6.5-hour adventure starts at 9:00 and 10:00 a.m. Call SamTrans in advance for reservations at (650) 508-6441.

The rest of the year, direct public transit isn't available. For more information, contact SamTrans at (800) 660-4287; www.samtrans.com. CalTrans road information is at (800) 427-7623; www.dot.ca.gov/hq/roadinfo. You can also call 511 or visit 511.org.

THE HIKE

Ah, the sound of the surf crashing against rocks, the squawk of seagulls, the wind whistling in the dunes . . . burps, gurgles, farts, and growls. No, it's not a fraternity beach party. These are the sounds of the Point of the New Year: Año Nuevo, the most popular beach on the West Coast, that is, for elephant seals. Here, the blubbery animals take a break from cruising the Pacific to breed and molt. And a peculiar sight they are, lying around on pretty Northern California beaches, bluffs, and dunes.

How much fun can you have watching apathetic 3,000-ton creatures lusting, sleeping, losing skin, and flipping sand over themselves? You might be surprised. Their story is fascinating. And inside the Wildlife Protection Area, along with the elephant seals, you may see harbor seals, California sea otters, and Steller sea lions.

For your first visit take a docent-led tour, available from December 15 through the end of March. Experienced and enthusiastic volunteer docents have a wealth of information about the seals, birds, and geology of the area.

The Point of the New Year was seen and named by Father Antonio de la Ascension, chaplain for the Spanish maritime explorer Don Sebastian Viscaino, on January 3, 1603. Before the Spaniards arrived, the native Quroste people, a group of Ohlone Indians, lived and fished on this shore for 12,000 years. On the beaches, you can still see remnants of their ancient shell mounds that served as both dumping grounds and graveyards.

The elephant seals have chosen a dramatic setting: sandy, flowered bluffs with scurrying rabbits and songbirds, cresting dunes, beaches that sparkle with mica, and fields of coastal plants like sand lupine and arroyo willow. Look closely because this place will be different the next time you visit. The dunes are constantly changing.

On the other side of the channel, you can see Año Nuevo Island, where today the seals live communally with sea lions and seabirds in a lovely old Victorian house built in 1904 for a resident lighthouse keeper. Between 1880 and 1920, hundreds of wooden-hulled steam schooners sailed the West Coast in dangerous conditions to haul lumber, farm products, and passengers between growing coastal towns. The federal government bought the island in 1870 and built a five-story lighthouse to help put an end to shipwrecks in the area. But still, the schooner *Point Arena* wrecked at Pigeon Point in 1913. Some of the wreckage drifted to the beach at Año Nuevo and was uncovered by storm waves in 1983. You can see part of the bow near the Año Nuevo Point Trail.

Elephant seal bulls live to battle. If you visit Año Nuevo late in November, you may see them fighting to determine dominance. Only 10 percent of the males actually get to mate, so they learn even as pups how to chest butt on the beach.

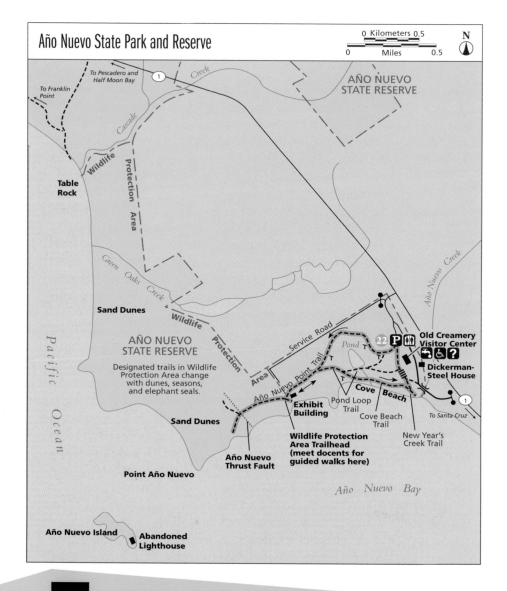

Elephant seals—mostly weaners—on the beach

Size is everything for the male elephant seal. Mature males can weigh up to 5,000 pounds.

In winter, you will likely witness mating or birth. Within three to five days of arriving, each female gives birth to a single pup. The mother vocalizes to the pup soon after it is born, so the baby will know her voice and be able to identify its mother among the hundreds of seals on the beach. If they are separated, there is a chance they won't come back together and the pup will starve.

Elephant seals were almost all wiped out by hunting and disease, but slowly, their population has been growing, so that we can enjoy these burping giants… along with a good day's hike.

MILES AND DIRECTIONS

0.0 Start from the parking lot. Follow signs to the visitor center, housed in the old Dickerman barn. The center features live video cameras of seal activity on beaches, information about other wildlife, geology, and plant life, and interactive exhibits. If taking a guided hike, meet on the deck in front of the barn. A ranger will direct you to Año Nuevo Point Trail, which goes back toward the parking lot and bends left at the trailhead.

0.7 Reach the junction with the Pond Loop Trail. Turn right (northwest), staying on the Año Nuevo Point Trail.

1.0 Arrive at the exhibit building, where you will find information on seals and sea lions. This is the entrance to the Wildlife Protection Area. If taking the guided walk, meet your docent here. Otherwise, you must have a permit to enter the area. For the next 0.5 mile, you'll hike dunes and beach among elephant seals. (*Note:* Stay 25 feet away from the animals.)

1.2 Reach Lawrence of Arabia Dune, the largest in Año Nuevo.

1.5 Cross the Año Nuevo Thrust Fault, a branch of the San Gregorio Fault Zone. Arrive at a viewpoint of Año Nuevo Island and the abandoned lighthouse cottage. Keep a lookout for the bow of the shipwrecked schooner *Point Arena*. There are several branches of trail here, only a few hundred feet long, providing different views of the seals' beach. Go back the way you came.

2.0 Arrive back at the exhibit building. Retrace your steps on the Año Nuevo Point Trail to the junction with the Pond Loop Trail.

2.3 Turn right (south) onto Pond Loop Trail.

2.4 Turn right (southeast) onto the Cove Beach Trail to Cove Beach. Continue southeast on Cove Beach Trail. Pass over New Year's Creek.

2.7 Turn inland (left/north) onto the New Year's Creek Trail.

3.0 Arrive back at the Dickerman barn and visitor center.

HIKE INFORMATION

Local Events/Attractions: Pigeon Point Light Station State Historic Park, 210 Pigeon Point Road, Pescadero, CA 94060; (650) 879-2120; www.parks.ca.gov
Accommodations: Pigeon Point Lighthouse Hostel, 210 Pigeon Point Road, Pescadero, CA 94060; (650) 879-0633; www.norcalhostels.org
Hike Tours: Año Nuevo State Reserve, (650) 879-2025; (650) 879-0227 for recorded information; (800) 444-4445 for reservations; www.parks.ca.gov

Elephant Seals' Annual Schedule

Breeding season: Males show up in late November and start fighting; females start arriving in late December and continue arriving until the end of February to give birth. By mid-March, the adults have mated and wean their pups by leaving. Weaners remain until late April to bask in the sun and learn to swim. A pup nurses for twenty-eight days, consuming a diet equivalent to seventy-five milkshakes a day.

Molting season: Juveniles and females come to molt from March through May; in early summer, subadult males show up to molt; in late summer, July and August, adult males arrive to change skins.

McNee Ranch State Park and Montara State Beach

McNee Ranch State Park (625 acres), adjacent to Montara State Beach, Gray Whale Cove State Beach, and Montara Mountain, offers a hillside climb with views and two short walks to caramel-colored beaches with wild, seething surfs. A stroll on the bluffs above the Cabrillo Highway, with glorious Pacific views, takes you to the historic McNee Ranch, in the shade of Monterey cypress and Monterey pine trees. Prepare to use those calves as you ascend both moderate and strenuous grades to the top of Montara Mountain (1,898 feet).

Start: The parking lot on the west side of Highway 1 across from Gray Whale Cove

Distance: 8.1 miles round-trip, out-and-back with a loop in the middle

Approximate hiking time: 4.5 hours

Difficulty: Mostly moderate, but strenuous in steep uphill sections

Trail surface: Sand and stairs lead to the beach. Single-track dirt trail through McNee Ranch, followed by dirt fire road and broken pavement with some steep portions. Trail floor becomes granite rock, then dirt and gravel at the top of Montara Mountain.

Other trail users: Equestrians and mountain bikers

Canine compatibility: Leashed dogs permitted

Land status: State park and beach

Fees and permits: No fees or permits required

Schedule: Open year-round daily from 8:00 a.m. to dusk

Maps: USGS Montara Mountain, CA. McNee Ranch State Park Office, Half Moon Bay, CA; (650) 726-8819

Trail contact: Half Moon Bay State Beach (the ranger station for McNee Ranch); (650) 726-8819; www.parks.ca.gov

Other: Dress in layers to compensate for lots of direct sunlight and sudden cold fog. Bring plenty of water, too, as there are virtually no facilities.

Finding the trailhead

By Car: The Gray Whale Cove parking lot is 3 miles south of the last stoplight in Pacifica (Linda del Mar) on Highway 1 (8 miles north of Half Moon Bay). Parking is on the left-hand side of the road (east). Signs read MCNEE RANCH. There is more parking 0.5 mile down Highway 1 at Montara State Beach.

THE HIKE

This hike starts with an optional venture down the wooden-railed steps to the small but dramatic Gray Whale Cove (a clothing-optional beach). In winter, you will probably have the beach to yourself. Until 2001, Gray Whale was known as Devil's Slide Beach, named for the Devil's Slide area where rock slides onto Highway 1 have taken out vehicles and blocked the road many times.

Why are slides so common here? The sparkling, camel-colored Montara Mountain granite, which makes up part of the floor and walls of the North Peak Trail, meets Paleocene sediments in the area, causing a crumbling effect. There's also the Pacific Ocean, wearing away the land's edge.

After enjoying the ocean view from the Gray Whale Cove Trail, a shaded road between rows of mature cypress and Monterey pines brings you to the flat valley of McNee Ranch. The bridge to the stables stretches over Martini Creek. Before the ranch days, Native Americans hunted and picked berries here, and in 1769, Don Gaspar de Portolá's scouting party camped here as they trekked north to discover the San Francisco Bay.

After California entered the Union in 1850, roads and railroads traversed McNee Ranch, opening up the coast to development, and remnants, including the broken pavement on Old Pedro Mountain Road, can be seen here. McNee Ranch became part of the empire of Duncan McNee, an early California land baron. During World War II, the U.S. Army moved onto the ranch, using it as a training ground. You can still see two of the bunkers.

The drought-tolerant natural grasses and chaparral on Montara Mountain act like superglue, holding the slopes together against erosion. The plant community changes subtly as you gain elevation. At the lower elevations, you find coastal scrub: coast sagebrush, seaside daisy, Pacific blackberry, and coast buckwheat. Next up is coastal chaparral, comprised of pink and white flowered manzanita (including the unique Montara manzanita), blue ceanothus, fuchsia, coffeeberry, and chinquapin. The marine chaparral at the highest elevation, consisting of manzanita, salal, and lupine, grows only in this location on the San Mateo coast. Native vegetation includes the endangered Hickman's cinquefoil, as well as San Francisco gumplant, Montara bush lupine, coast and San Francisco wallflowers, and coast rock cress.

Claiming the area under a Mexican land grant, prominent San Franciscans Francisco Guerrero, one of the early mayors of San Francisco, and rancher Tiburcio

Velasquez brought cattle to graze these hillsides. That land grant still exists today, the only one left in the state and one of the largest undeveloped properties on the San Francisco peninsula: Rancho Corral de Tierra. The plan for this rich area of mountain, watershed, and farmland, now under the protection of the Peninsula Open Space Trust (POST), is to give the open space over to the Golden Gate National Recreation Area. Already the largest urban national park in the world, Rancho Corral de Tierra increases the recreation area's size by over 5 percent. Hikers can venture onto these restricted access trails, 6,700 glorious continuous acres mostly on the untrodden south face of the mountain, but to hike beyond North Peak, you must obtain permission. Call POST at (650) 854-7696; www.openspacetrust.org.

In the late winter, bring binoculars to spot gray whales in the Pacific on their migration north. Watch for Anna's and ruby-throated hummingbirds hovering to feed from sticky monkeyflowers in summer and berry blossoms anytime of year. Besides a healthy raptor population, large black ravens add a Poe-like eeriness on foggy days. Look for tracks of coyotes, fox, bobcats, deer, raccoons, and brush rabbits on the trail. Mountain lions, though present, are rarely sighted.

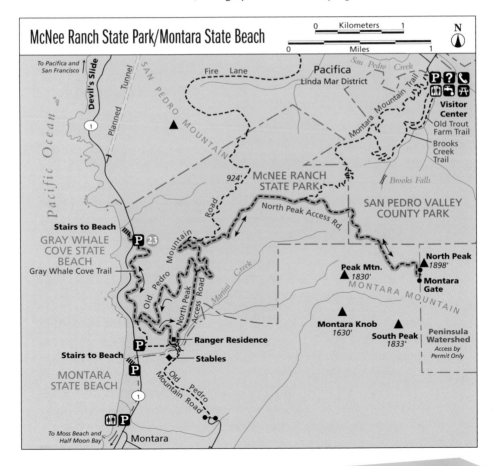

Pampas grass in front of Montara Mountain

MILES AND DIRECTIONS

0.0   Start in the parking lot across the street from Gray Whale Cove State Beach. Cross the street carefully to visit cove. Turn right past the green shack and restrooms to the staircase that leads to the beach. (*Note:* Gray Whale Cove Beach is clothing-optional. Watch for dangerous surf, recurring riptides, and sleeper waves.)

0.3   Reach Gray Whale Cove Beach. Come back up the stairs, retracing your steps. Cross the highway carefully.

0.6   Walk to the trailhead for McNee Ranch at the south end of the parking lot. An interpretive sign with the park map marks the start of single-track Gray Whale Cove Trail. (*Note:* The trail can flood after rain.)

1.2   Reach a viewing bench on the bluff.

1.5   Veer right (southeast) onto the connector trail to North Peak Access Road (toward McNee Ranch) at Old Pedro Mountain Road junction. This is a multiuse trail.

1.8 The trail winds down and meets paved North Peak Access Road. Turn left (north).

1.9 Pass the ranger residence on the left (north) and the bridge to the stables on the right (south). Go through the gate, starting uphill on the double-track, dirt North Peak Access Road.

2.4 The trail splits; stay right (northeast) on North Peak Access Road, past unmarked Old Pedro Mountain Road to San Pedro Mountain. The trail to North Peak becomes a maintained dirt fire road.

3.3 Stay right, continuing on North Peak Access Road to the top of Montara Mountain. The trail to the left (northeast) is Montara Mountain Trail, which leads to San Pedro Valley County Park.

4.4 Reach the North Peak of Montara Mountain (1,898 feet). Beyond this point a gate blocks the fire road, which continues on the permit-only San Francisco Water Department Peninsula Watershed. When this area becomes part of the Golden Gate National Recreation Area, it will probably become more accessible to hikers, an exciting prospect. Note the repeater stations on the peak (used for relaying signals from cellular phones, radios, etc.). Return the same way down North Peak Access Road.

5.5 Pass Montara Mountain Trail again, staying left (west) on North Peak Access Road.

6.4 After about 0.1 mile of broken paved trail, turn right (west) onto the single-track, dirt Old Pedro Mountain Road trail, marked by two wooden posts on either side of the path. The path widens, then becomes single-track again. There are steep downhill sections. Follow the trail to Gray Whale Cove Trail.

7.2 Reach the junction with Gray Whale Cove Trail. Turn right (north) to head to the parking lot across from Gray Whale Cove State Beach.

8.1 Arrive back at the parking lot.

Option: After your hike, you can drive 1 mile south to Montara State Beach.

HIKE INFORMATION

Local Information: Half Moon Bay Coastside Chamber of Commerce and Visitors' Bureau, 235 Main Street, Half Moon Bay, CA 94019; (650) 726-8380; www.halfmoonbaychamber.org

Hike Tours: McNee Ranch State Park Office, Half Moon Bay; (650) 726-8819 Save Our Shores; (415) 726-3123; (415) 726-9525; (415) 949-0708

Tide Information: tidesandcurrents.noaa.gov

James V. Fitzgerald Marine Reserve:
The Tide Pool Loop

This hike takes some planning. You only want to walk on the beach part of this loop at low tide (1 foot or under). Awaiting you there is the longest intertidal reef in California, an unforgettable experience. But even if you arrive at high tide, you can enjoy a walk along coastal bluffs with Pacific views, passing over a creek and through a grove of old, tall cypress trees shaped by the salty winds. A short stint past the wood-framed homes and the haunted favorite haunt, Moss Beach Distillery, takes you to a trail on open space through seaside scrub and grassland along the cliffs. Over the ridge to the east is the fishing harbor of Pillar Point and a trail through a bird watcher's paradise.

Start: James V. Fitzgerald Marine Reserve Information Center, on the corner of California Avenue and North Lake Street in Moss Beach
Distance: 3-mile loop
Approximate hiking time: 2.5 hours
Difficulty: Moderate
Trail surface: Single-track, dirt trail along bluffs, roadside walking, a paved trail down to the marsh; a couple of miles on sandy and rocky beach; tide pools
Other trail users: Hikers only on beach; mountain bikers and equestrians on bluffs
Canine compatibility: Dogs not permitted; delicate wildlife reserve
Land status: Marine reserve
Fees and permits: The trail between Ocean Boulevard and Pillar Point is a Peninsula Open

Space Trust (POST) restricted access trail. Call POST at (650) 854-7696 to obtain permission.
Schedule: Open daily from dawn to dusk
Maps: USGS Montara Mountain; Half Moon Bay. James V. Fitzgerald Marine Reserve, P.O. Box 451, Moss Beach, CA 94038; (650) 728-3584; www.fitzgeraldreserve.org
Trail contact: James V. Fitzgerald Marine Reserve, P.O. Box 451, Moss Beach, CA 94038; (650) 728-3584; www.fitzgeraldreserve.org
Other: To determine low tides, search online for "low tide, Half Moon Bay," or call the ranger station at the Fitzgerald reserve. There is a restroom and information kiosk, which is sporadically attended, at the trailhead.

Finding the trailhead
By Car: Take Highway 1 to Moss Beach. Turn west onto California Avenue (following signs for the marine reserve). Turn right (northwest) at the end of California Avenue onto North Lake Street and immediately right into the parking lot on the corner.

THE HIKE

This stretch of coastline was officially protected as a reserve in 1969 and named James V. Fitzgerald Marine Reserve for a San Mateo County board member involved in the process. Some 100,000 people explore the tide pools each year, most of them schoolchildren on field trips. With thirty acres of marine habitat, more than 400 species of animals, and 150 plant species revealed by the low tides, it makes a fantastic classroom. Docents (adults and high school students) teach kids about tides and offer guided tours on the weekends to the public.

Scientists studying the shallow marine shelf have discovered twenty-five plant and invertebrate species, as well as a few endemic ones, living nowhere else but here. They include a worm, a type of seaweed, and a shrimp that lives in the gut of a sea anemone. Species are still being catalogued. At times, some 300 harbor seals haul themselves out on the beaches. Always stay at least 300 feet away from the seals for your safety and theirs. The best time to see the tide pools is at minus tide, on the days following a full moon. If you come at high tide, only a short hike on the bluff is accessible.

Walking through the cypress grove

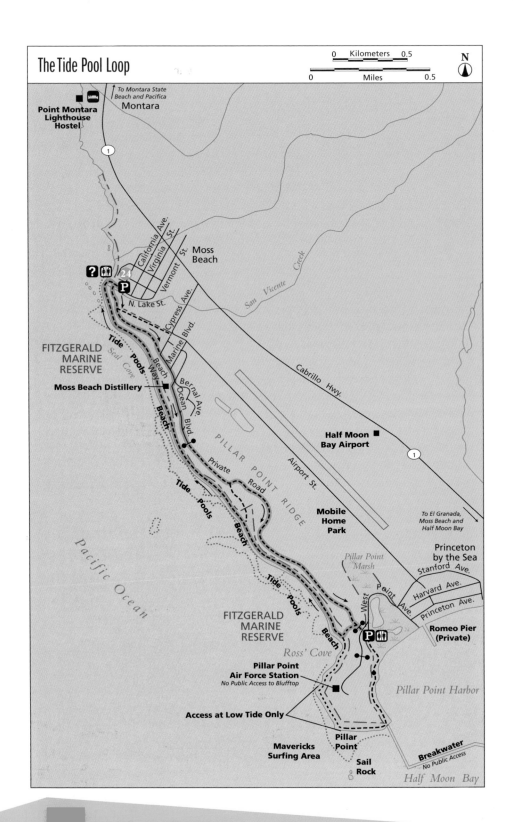

The Tide Pool Loop

Kilometers 0 — 0.5
Miles 0 — 0.5

N

Point Montara
Lighthouse
Hostel

To Montara State
Beach and Pacifica
Montara

1

California Ave.
Virginia St.
Vermont St.
Moss
Beach

San Vicente Creek

? 24 P

N. Lake St.

Cypress Ave.

FITZGERALD
MARINE
RESERVE

Tide
Pools

Seal Cove

Beach Way

Marine Blvd.

Cabrillo Hwy.

Moss Beach Distillery

Ocean Blvd.

Bernal Ave.

Beach

PILLAR POINT RIDGE

Half Moon
Bay Airport

1

Private Road

Tide
Pools

Beach

Airport St.

Mobile
Home
Park

To El Granada,
Moss Beach and
Half Moon Bay

Pacific Ocean

Tide
Pools

Beach

Pillar Point
Marsh

Point Ave.

Princeton
by the Sea
Stanford Ave.

Harvard Ave.

Princeton Ave.

FITZGERALD
MARINE
RESERVE

West

P

Romeo Pier
(Private)

Ross' Cove

Pillar Point
Air Force Station
No Public Access to Blufftop

Pillar Point Harbor

Access at Low Tide Only

Mavericks
Surfing Area

Pillar
Point

Sail
Rock

Breakwater
No Public Access

Half Moon Bay

The featured hike starts on the bluff with some interesting landmarks. The cypress forest was planted as a windbreak by coastal farmers and ranchers around World War I. Cypress and eucalyptus trees were the most popular trees for this purpose on the Northern California coast, both fast growing and able to withstand extreme weather conditions.

The lore of the Moss Beach Distillery gives you some insight into the colorful past of the San Mateo coast. During Prohibition, the coast was an ideal spot for rum running, bootleggers, and speakeasies that sold illegal booze to thirsty clients. One of the most successful speakeasies of the era was Frank's Place, built by Frank Torres in 1927 on the cliffs near Moss Beach. Frank's Place became a popular nightspot for silent film stars and politicians from the city. Under cover of darkness and fog, illegal whiskey was landed on the beach below the restaurant, dragged up the steep cliffs, and loaded into waiting vehicles for transport to San Francisco. The distillery is also famous for its resident ghost, the Blue Lady, an old customer from the speakeasy days. She was evidently drowned, and the culprit never caught, though a jilted lover was a suspect.

The trail heads back onto the bluffs where Ocean Boulevard meets Bernal Avenue, taking you onto Peninsula Open Space Trust (POST) restricted access trails. You can obtain permission to hike here by calling POST or going to their Web site (650-854-7696; www.openspacetrust.org).

Pillar Point, with its 175-foot crown, was once called Snake's Head for its unique shape. The Costanoans gathered shellfish at its base 5,800 years ago. Spaniards, Mexicans, and Americans grazed cattle on its hillsides from 1790 through the 1890s. Portuguese whalers used the high point as a lookout for humpback whales. Not until World War II did buildings appear on the point, when it became an observation post linked to the harbor defenses of San Francisco. Today, Pillar Point is still an active U.S. Air Force base, with soldiers stationed in the 120-foot tower and its giant dish, 80 feet in diameter, still tracking military activity over long distances.

The trail from West Point Avenue passes through the Pillar Point Marsh, home to 151 species of birds. You can also watch—with binoculars—the surfers at Mavericks, famous for 100-foot waves that are the delight of professional surfers. During low tide, you can walk around the base of the point for up to 3.5 miles of lovely beach walking and tide pools.

Marine Mammal Center

The Marine Mammal Center often uses the reserve as a place to reintroduce harbor seals, sea lions, and other ocean creatures that have been rehabilitated after injury to the wilds of the Pacific. Call the Marine Mammal Center (415-289-7325) to find out about scheduled releases; it's a great thing for kids to see. The Web site is www.marinemammalcenter.org.

0.0   Start from the parking lot at the marine reserve information kiosk. Turn left (south) onto North Lake Street. Just past the parking lot, on the right, watch for a dirt trail that leads over the creek (going west). There are several trails heading up to the bluff. Take the well-worn trail on the right.

0.1   A single-track dirt trail beside a split-wood safety fence heads south along the cliffs. Looking along the line of the bluffs south, you can see the Moss Beach Distillery out on a short point.

0.3   Pass palm trees and back into some woods.

0.4   At the corner of Beach and Cypress, continue south, walking on the side of Beach Way past coastal houses. Seal Cove Inn is on the left. Stay on Beach Way heading south, past the stop sign at Marine Boulevard. Follow signs to Moss Beach Distillery.

0.5   Arrive at the Moss Beach Distillery, where Beach Way meets Ocean Boulevard. Continue south past the parking lot on Ocean Boulevard. A small paved road leads uphill, where you'll find views of Pillar Point. The cement pillar in the water is a sighting to range artillery from Pillar Point, one of eighty including landmarks and lighthouses.

0.9   Ocean Boulevard meets Bernal Avenue and dead-ends at a field. Take the dirt trail heading south. There are many social paths, so make your way carefully. Follow the cliffs toward Pillar Point. You can see several areas where the cliffs have fallen away, so do not stand right on the edge. Views of Montara Mountain and open beyond Pillar Point.

1.4   Turn right onto a dirt path down to the beach. Watch your footing.

1.5   Reach Ross' Cove (formerly Whalers' Cove) on the north side of the point, a favorite surfing spot. To the southwest, beyond Bird Rocks, is the famous Mavericks surfing spot (named for a surfer's dog). This is best viewed from the south side of Pillar Point, but hard to see in general. Turn north up the beach to enjoy the tide pools.

2.0   Reach Frenchman's Reef. Continue along beach.

2.5   Arrive at Seal Cove.

3.0   Reach San Vicente Creek, which runs into the ocean. Carefully cross the creek and climb up rocks on other side. (*Note:* This is the most strenuous part of the hike when the tide is in. An alternative route is a path up to the cypress grove.) Turn inland for a brief walk to the parking lot.

Options: The marine reserve continues north all the way to Montara Lighthouse, another 0.9 mile, if you want a longer hike on the beach and a look at the light-house, which now houses an international youth hostel. Montara State Beach starts beyond it.

You can also take the trail left (east) at the 1.4 mile-mark, down to the parking lot. Turn right onto the paved pathway, right (north) again onto West Point Avenue, and out onto a trail that visits the marshland and piers of Pillar Point Harbor. This adds 1 mile round-trip to the hike. In very low tide only, it is possible to walk the beach around Pillar Point. Proceed with caution.

To shorten the hike, take the stairs down to the beach near the palm trees (0.3 mile from the trailhead) to create a 0.5-mile loop.

HIKE INFORMATION

Local Information: Half Moon Bay Coastside Chamber of Commerce and Visi-tors' Bureau, 235 Main Street, Half Moon Bay, CA 94019 (650) 726-8380; www.halfmoonbaychamber.org

Hike Tours: James V. Fitzgerald Marine Reserve, P.O. Box 451, Moss Beach, CA 94038; (650) 728-3584; www.fitzgeraldreserve.org

Tide Information: www.tides.info or tidesonline.com (search Princeton/Half Moon Bay)

Taking Care of Tide Pools

Twice a day, retreating tides leave seashore life clinging to the rocks. Intertidal plants and animals are well adapted to this changing world of surf and sand but have no defense against humans. Therefore, whenever you are tide pool-ing, observe the following guidelines:

1. The best way to observe tide pools is to sit quietly until animals emerge from their hiding places and resume their activities. Watch out for the rising tide.

2. You may touch marine life, but DO NOT pick it up or place it in a container. If you do, it will die. Examine it in the place that you find it.

3. Watch your step! Walk carefully around the tide pools for your own safety and to spare the marine life underfoot.

4. Any rocks that get moved should be replaced with the seaweed side up. Life on the bottom of the rocks will die when exposed to sun and air. Avoid moving rocks whenever possible.

5. Shells and rocks are a natural part of the areas. Many serve as future homes for creatures such as hermit crabs. DO NOT COLLECT SHELLS, VEGETATION, ROCKS, OR MARINE LIFE IN THE RESERVE.

San Pedro Valley Park

San Pedro Valley Park, nestled between the northernmost Santa Cruz Mountains and the foothills of Pacifica, is protected from harsh coastal winds and weather, a place to breathe easy. Three freshwater creeks flow under the shade of willows, oaks, and dogwoods, supporting fish and riparian flora and fauna. Eight different trails offer chaparral with views, meadows of deer and wildflowers, hillside grasslands, herbal eucalyptus groves, and a waterfall. People have enjoyed the peaceful scenery here for thousands of years; with the addition of picnic areas and an interesting visitor center, you can spend the day doing the same.

Start: In the parking lots by the San Pedro Valley Park Visitor Center
Distance: 6.1-mile loop
Approximate hiking time: 3 hours
Difficulty: Moderate
Trail surface: Single- and double-track dirt trails, a couple of wooden bridges, and some paved path
Other trail users: Bikers on Weiler Ranch Road
Canine compatibility: Dogs not permitted
Land status: County park
Fees and permits: A $5 fee is levied for parking

Schedule: Open daily from 8:00 a.m. to dusk
Maps: USGS Montara Mountain. San Pedro Valley Park, 600 Oddstad Boulevard, Pacifica, CA 94044; (650) 355-8289; www.co.sanmateo.ca.us (go to the parks department link). San Mateo County Parks and Recreation, 455 County Center, 4th Floor, Redwood City, CA 94063; (650) 363-4020
Trail contact: San Pedro Valley Park, 600 Oddstad Boulevard, Pacifica, CA 94044; (650) 355-8289; www.co.sanmateo.ca.us (go to the parks department link)

Finding the trailhead

By Car: From Highway 1 in Pacifica, turn east onto Linda Mar Boulevard (at the stoplight). Where Linda Mar ends, turn right (south) onto Oddstad Boulevard and proceed 1 block to the park entrance. Turn right (southeast) up the hill into the park, pay at the kiosk, and park in either lot. (You have to pay the fee even when the kiosk is unattended, so bring $5 in change.)
By Public Transportation: SamTrans runs buses from the Daly City and Colma BART stations to the Linda Mar stop. From Linda Mar, you can transfer to local service, which stops at Linda Mar and Oddstad Boulevards, a half block from the park entrance. For trip planning and more information, call SamTrans at (800) 660-4BUS (4287) or dial 511; visit www.samtrans.com or 511.org.

THE HIKE

t's easy to see why people have gathered in this valley for centuries. The south and middle forks of San Pedro Creek flow year-round and provide safe spawning areas for migratory steelhead trout. Brooks Creek during the rainy winter months puts on a show, with Brooks Falls splashing down 175 feet in three tiers. The Middle Valley is an artist's palette with springtime wildflowers: California poppies, suncups, buttercups, wild mustard, and wild radish. At dusk, brush rabbits cautiously hop out of hiding to feed. Black-tailed does and fawns munch contentedly on flowers.

The Costanoan Indians had a seasonal camp here for possibly thousands of years. In 1769, Spanish explorer Gaspar de Portolá and his men arrived here sick and exhausted. Their expedition, which was supposed to end at Monterey, had missed the target, and they had walked on. They stumbled into this valley and set up camp. It was so peaceful and rejuvenating, they stayed a while, and it was from this camp that Portolá's scout, Sergeant Jose Francisco Ortega, set out to explore the area and, climbing Sweeney Ridge, saw the San Francisco Bay for the first time.

Around the turn of the twentieth century, wealthy San Franciscans constructed palatial summer homes on the coast side. Not long ago, cattle still ruminated on the hillsides, and commercial farmers harvested crops of pumpkins and artichokes in the meadows. A fellow named John Gay operated a trout farm on the south fork of San Pedro Creek until 1962, when rainstorms washed out his operation.

In the early 1950s, developer Andres Oddstad bought up seven of the ranches in the San Pedro Valley and started construction on tract homes in Linda Mar. By 1957, nine hamlets along 6 miles of coastline incorporated as the city of Pacifica, Spanish for "peace." The new community found the natural meadows and hillsides a backyard paradise. With a citywide vote, the citizens donated as much open space as possible to the National Park Service and the county. As a result, Pacifica's population hasn't grown significantly in thirty years, and back at the end of Odd-stad Boulevard are 1,150 acres of serene valley, hillsides, and cascading streams.

Of course nothing is perfect. Poison oak grows heartily along with everything else in the park. Fog can roll in, blocking views and chilling the bones. The park has great group picnic sites, but that means there are often crowds of people here on the weekends. Pooches have to stay home. Small portions of Hazelnut Trail, though under repair, are rutted by rain runoff, and deer paths on the Valley View Loop require that a hiker pay attention to stick to the main trail.

These considerations are slight, however, compared with the hiking possibilities. If hiking with young children, the nature trail and a tour of the visitor center make a nice outing. The Brooks Falls Loop is a short 2 miles. With two cars, a wonderful option is hiking the Montara Mountain Trail through McNee Ranch and ending at Montara Beach for a picnic. The featured hike takes in a little bit of everything for a satisfying loop.

MILES AND DIRECTIONS

0.0 Start at the visitor center in San Pedro Valley Park and walk toward the trailhead for Plaskon Nature Trail. Cross the bridge. After about 30 yards, turn right (southeast) onto the signed Hazelnut Trail. The trail ascends the hill on switchbacks.

1.2 Higher up the trail, you enter the drier sandstone area where rare Montara manzanita and giant golden chinquapin grow beside coyote brush, toyon, and coffeeberry. Continue on Hazelnut Trail, which eventually heads east on switchbacks down to the valley.

3.3 Turn left (west) onto Weiler Ranch Road.

3.6 Turn right (north) onto Valley View Trail. Valley View traverses south-facing slopes above the valley. Be careful of rocks on the trail and watch for the scat and footprints of coyotes and other critters. The trail rises, then descends.

5.0 The Valley View Trail ends. Turn right (west) onto Weiler Ranch Road, then left (north) onto the park service road, heading toward the visitor center. The road crosses the middle fork of San Pedro Creek and passes by the Walnut Grove Group Picnic Area. Continue on the service road to the north parking lot.

5.2 Continue on the sidewalk past the visitor center to the end of the south parking lot. Take the Old Trout Farm Trail (0.8-mile long).

5.3 On the Old Trout Farm Trail, you will pass the picnic area on the left and, near the beginning of the trail, a couple of tanks, the remains of John Gay's trout farm.

5.5 At the hairpin turn, the trail looks up the ravine at Brooks Falls.

5.6 At the junction with the Brooks Creek Trail, stay right (north) on the Brooks Falls Overlook Trail. For a different view of the falls, turn left (west) and head to a bench about 0.3 mile up the trail.

6.1 Arrive back at the parking lots and visitor center.

Option: From the intersection with the Valley View Trail at 3.6 miles, you can continue west on Weiler Ranch Road back to the visitor center for a 4.3-mile loop.

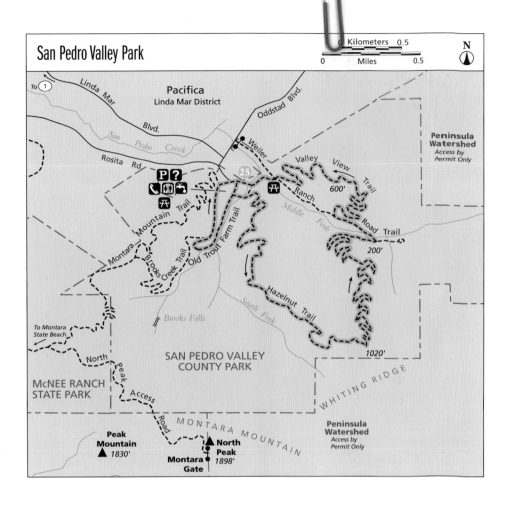

San Pedro Valley Park

To ①

Linda Mar

Pacifica
Linda Mar District

Oddstad Blvd.

Blvd.

San Pedro Creek

Rosita Rd.

Peninsula Watershed
Access by Permit Only

Weiler

Valley View Trail

25

600'

Ranch

Road Trail

Middle Fork

200'

Montara Mountain Trail

Brooks Creek Trail

Old Trout Farm Trail

Hazelnut Trail

South Fork

Brooks Falls

1020'

To Montara State Beach

North

SAN PEDRO VALLEY COUNTY PARK

WHITING RIDGE

McNEE RANCH STATE PARK

Peak Access Road

MONTARA MOUNTAIN

Peninsula Watershed
Access by Permit Only

Peak Mountain ▲ 1830'

▲ North Peak

Montara Gate

1898'

HIKE INFORMATION

Local Information: Pacifica Chamber of Commerce and Visitor Center, 225 Rockaway Beach, #1, Pacifica, CA 94044; (650) 355-4122 or (650) 355-6949; www .pacificachamber.com

Local Events/Attractions: Milagra Ridge (protected habitat hiking in the Golden Gate Recreation Area), 600 Sharp Park Road, Pacifica, CA 94044; www.nps.gov .goga

Sanchez Adobe Historic Site, 1000 Linda Mar Boulevard, Pacifica, CA 94044; (650) 359-1462; www.co.sanmateo .ca.us (follow links to the parks department)

Hike Tours: San Pedro Valley Park, 600 Oddstad Boulevard, Pacifica, CA 94044; (650) 355-8289; www.co.sanmateo.ca.us (follow links to the parks department)

San Pedro Valley Park **161**

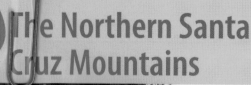

The Mother of the Forest (Hike 6)

You're up on Skyline Boulevard (Highway 35), sun shining through the windshield. Motorcyclists ride in posses on Sunday mornings to the famous Alice's Restaurant at Saratoga Gap. They have one destination, but for you, the hiker, your quest could take years: to explore all the parkland and open space accessible from this one road.

Skyline Boulevard follows the ridge of the northern Santa Cruz Mountains. Sloping down to eastern valleys and western coastline are tens of thousands of acres and hundreds of miles of trails through thick forests, scrub, and grassland.

The Midpeninsula Regional Open Space District alone has saved 46,500 acres in twenty-six preserves where sawmills once stood. Soda Gulch Trail in Purisima Creek Redwoods Open Space Preserve provides a meditative stroll through giant redwoods. Portola Redwoods has its Old Tree Trail and out-of-the-way campgrounds. Castle Rock State Park, aside from its groves of madrones and black oak trees, has amazing rock outcroppings. Rock climbers gather around Goat Rock to practice maneuvers. Big Basin State Park has the largest continuous stand of ancient coast redwoods south of San Francisco, some up to 2,000 years old. The waterfalls on Berry Creek Falls Trail are some of the most memorable in the Bay Area.

Sawmills made their first appearance in these vast forests back in 1849. But the steep mountains and tight gullies that keep the redwoods protected from wind and sun also protected a lot of them from becoming timber. The mills only operated when prices were high enough to compensate for the cost of hauling the lumber out. Cutting is still happening on private land today, but the happy consequence of the difficult terrain is that much of the forest has been saved.

California's coastal mountain range formed when the North America Plate, supporting the continent, and the Pacific Plate, under the Pacific Ocean, collided and began rubbing past each other along the San Andreas Fault line, which follows Stevens Creek east of the Santa Cruz Mountains. The pressure caused the folding of the sea floor and formed an almost continuous series of ranges and valleys the length of California, separating the coast from the great Central Valley and the deserts of the interior. The mountainous barrier is what causes the weather pattern most important to the redwoods: fog. The line where thick forests end and scrub and grasslands begin marks the fog line. Where the fog settles, you have green mixed forest up to the top of the ridge and slightly over the top where the fog spills, but then, suddenly, grasslands and scattered drought-resistant live oaks take over. You can find all of these habitats in the parks off Skyline Boulevard.

> The parks off Skyline Boulevard offer tens of thousands of acres and hundreds of miles of trails through thick forests, scrub, and grassland.

Big Basin Redwoods State Park: Berry Creek Falls Trail Loop

This 11-mile loop is a satisfying jaunt through the largest continuous stand of ancient coast redwoods south of San Francisco. Following the contours of the hillside, the Sunset Trail brings you through several deep canyons and cascading creeks. Berry Creek Falls Trail takes you past a series of waterfalls and through a deep basin. The Golden Cascade and Silver Falls feature just that: manes of silver water against golden earth. Berry Creek Falls is a 60-foot vertical sheet of white water falling down dark glistening rocks. Out of the canyon, the Skyline to the Sea Trail takes you through lush canyons past downed trees and more red giants.

Start: In the main parking lot across from Big Basin Redwoods State Park headquarters

Distance: 11.6-mile loop

Approximate hiking time: 6 hours

Difficulty: Strenuous due to the distance; the trail slopes are moderate

Trail surface: Single- and double-track dirt trail

Other trail users: Hikers only

Canine compatibility: Dogs not permitted

Land status: State park

Fees and permits: $6 for parking

Schedule: Open daily from 6:00 a.m. to 10:00 p.m.

Maps: USGS Big Basin. Big Basin Redwoods State Park and California Department of Parks and Recreation, 21600 Big Basin Way, Boulder Creek, CA 95006; (831) 338-8860; www.bigbasin .org or www.parks.ca.gov

Trail contact: Big Basin Redwoods State Park and California Department of Parks and Recreation, 21600 Big Basin Way, Boulder Creek, CA 95006; (831) 338-8860; www.bigbasin.org or www.parks.ca.gov

Other: The park has 148 campsites and several backpacking camps.

Finding the trailhead

By Car: From Highway 17, exit at Mount Hermon Road (at the sign for Big Basin). Stay right on Mount Hermon Road, which ends at Graham Hill Road. Turn right (north) at this light. You will immediately come to another signaled intersection with Highway 9); turn right (north) again. Stay on Highway 9 north for 15 miles. In the town of Boulder Creek, turn left (west) at the stop sign onto Highway 236/Big Basin Way. Stay on this highway for 9 miles to Big Basin Redwoods State Park. Proceed to the park headquarters.

By Public Transportation: Contact BART (www.transitinfo.org); SamTrans (800-660-4BUS (4287); www.samtrans.com); or Santa Clara Valley Transportation Authority (408-321-2300; www.vta.org) for public transportation options to the park.

THE HIKE

"These trees, because of their size and antiquity, are among the natural wonders of the world and should be saved for posterity."
—Photographer Andrew P. Hill, Savior of Big Basin, circa 1900

Beside the visitor center, a slice of an ancient redwood tree tells the first story of many on this hike. It sprouted in the year 544 during the Byzantine Empire and was already 1,392 years old when the park opened in 1902, the first state park in California. The early conservation effort that resulted in the park's creation came from photographer Andrew P. Hill, who started the Sempervirens Club to protect these redwoods. Today, the club is still hard at work protecting forests for future generations.

Big Basin Visitor Center

The Ohlone Indians lived around Big Basin for nearly 10,000 years. They believed the trees to be spirit beings, part of a divine race that existed before humans who taught people the proper way to live among the redwoods. Even their houses, made out of planks split from fallen redwoods over pits, were understood to be living bodies. Grizzlies, whom the natives respected and feared, lived in the dense ravines. Other than mushrooms, there wasn't a lot the Ohlones needed in the shadowy woods, so they pretty much left them alone. Sometimes their controlled burns in the grasslands reached the forest, but the redwoods always withstood the flames.

When Portolá's Spanish expedition came through in 1769, the men, sick with scurvy, camped at the mouth of Waddell Creek and gorged themselves on berries. With their miraculous recovery, they named the valley Cañada de la Salud or Canyon of Health.

Logging of the redwoods happened at a frantic pace after the gold rush as cities rose in the Bay Area. The resources seemed endless. Frustrated miners and others seeking a new life became lumbermen, living and working in the forests in a rough and isolated existence.

Single-track and double-track trails take you through cool canyons, following the contours of the hills. They meander by fern-lined creeks and immense tangled roots of fallen trees. This vast stand of giant redwoods, with their orangutan fur and citrus-scented needles, is overwhelming in scale. The mixed woodland also features very mature Douglas fir and tanbark oak trees, their trunks covered with soft, hairy moss. This landscape is uninterrupted for miles, except for the occasional orange monkeyflower, yellow banana slug, wild strawberry, or colorful mushroom that grows beside the trail. Bridges take you over gurgling streams. Natural sulfur in a couple of the creeks causes some sharp smells. In the rainy season, marshes serve as breeding grounds for California newts.

After the Berry Creek crossing, this route climbs to the edge of the forest, where startling afternoon sun blanches the scene for a tenth of mile. Here you find knobcone pines, manzanita, and soft, dry sandstone. Most of the animals in the park live in chaparral like this, in the coastal valleys or oak groves. Foxes, coyotes, bobcats, opossums, and the rare mountain lion share this area with hunting raptors, brush rabbits, lizards, and western rattlesnakes.

Back in endless woodland, you eventually reach the Berry Creek Falls Trail, which features almost continuous waterfalls. Golden Cascade, so named for the gold sandstone earth that forms the 20-foot slide beneath the falls, is followed by the two cascades of Silver Falls. A meditative walk beside Berry Creek brings you to 60-foot Berry Creek Falls, splashing bridal veil–fashion into the creek below.

The lush Skyline-to-the-Sea Trail, following Kelly and Timms Creeks, takes you back to the Redwood Trail Loop, a great finale to the day. A guide purchased from the visitor center leads you to redwood fairy circles and burls, the Chimney Tree, and the largest redwoods in the park.

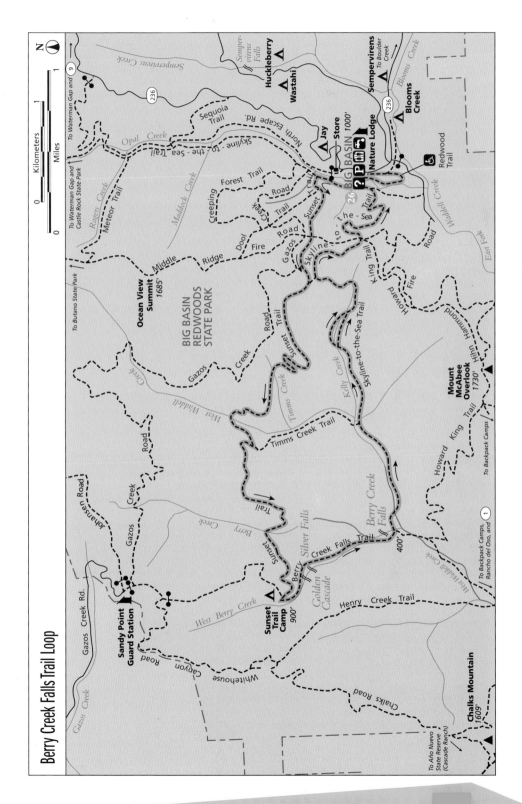

Berry Creek Falls Trail Loop

MILES AND DIRECTIONS

0.0 Start at the parking lot outside park headquarters. (*Note:* Before starting the hike, check out the visitor center and the redwood tree display beside it. Maps cost $3, self-guiding nature guides for the Redwood Trail are 25 cents.) Look for the trailhead for the Redwood Nature Trail on the side of the parking lot opposite the park headquarters. Go straight (west): You will take the Redwood Nature Trail as a cool-down walk after the main hike.

0.1 Past the restrooms is the start of the Skyline-to-the-Sea Trail, connecting to most other trails. Cross the bridge over Opal Creek to the trailhead. Turn right (north) onto the Skyline-to-the-Sea Trail toward Sunset Trail. It becomes a single-track dirt trail beyond the creek.

0.3 Stay to the left (west) on the Skyline-to-the-Sea Trail toward the Dool Trail.

0.4 Reach the trailhead for the Dool Trail. Turn left onto the Dool Trail for 0.1 mile to the Sunset Trail. Redwood Creek is on the right (north).

0.5 The trail splits. Turn left (west) onto the Sunset Trail toward Middle Ridge Fire Road.

1.3 Reach the trailhead for the connector trail. Continue straight (west) on Sunset Trail toward Timms Creek Trail. The trail goes through redwood groves and over hills. Cross several bridges, one of them over West Waddell Creek.

3.9 At the trailhead for the Timms Creek Trail, make a sharp turn right (uphill), continuing on Sunset Trail (a sign reads TO THE SUNSET TRAIL CAMP).

5.4 Cross Berry Creek. The trail begins to climb, then crosses the ridge.

5.5 At the turnoff to the Sunset backpacking camp, continue straight (west) on Sunset Trail to Berry Creek Falls Trail.

5.6 Head around a bend; you are now on Berry Creek Falls Trail. Reach Golden Cascade (so named for the gold sandstone that forms the 20-foot slide beneath the falls). This is followed by the two cascades of Silver Falls, so that you have 0.1 mile of continuous waterfalls. Follow the trail down rock stairs right beside the falls.

6.4 Reach Berry Creek Falls.

6.5 Arrive at a trailhead at a bridge. Turn left (east), over the bridge, toward Big Basin headquarters. You are now on the Skyline-to-the-Sea Trail, which heads uphill, with some flat areas and short descents, all the way back to the trailhead.

Logger Legends and Big Basin Place Names

Waddell and West Waddell Creek—William White Waddell (b. Kentucky, 1818) arrived in Santa Cruz County in 1851 and built sawmills. One, along with a tram-way and a wharf, was along the creek that now bears his name. They burned down. Waddell died in 1875 from complications of injuries resulting from a bear attack—the bear ripped one of his arms off. Every Halloween there's a special night hike in Big Basin titled, "The Missing Arm of William Waddell."

Berry Creek—Berry Creek was named for an old lumberman, Tilford George Berry, probably an employee of Waddell's. Tilford, from Indiana, built a cabin at the base of the lower Berry Creek Falls in the mid-1860s. He mysteriously disappeared during the next decade, and finally, in 1890, his bones were found in the chaparral above Boulder Creek.

Dool Trail—William H. "Billy" Dool served as warden of Big Basin from 1911 until 1932. A Canadian, naturalized in Santa Cruz County in 1888, he was also a butcher, with a shop on what is now Central Avenue near Big Basin Way.

Hihn Hammond Road—Originally built in 1917 by the Hihn Hammond Lumber Company, it is a retired logging road.

Timms Creek—George Timms was a squatter and timber claimant who had a cabin in an opening in the woods near the present Gazos Creek Road. Like many of the mountain men around here, Timms was a hard drinker and occasionally had delirium tremens (the DTs). Around 1884 he disappeared, leaving the basin's greatest mystery behind him. Three different stories pointed to murder, but none had sufficient factual evidence to make an accusation.

Kelly Creek—This short creek is named for Dr. Thomas Kelly, a surgeon in the Civil War who took up a timber claim in the area in the 1870s. The Kelly Cabin became a well-known rendezvous for hunters. He died in his bed in 1906 at the age of seventy.

6.6 The trail passes over West Waddell Creek and follows the creek uphill. There are several old-growth trees on this trail.

7.5 Continue straight (east) on the Skyline-to-the-Sea Trail as you pass the trailhead for Timms Creek Trail. The trail now follows Kelly Creek.

8.1 The trail splits; take either branch. The lower trail passes over the creek and back; the upper trail goes along the ridge and passes through the burned-out base of a tree.

8.3 The two trails rejoin. Continue east on the Skyline-to-the-Sea Trail.

9.2 At the trail junction, turn right (east) to stay on Skyline-to-the-Sea Trail. This is also a connector to the Hihn Hammond Road. The other leg goes north to the Sunset Trail.

9.6 Turn left (east) and pass over the Middle Ridge Fire Road, continuing downhill and east on the Skyline-to-the-Sea Trail.

10.7 Take the bridge, continuing straight east back to the park headquarters (to the right is the Skyline–Hihn Hammond trail connector).

11.0 Turn right, back over the bridge, to the start of the hike. Past the restrooms, turn right (south) between split-rail fencing to the Redwood Trail Loop, a great finale to the day. Pass great examples of a redwood circle (or fairy circle), redwood burls, the burned-out Chimney Tree, the Father of the Forest, and the Mother of the Forest. You'll also see the memorial to Andrew Hill, who helped to preserve these redwoods as parkland.

11.6 Arrive back at the parking lot.

HIKE INFORMATION

Local Information: Santa Cruz County Conference and Visitors Council, 1211 Ocean Street, Santa Cruz, CA 95060; (831) 425-1234 or (800) 833-3494; www.santacruzca.org

Local Events/Attractions: Natural Bridges State Beach, West Cliff Drive, Santa Cruz, CA 95060; (831) 423-4609; www.parks.ca.gov

Seymour Marine Discovery Center, University of California, Santa Cruz, 100 Shaffer Road, Santa Cruz, CA 95060; (831) 459-3800; www2.ucsc.edu/seymourcenter

Hike Tours: Big Basin Redwoods State Park and California Department of Parks and Recreation, 21600 Big Basin Way, Boulder Creek, CA 95006; (831) 338-8860; www.bigbasin.org or www.parks.ca.gov

Castle Rock State Park

Castle Rock State Park is on one of the highest ridges in the Santa Cruz Mountains. The hike features great variety: cool, dark mixed forests, creeks and a seasonal waterfall, dry, manzanita-lined ridges, grassy hills, oak savanna, and above all, rock formations. The boulders come in amazing shapes, with curves, crevices, and caves. On weekends, you will see climbers navigate their way up 90-degree rock faces with chalky fingers. The giant boulder that gives the park its name sits in high woodland toward the end of the hike. There are interpretive exhibits and scenic overlooks that show off the park's 5,300 acres and over 50 miles of hiking paths.

Start: From the Saratoga Gap Trailhead in the Castle Rock main parking lot on Highway 35 (Skyline Boulevard)

Distance: 6.1-mile loop

Approximate hiking time: 3 hours

Difficulty: Moderate, with strenuous (but safe) passes over rock near a sheer cliff

Trail surface: Single- and some double-track dirt trail; rocky paths passing between giant boulders

Other trail users: Hikers only

Canine compatibility: Dogs not permitted

Land status: State park

Fees and permits: Parking fee is $6.

Schedule: Open daily from 8:00 a.m. to dusk

Maps: USGS Castle Rock Ridge. Castle Rock State Park, 15000 Skyline Boulevard, Los Gatos, CA 95033; (408) 867-2952; www.parks .ca.gov. Big Basin Redwoods State Park and California Department of Parks and Recreation, 21600 Big Basin Way, Boulder Creek, CA 95006-9064; (831) 338-8860; www .parks.ca.gov

Trail contact: Castle Rock State Park, 15000 Skyline Boulevard, Los Gatos, CA 95033; (408) 867-2952; www.parks.ca.gov/?page_id=538

Other: Bring water (limited facilities) and dress in layers.

Finding the trailhead

By Car: From Highway 92 westbound in San Mateo, turn south onto Skyline Boulevard (Highway 35). Travel approximately 25 miles to the junction of Highways 35 and 9 (Saratoga Gap). Continue on Highway 35 another 2.5 miles south. Look for the brown sign on the right (west) for Castle Rock State Park. Turn right (west) into the packed dirt parking lot.

By Public Transportation: There's no direct way to the park. Contact BART for more information (www.transitinfo.org). SamTrans information is available by calling (800) 660-4BUS (4287) or visiting www.samtrans.com. The Santa Clara Valley Transportation Authority is at (408) 321-2300; www.vta.org.

THE HIKE

The trail starts creekside in a shady redwood, oak, and bay woodland, with lichen-covered rocks against the hillsides. Costanoan Indians used to hike this trail from their coastal villages to gather acorns produced by the park's plentiful oak trees. Rangers have found arrowheads and other faint traces of their travels through Castle Rock. After the Civil War, farmers and dairy cattle ranchers settled in the hills around Castle Rock.

Just over a wooden bridge on the Saratoga Gap Trail, the sound of running water crescendos. An observation platform allows you to stand at the top of Castle Rock Falls and watch the water drop approximately 60 feet down onto the rocks below. This seasonal waterfall is best after storms.

The trail descends through oak scrub dotted with sticky monkeyflower and wild strawberries. In spring, the park offers a surprising display of wildflowers. Coral bells, chickweed, hedge wood rose, and California fuchsia decorate the banks of the creek. Dryer areas host lots of orange California poppies and Indian paintbrush, with blossoms like red sparklers that stay around through most of summer, providing perches for cabbage butterflies.

The trail rises onto rocky ridges high above wooded ravines with spectacular views of the park and Pacific. A safety cable helps hikers climb a set of narrow stone steps on the cliff. This rite-of-passage brings you to Goat Rock. The pockets, patterns, and protrusions of Goat Rock look like part of an alien landscape. The intricate patterns in the sandstone, called stone lace and honeycomb, are the result of what geologists call "chemical weathering."

The rock formations are an intriguing sight in the park. Climbers often compare the Castle Rock boulders to those in Fontainebleau, France, though the Santa Cruz rocks, mostly less than 12 feet tall, are small in comparison. They use them to boulder, practicing maneuvers without the protection of a rope. If the boulder is tall, the climbers place a landing pad on the ground below. They have christened the rocks with wonderful names, such as Duct Tape, the Domino, the Ecoterrorist, Parking Lot Rock, Ten Arrows, Deforestation, Lost Keys Boulder, and the Beak.

Beyond Goat Rock, an interpretive shelter shares interesting information about park life and history. Back in the woods, you walk through the largest stand of black oak left in the Bay Area. Blanched boulders sit in groves of orange-red

Goat Rock, a victim of chemical weathering

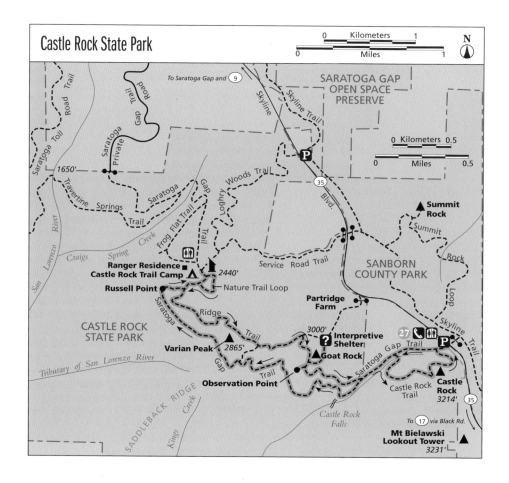

Castle Rock State Park

madrones against blue sky. The popular climbing rock, Castle Rock, sits near the park entrance among trees, reaching to 3,214 feet on the highest rise.

Castle Rock became a park thanks to a boy named Russell Varian. Young Russell fell in love with the big boulders. He dreamt of preserving the land around them as a public park for all to enjoy. As an adult, he took steps to buy the land himself and donate it to the state park system. As he was about to buy the land in 1959, he died. His friends finished the process, purchasing the first twenty-seven acres. The state officially opened the park in 1968 with 513 acres. Today it has 5,200 acres.

MILES AND DIRECTIONS

0.0 Start at the Castle Rock main parking lot on Skyline Boulevard. Follow the Saratoga Gap Trail, which follows the creek (flow is seasonal) and passes over a wooden bridge.

0.2 Pass by the trailhead to Castle Rock. (*Note:* The end of the hike brings you back to this point and to the stone chateau.) Continue west on the Saratoga Gap Trail. Pass the memorial grove.

0.6 At a split in the trail, stay left (southwest), continuing on the Saratoga Gap Trail. The fork on the right (northwest) is the return route, on Ridge Trail.

0.8 Reach Castle Rock Falls and an observation platform. The trail descends through oak scrub. (*Note:* Poison oak bushes add color in the fall—and winter, too, with bare red branches. Don't touch!) Then you find yourself climbing a moderate grade into sunshine where coyote brush, coffeeberry, and manzanita plants grow beside the trail. You get your first views of the lush hillsides and canyons. The trail follows the edge of the cliff. Back by the creek, another bridge takes you across where there is a resting bench. If you hear gunfire as you continue, do not be alarmed. The shots are echoing through the canyon from the Los Altos Rod and Gun Club. This noise, audible from the campground, has been a source of controversy since at least 1998.

1.3 Continue straight (west) on the Saratoga Gap Trail past the trailhead for a connector path to Ridge Trail. Turning on this path reduces the hike to 3.1 miles.

1.5 There's a flat rock with a rocky shelf above it hanging over the cliff that would make a quiet place to drink water, admire the view, and dangle your feet.

2.0 The trail crosses over a cliff (a cable gets you safely across). After the 2.3-mile trail marker, the route heads west through a madrone grove.

2.5 Pass posts 13 and 14 of the self-guided Danny Hannavan nature trail, then come to the trailhead for the Ridge Trail. Before heading uphill, bear right, crossing over the bridge toward the picnic area. Follow the trail to post 20. (*Note:* Contact the park for the nature trail brochure. The trail memorializes a Boy Scout.)

2.6 At the trailhead for Saratoga Gap Trail, turn left (north) to the campground and park office. Return to this spot, heading in the opposite direction, on the self-guided nature trail loop.

2.7 Arrive back at the split for the Ridge Trail and the Saratoga Gap Trail. Bear left (southwest), ascending the Ridge Trail.

3.0 The trail leads to the ridge (a rock-climbing boulder is to the right).

3.8 Pass the trailhead for a connector trail, staying left (east) on the Ridge Trail.

3.9 The Emily Smith Bird Observation Point is to the right (west). Detour to the observation point to spot raptors, ravens, and vultures, Steller's and western scrub jays, chestnut-backed chickadees, wrentits, dark-eyed juncos, and sparrows. Be sure to bring binoculars. Return to the Ridge Trail to continue the hike.

4.1 Take the side trail left (north) 0.2 mile to Goat Rock.

4.3 Arrive at Goat Rock. This is the backside of the rock. Turn right (east) and detour to the scenic overlook. Return to Goat Rock.

4.4 From Goat Rock continue east on the Ridge Trail toward the parking lot. In about 0.1 mile, reach the trailhead for the interpretive shelter; turn left (north) onto the path to the shelter. A rock cave is on the right.

4.5 Reach the interpretive shelter. Return 0.1 mile to the Ridge Trail.

4.6 Turn left (east) onto the Ridge Trail toward the parking lot. Take the stairs down to watch climbers challenge the face of Goat Rock. Pass other boulders. The trail once again opens up to views before heading back into woodland.

5.0 At the junction with the Saratoga Gap Trail, cross the bridge.

5.5 At the trailhead for Castle Rock, turn right (south). The trail heads through thick Douglas fir forest.

5.8 Arrive at Castle Rock. The trail leads around the rock and becomes fire road–width.

5.9 Turn right at the trailhead for the parking lot. The single-track trail heads downhill to the starting point.

6.1 Arrive back at the parking lot.

Option: If you are looking for a rewarding backpacking trip, try the three-day, 30-mile Skyline-to-the-Sea Trail, which starts at the trailhead for Saratoga Gap and heads through Castle Rock and Big Basin Redwoods State Parks before ending at the sea by Año Nuevo. It's mostly downhill.

HIKE INFORMATION

Local Information: Los Gatos Chamber of Commerce, 349 North Santa Cruz Avenue, Los Gatos, CA 95030; (408) 354-9300; www.losgatoschamber.com
Town of Woodside, 2955 Woodside Road, Woodside, CA 94062; (650) 851-6790; www.woodsidetown.org
Hike Tours: Castle Rock State Park, 15000 Skyline Boulevard, Los Gatos, CA 95033; (408) 867-2952; www.parks.ca.gov

Portola Redwoods State Park

A hike in Portola Redwoods State Park takes you past an ancient 300-foot redwood tree, through first- and second-generation redwood forest, and down shady paths under mixed evergreens lined with ferns and western azaleas. The ample creeks support crawdads and steelhead trout and are the centerpieces of stories of the old lumber days in the canyon. A nature trail guides you to details about the forest. Perhaps the best thing about Portola is that the crowds don't seem to gather here, so you may have the 18 miles of trails to yourself.

Start: In the parking area on the road to the Campfire Center

Distance: 5.4-mile loop

Approximate hiking time: 2.5 hours

Difficulty: Moderate

Trail surface: Well-maintained dirt trail, a nature trail, and small stints on a service road and main road

Other trail users: Equestrians

Canine compatibility: Leashed dogs permitted

Land status: State park

Fees and permits: Parking fee $6

Schedule: Open daily from 8:00 a.m. to dusk

Maps: USGS Woodside; La Honda. Portola Redwoods State Park, 9000 Portola State Park Road, P.O. Box F, La Honda, CA 94020; (650) 948-9098; www. parks.ca.gov

Trail contact: Portola Redwoods State Park, 9000 Portola State Park Road, P.O. Box F, La Honda, CA 94020; (650) 948-9098; www .parks.ca.gov

Other: In spring and early summer, repellent to ward off mosquitoes is highly recommended.

Finding the trailhead

By Car: From Highway 35 (Skyline Boulevard), turn west onto Alpine Road. Go 3 miles and turn left (south) onto Portola State Park Road. Pass the park office, cross the bridge, and take the first right toward the Campfire Center. Parking is immediately on the right. If the lot is full, head back toward the park headquarters, turn right into the Tan Oak picnic area, and park there.

By Public Transportation: There's no direct way to the park. Contact BART for more information (www.transitinfo.org), or call the SamTrans information line at (800) 660-4BUS (4287); www.samtrans.com.

Old Tree Trail

THE HIKE

Within Portola Redwood State Park's rugged basin, quiet trails cross Peters Creek and Pescadero Creek and curve and climb through the canyons under the foliage of redwoods, Douglas firs, live oak, madrone, and hazelnut trees. Sunlight drifts down through needles, spotlighting the leaf-carpeted forest floor. Spiderwebs glisten after bathing in fog. Shelf fungi hang on logs and rocks. Mushrooms push up through the dark soil as banana slugs inch their way across the trails.

On the Old Tree and Slate Creek Trails, dead tree trunks in varied states of decay have fallen every which way. Stumps are a reminder of logging days, and charred bark tells the story of the many fires to sweep through the canyon, one every sixty years or so. The last blaze to clean up the basin was in 1989. It finally took down the park's Shell Tree on the Sequoia Nature Trail. It was 2,000 years old and had survived some thirty fires during its long life.

The Summit Trail takes you through a woodland of mostly live oaks and madrones. False Solomon's seal, trillium, and wood fern grace the hillsides. In spring, the huckleberry bushes flower. Reclusive winter wrens and American robins hop through the brush. Steller's jays and ravens squawk from branches. Gray squirrels scamper up tree trunks. Heading downhill, the trail returns you to the redwood basin and the Iverson Trail.

Iverson Trail takes the name of the first settler here, Christian Iverson, a Scandinavian immigrant who worked as a Pony Express rider and shotgun guard. Iverson lived on two parcels of land on Pescadero Creek in the 1860s in a hand-split redwood cabin. The cabin stood for over 120 years until the Loma Prieta earthquake of 1989 finally brought it down. Planks piled beside the trail serve as a memorial to the site. Iverson Trail also takes you to seasonal Tiptoe Falls, with water pouring over a 6-foot shelf of rock.

On the Slate Creek Trail, you have the option of visiting the Page Mill site. Here, the men made shingles and cut tan oak for use in the tanneries, where slabs of dried wood were pulverized and boiled in water to make liquid tannic acid. Redwoods now grow through what was once a mill platform or tramway.

The campgrounds are a great place to spend the night. If hiking with kids, the Sequoia Nature Loop makes a fun short hike. The $2 park map includes the guide for the nature trail and is worth buying. Backpack camps and many longer trails are available. Paths connect to Long Ridge Open Space Preserve and Pescadero Creek County Park.

Note: As of 2008, work was still underway to clear a closure at the service road and bridge from a 2005 log jam. This severed the connection from Summit Trail to Iverson Trail. Check on the trail status with the rangers when planning your hike.

MILES AND DIRECTIONS

0.0   Start from the parking area, walking toward the Campfire Center until you see the trailhead on the left. Turn left onto Old Tree Trail.

0.3   Reach the Old Tree, which is 300 feet tall, 12 feet in diameter, and probably between 1,500 and 2,000 years old. Yet its shallow roots are only about 10 feet below the ground, connected to other trees in the area in a family system. It is among the tallest redwoods on the peninsula. Turn around and head back the way you came.

0.5   At the trailhead for the Slate Creek Trail, turn right (north). The single-track trail goes uphill and over a seasonal creek.

0.9   Stay right (north, then east) on the Slate Creek Trail.

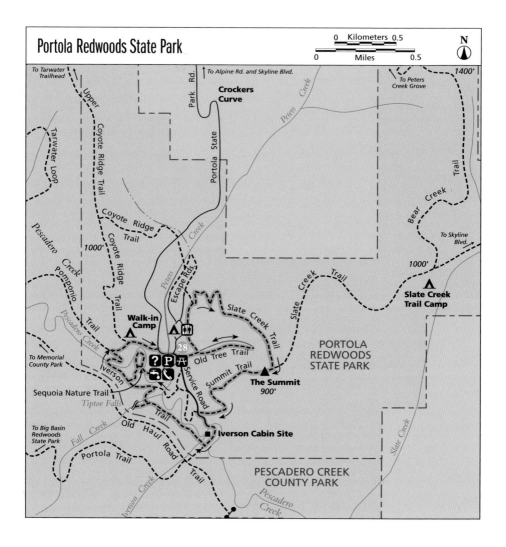

Portola Redwoods State Park

0 Kilometers 0.5

0 Miles 0.5

N

To Tarwater Trailhead

To Alpine Rd. and Skyline Blvd.

Crockers Curve

Park Rd.

Portola State

Peters Creek

To Peters Creek Grove

1400'

Upper Coyote Ridge Trail

Tarwater Loop

Pescadero Creek

Pomponio

1000'

Coyote Ridge Trail

Coyote Ridge Trail

Peters Creek

Escape Rds.

Bear Creek

Bear Creek Trail

To Skyline Blvd.

1000'

Slate Creek Trail Camp

Slate Creek Trail

Slate Creek Trail

Walk-in Camp

Pescadero Creek Trail

Iverson Trail

28

Old Tree Trail

Summit Trail

The Summit 900'

PORTOLA REDWOODS STATE PARK

To Memorial County Park

Sequoia Nature Trail

Tiptoe Falls

Service Road

To Big Basin Redwoods State Park

Fall Creek

Old Haul Road

Iverson Cabin Site

Portola Trail

Iverson Creek

Pescadero Creek

Slate Creek

PESCADERO CREEK COUNTY PARK

1.8   At the junction with Summit Trail, turn right (west) onto the Summit Trail. The single-track trail becomes winding, with switchbacks and stairs. Past the water tanks, the path widens to double-track and ends at the service road.

2.6   Turn left (south) onto the service road. It crosses Iverson Creek and curves past the Iverson Cabin site.

3.0   At the Iverson Trailhead, turn right (west). Pescadero Creek is on the right (northeast).

3.6   Turn left (west) to view Tiptoe Falls. Bear left (north) to continue on the Iverson Trail, which follows the curve of the creek.

3.9 Continue on Iverson Trail, taking the left (west) fork. To shorten the hike by 1.1 miles, turn right (east) onto the Sequoia Nature Trail and follow it back to the car. Otherwise, cross the bridge over Pescadero Creek. If you are visiting in winter or early spring, look for spawning steelhead trout in the creek. On the other side of the bridge, the trail continues through a redwood grove.

4.2 Turn right at the junction with the Pomponio Trail, staying east on the Iverson Trail.

4.3 At the junction with the Coyote Ridge Trail, turn right (east), continuing on the Iverson Trail.

4.4 The Iverson Trail ends at the park road across from the Madrone picnic area. Turn right (east), walking a short distance along the park road to park headquarters.

4.5 To the right (west) of park headquarters, follow signs to the Sequoia Nature Trail.

4.7 Stay to the right, remaining on the Sequoia Nature Trail.

4.8 Cross the footbridge and turn left at marker #8 to do the loop. At the trail junction with the Iverson Trail, bear right toward marker #9.

5.0 Back at marker #8, bear left back the way you came, crossing the bridge and returning to the visitor center.

5.3 Turn right onto the park road and walk beside it, crossing the bridge.

5.4 Turn right onto the road to the Campfire Center, with the parking area on the right.

Option: From the intersection of the Slate Creek Trail and the Summit Trail at 1.8 miles, you can continue another 1.4 miles east on the Slate Creek Trail to check out the Page Mill site.

HIKE INFORMATION

Local Information: San Mateo County Convention and Visitors Center, (650) 348-7600; www.sanmateocountycvb.com

Local Events/Attractions: La Honda Faire and Music Festival, held in mid-June in La Honda Gardens, 8865 La Honda Road, La Honda, CA 94020; (650) 747-0640; www.la-honda-faire.org

Hike Tours: Portola Redwoods State Park, 9000 Portola State Park Road, P.O. Box F, La Honda, CA 94020; (650) 948-9098; www. parks.ca.gov

Purisima is one of the gold nuggets in the bounty of the Midpeninsula Regional Open Space District. The trails in this 3,117-acre westernmost preserve take you through deep canyons under towering redwoods with creeks gurgling and cascading between rich banks of ferns and sorrel. Paths also traverse grassy, oak-scattered hills and ridges with inspiring views. Some of these trails follow the old mill roads of Purisima's logging past. A moderately strenuous climb is an unavoidable part of almost any hike in Purisima, except the wheelchair-accessible Redwood Trail.

Start: From the North Ridge Trailhead on Skyline Boulevard. You also can start the same loop at Higgins Purisima Road off Highway 1 just south of Half Moon Bay

Distance: 9.9-mile loop

Approximate hiking time: 5 hours

Difficulty: Moderate, with a 1,600-foot gradual ascent

Trail surface: Well-maintained single- and double-track dirt trails

Other trail users: Bicyclists and equestrians in summer only; hikers only on the Soda Gulch Trail

Canine compatibility: Dogs not permitted

Land status: Open space preserve

Fees and permits: No fees or permits required

Schedule: Open daily from 8:00 a.m. to dusk

Maps: USGS Woodside. Midpeninsula Regional Open Space District, 330 Distel Circle, Los Altos, CA 94022; (650) 691-1200; www .openspace.org

Trail contact: Midpeninsula Regional Open Space District, 330 Distel Circle, Los Altos, CA 94022; (650) 691-1200; www .openspace.org

Other: Bring your own water, though you can find all other basic facilities at the trailhead.

Finding the trailhead

By Car: From Skyline Boulevard (Highway 35) about 4.5 miles south of Highway 92, look for the sign for the Purisima preserve, and turn right (west) into the parking lot (parking for twenty cars). If you start the hike in Half Moon Bay, take Highway 1 for 1 mile south of Half Moon Bay and turn left (east) onto Higgins Purisima Road. Drive 4.5 miles, just past the short white bridge and before the road horseshoes onto Purisima Creek Road. The parking lot is on the left (north) with room for ten cars.

By Public Transportation: Currently, no public transportation is available to the trailhead. However, routes change frequently. Go to 511.org or www .transitinfo.org, or call 511 or SamTrans at (800) 660-4BUS (4287).

Soda Gulch on the trail

THE HIKE

n Spanish, *purisima* means "the most pure," and this is one of those hikes that has a purifying quality. The Spanish named the creek and canyon to honor the Virgin Mary. But it is also the magic of the redwood trees that creates the effect. These ancient trees once dominated all of the Northern Hemisphere but are now limited to the coastal range between Monterey and southern Oregon, thriving in the cool, foggy summers and mild winters. Beside the flowing creeks several kinds of ferns prosper: sword fern, with serrated edges on its leaves western wood fern, and the lacy bracken fern.

These meandering trails are truly a gift from the Midpeninsula Open Space District, which was formed by residents of the Portola Valley who wanted to stop the development of million-dollar homes on the pristine ridge of the Santa Cruz Mountains. Formed in 1972, today the district manages over 46,500 acres of public land in twenty-six open-space preserves and continues to grow.

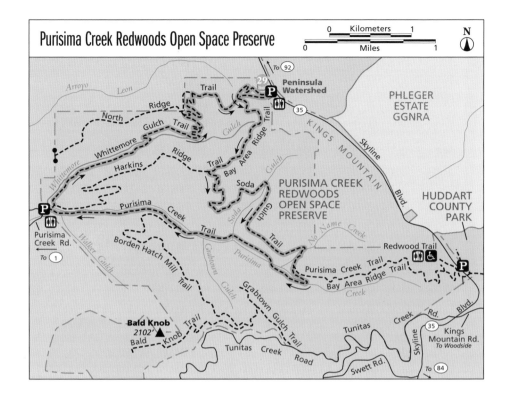

Purisima Creek Redwoods Open Space Preserve

Previously, lumber companies owned much of the acreage, cutting down redwoods for siding, fencing, and furniture from the gold rush up to 1970. The first boom was after the gold rush, with folks settling into the new Golden West. Loggers used handsaws and axes to fell trees. One giant redwood took them a week to cut down, according to the park brochure. Virgin trees, some 1,000 years old, were as large as 20 feet in diameter.

Transportation of the lumber was difficult. Oxen dragged the logs to the creekside mills down "skid trails," roads with greased logs across them. Mill workers then blasted the logs with dynamite to split them into manageable pieces. Powered by waterwheels, the mills "gulched out" the wood, cutting them into shingles to take over the steep canyon walls to Redwood City to be shipped to San Francisco. Running the mills was expensive, so they only operated when the prices were high.

Another lumber boom happened after the Great San Francisco Earthquake of 1906. Half of the city needed to be rebuilt, and new cities around the Bay grew. By then, "donkey engines," machines that pulled a tree down easily to the mill, replaced the tired oxen. Steam power replaced the waterwheels. There was dairy ranching here, too, and hog farms. They have been replaced by the scattered ranches you can see in the western valley.

After the virgin redwoods were cut down, a forest of second-generation trees grew in their place. Using controlled burns to singe away the undergrowth for easier access to the trees, the loggers actually aided their growth. The fire discouraged competition, making it easier for new redwoods to get started. Other than some burn stains, redwoods withstand most fires. These trees are about one hundred years old.

Along Soda Gulch Trail, giant stumps not only host moss and mushrooms, but often a circle of tall, straight, second-generation redwoods, sprouted from the roots of the mother tree. These circles are called "fairy rings" or "family circles." Some people consider them sacred places, spots for inspiration, meditation, or rejuvenation.

Painted bluish white lines on trunks indicate trees that were to be cut, but were saved by the acquisition of the park. These ghostly marks are a reminder of how tenuous the public hold on open space is, and that, as times change, we must remain vigilant to protect it.

MILES AND DIRECTIONS

0.0 Start at the parking lot for the North Ridge and Harkins Ridge Trailheads. Go through the gate to start the hike on the Harkins Ridge Trail (also the Bay Area Ridge Trail). The first 0.5 mile is a hikers-only trail.

0.5 Reach the junction with North Ridge Trail. Continue straight on the Harkins Ridge Trail, heading downhill on a double-track dirt track through mixed woodland with views of Half Moon Bay and Pillar Point. Look carefully beyond Pillar Point for the white caps of Mavericks, the famous surfing spot.

The Purchase of Purisima

When acquiring the land to create this park, the open space district discovered something odd. In 1900, *Collier's* magazine had a special promotion: buy a subscription and get a parcel of land in the Santa Cruz Mountains. People ordered the magazines and the deeds were handed out. They were mostly forgotten over time. When the district contacted the descendants of the Collier's readers, most didn't even know they owned the land. There was good news and bad news. The good news was the land was theirs. The bad news was they were liable for all the back taxes from 1900. Given the choice, most agreed to donate their parcels to the district for a tax break.

1.4 Reach the trailhead for the Soda Gulch Trail. Turn left (south) onto the single-track, hikers-only trail, which leads into one of the deepest parts of the redwood forest.

2.4 As you cross the bridge over Soda Gulch, look to the right at a pile of roots, rocks, and mud washed down into the creek during heavy rain in 2000. Continue on the Soda Gulch Trail.

4.0 Reach the trailhead for the Purisima Creek Trail, which splits. Take the fork to the right (west). After crossing the creek around the bend, you next cross No-Name Creek. The clearing is the site of Hatch Mill. Cross Purisima Creek several times as you proceed.

5.3 Pass the trailhead for the Borden Hatch Mill Trail, continuing on Purisima Creek Trail to the right (northwest). The path continues to follow the creek.

6.3 Reach the trailhead on the Higgins Purisima Road. Half Moon Bay is about 5.5 miles away. Turn right (east) and cross the bridge onto the Whittemore Gulch Trail. On the other side of the bridge, go left (northeast) (You can shorten the loop to around 7 miles by turning right onto the Harkins Ridge Trail.) Ascend on the Whittemore Gulch Trail through redwoods, bigleaf maples, red alderberries, and Douglas firs. The trail zigzags uphill through chaparral. (*Note:* Watch out for poison oak. It's beautiful in the fall, but always keep your distance.)

8.5 Continue straight on the Whittemore Gulch Trail, passing the bridge that crosses to the North Ridge Trail.

9.1 Whittemore Gulch Trail dead-ends at the North Ridge Trail. Turn right (east).

9.6 Reach the junction with the Harkins Ridge Trail. Continue straight on the North Ridge Trail.

9.9 Arrive back at the gate and parking lot.

Option: If you have two cars, park one at the trailhead for the Purisima Creek Trail and the Redwood Trail. When you reach the intersection of the Soda Gulch Trail and the Purisima Creek Trail at the 4-mile mark, turn left (east) at this junction for a 5-mile point-to-point hike.

HIKE INFORMATION

Local Information: Town of Woodside, 2955 Woodside Road, Woodside, CA 94062; (650) 851-6790; www.woodsidetown.org

Hike Tours: Midpeninsula Regional Open Space District, 330 Distel Circle, Los Altos, CA 94022; (650) 691-1200; www.openspace.org

29

Banana Slugs (*Ariolimax columbianus*)

Almost any walk through redwood forests includes stepping around these yellow, slimy creatures. Because of the banana slug's association with the giant redwoods and its unique characteristics, Bay Area hikers have a great affinity for it. The University of California, Santa Cruz even declared the banana slug its mascot.

Some slug facts:
- The banana slug has few natural enemies.
- Its slime is anesthetic, a bit like novocaine.
- Slug slime can take away the sting from nettles.
- The banana slug has both male and female reproductive organs; in mating, banana slugs cross-fertilize.
- It has a tongue with 27,000 teeth and rasps its food.
- A slug goes about .007 miles an hour.
- A slug can stretch out eleven times its normal length.
- Slugs mark their own scent so they can find their way home after dark.
- Banana slugs were a food source for the Yurok Indians (Yuck!).

A banana slug on Dipsea Trail

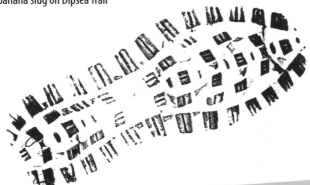

Honorable Mentions

F. Huddart Park and Phleger Estate

The best access to Phleger Estate (1,232 acres) is through Huddart County Park (973 acres), near the town of Woodside. Both parks climb from the foothills up into the northern Santa Cruz Mountains. There are five picnic areas, three covered shelters, day and overnight camps, an amphitheater, and an archery club. Trails are popular with equestrians and runners. You can find family trails like the Chickadee Trail, or long, expert loops through both parks climbing 1,900 feet.

A great 9-mile loop starts at the Crystal Springs Trail in Huddart, joins Richards Road, and turns onto the Miramonte Trail to enter Phleger Estate. The Mount Redondo Trail meets Lonely Trail. The Lonely Trail takes you a few hundred feet below the Kings Mountain Fire Department and Skyline Boulevard. Richards Road takes you down quickly to the Skyline Trail and Crystal Springs Trail. Crystal Springs links to the hikers-only Dean Trail. It once more intersects with Crystal Springs Trail and returns you to the start.

To reach the parks from Interstate 280 in San Mateo County, turn west onto Woodside Road (Highway 84) toward the town of Woodside. Drive about 1.5 miles through town. Turn right onto Kings Mountain Road. Proceed up the hill to the main park entrance. For more information contact Huddart Park, 1100 Kings Mountain Road, Woodside, CA 94062; (650) 851-1210 or (650) 363-4020; www.co.sanmateo .ca.us, click on Parks; Phleger Estate, (650) 556-8642; www.nps.gov/goga.

G. Wunderlich Park

Meadows, woodlands, flowing creeks, and an early-twentieth-century horse stable are some of the features that make Wunderlich Park fun. The 942 acres of steep mixed forest and grassland can be explored on a number of well-maintained loop trails, with sections following old logging and ranch roads. You can combine it with hiking through Huddart Park, or cross Skyline on its high ridge into El Corte de Madera Open Space Preserve. No bikes are allowed in the park, but equestrians frequent the trails.

The Alambique Trail passes the fine, large stable built by James A. Folger II (of coffee fame). The stable is still in operation, though Folger's elegant summer mansion has moved. The Alambique Trail passes through redwoods and mixed woodland. At Alambique Flat, turn right onto the Oak Trail under the dappled shade of oak woodland, popular with birds. A left onto the Meadow Trail takes you to "The Meadows," an open grassland with hawks hunting for field mice and moles. With a right onto the Bear Gulch Trail, you pass through a large Douglas fir grove. Stay to your left at Redwood Flat for a shady, cool walk through second- and third-growth redwoods on the aptly named Redwood Trail. A right onto Bear Gulch Trail again brings you back to the start (about 5 miles).

The park takes its name from contractor Martin Wunderlich, who bought the land from the Folgers and deeded the acreage to San Mateo County for use as a park and open space. It is open daily from 8:00 a.m. to sunset.

To reach the park from I-280, take the Woodside Road/Highway 84 exit west toward Woodside, then past the town about 4 miles. Turn right into the main park entrance. Wunderlich Park can also be accessed from Highway 35 (Skyline Boulevard). For more information contact Wunderlich Park, 4040 Woodside Road, Woodside, CA 94062; (650) 851-1210; www.co.sanmateo.ca.us, click on Parks.

H. Windy Hill Open Space Preserve

The first park acquired by the Midpeninsula Open Space District is named for its distinctive, breezy, grass-covered hilltop. But within its 1,308 acres, it has a lot more than what you see from Highway 35. Aside from its waving grasslands and spectacular views, you can find redwood, fir, and oak forests on the 12 miles of trails. Hamms Gulch, Eagle Razorback Ridge, and Lost Trail make an 8-mile loop. Kite flyers favor the ridge, and occasionally you may see a paraglider or remote control glider soaring above the eastern hills.

Windy Hill Open Space Preserve is located in the town of Portola Valley. The main parking area is on Skyline Boulevard (Highway 35) 2.3 miles south of Highway 84 (La Honda Road), or 4.9 miles north of Page Mill Road. Additional roadside parking is available along Skyline Boulevard. For access to the lower portion of the preserve, park at the Portola Valley Town Hall and follow the town trails to the preserve. To get more information contact Midpeninsula Regional Open Space District, 330 Distel Circle, Los Altos, CA 94022; (650) 691-1200; www.openspace.org.

I. Russian Ridge Open Space Preserve

These 1,822 acres provide a wildflower show, one of the best in the area. Its blown-grass hillsides, numerous springs creating the headwaters of Mindego and Alpine Creeks, diverse plant life, and miles of forest edge make it a popular habitat for animals, including the elusive mountain lion. It's also one of the best South Bay parks for watching raptors. Red-tailed hawks, turkey vultures, Cooper's hawks, sharp-shinned hawks, and golden eagles all soar above the 8 miles of trails in the preserve. You can extend your hike by crossing Highway 35 into little wooded Coal Creek Preserve (493 acres), one of the newest in the Midpeninsula Open Space District, or cross Alpine Road into Skyline Ridge Open Space Preserve.

The parking area is located at the intersection of Skyline Boulevard (Highway 35) and Alpine Road. Additional parking is located at the Caltrans Vista Point on Skyline Boulevard. You can reach Coal Creek Open Space Preserve from the vista point or farther north along Skyline Boulevard at Crazy Petes Road. Coal Creek is also accessible to hikers, bicyclists, and equestrians from Alpine Road. For more information contact Midpeninsula Regional Open Space District, 330 Distel Circle, Los Altos, CA 94022; (650) 691-1200; www.openspace.org.

J. Skyline Ridge Open Space Preserve

Within Skyline Ridge's 2,143 acres, you will find ridgetop vistas, expansive meadows, a pond for nature study, a quiet lake frequented by migrating birds, and the David C. Daniels Nature Center, open on weekends. Ten miles of trails also offer views of the Lambert Creek watershed, Butano Ridge, and Portola Redwoods State Park. Two 1-mile trails are accessible to wheelchairs and baby strollers, circling Horseshoe Lake and Alpine Pond.

The preserve's entrance is located about 1 mile south of the intersection of Skyline Boulevard (Highway 35) and Alpine Road. Equestrian parking is also available here. For convenient access to the nature center, park in the Russian Ridge Open Space Preserve parking lot, located at the corner of Alpine Road and Skyline Boulevard, and walk through the tunnel to the preserve. For more information contact Midpeninsula Regional Open Space District, 330 Distel Circle, Los Altos, CA 94022; (650) 691-1200; www.openspace.org.

K. Monte Bello Open Space Preserve

Aptly named, Monte Bello, Italian for "beautiful mountain," is one of the district's richest parks for wildlife and diverse ecosystems. Rolling grasslands, thickly forested canyons, inspiring vistas, and the most impressive riparian

Red-tailed hawk © Shutterstock

habitat in the Santa Cruz Mountains constitute the preserve's 3,133 acres. Fifteen miles of trails take you along Monte Bello Ridge and Black Mountain, from which you can view the whole Santa Clara Valley and Mount Hamilton. Through Stevens Creek Canyon, follow the flowing creek along the San Andreas Fault, enjoying the shade of Douglas firs. From the Stevens Creek Nature Trail, you can see Mount Umunhum and Loma Prieta, the epicenter of the 1989 earthquake. By crossing Page Mill Road, you can extend your earthquake study in Los Trancos Open Space Preserve on the self-guided San Andreas Fault Trail. With a Los Trancos brochure (available at the park entrance or district office), this is a fascinating and educational walk, great for families. Trails also connect to Upper Stevens Creek County Park and down into Rancho San Antonio Open Space Preserve. The backpack camp at Black Mountain is a good first stop on a backpack trip from the valley to the coast.

The preserve's main vehicle entrance is on Page Mill Road, 7 miles west of I-280 and 1 mile east of Skyline Boulevard. Parking is available for forty-five cars. For more information contact Midpeninsula Regional Open Space District, 330 Distel Circle, Los Altos, CA 94022; (650) 691-1200; www.openspace.org.

L. Upper Stevens Creek County Park

Madrone and Douglas fir forests, sunny south-facing grasslands, mixed chaparral of sage and manzanita, lovely shaded creekbeds, and the peak of Table Mountain (1,852 feet) await the hiker in this 1,095-acre Santa Clara County park. About 11 miles of trails take you through this wildlife habitat for deer, rabbits, bobcats, and raccoons.

Stevens Creek Park is located along Stevens Canyon Road and Mount Eden Road in the foothills between Saratoga and Cupertino. There are several entrances. To access the park from Cupertino, take I-280 to the Foothill Expressway. Follow Foothill Boulevard west 3 miles to the northern park entrance (Foothill Boulevard changes into Stevens Canyon Road as it crosses McClellan Road). Public transit is available. For more information contact The Stevens Creek County Parks, 11401 Stevens Canyon Road, Cupertino, CA 95014; (408) 867-3654 (Stevens Creek County Park) or (408) 867-9959 (Upper Stevens Creek).

M. Rancho San Antonio Open Space Preserve and County Park

Combined, these two adjacent parks provide 3,965 acres of oak woodland, cool fern-banked ravines beside babbling creeks, soft open meadows full of lupine, poppies, and blue-eyed grass, hillsides of chaparral, and ridgetops that open to views. Along the extensive 23-mile trail system, you can create short family loops and longer, more challenging routes, including a climb to the top of Black Mountain (2,800 feet).

A great family feature is Deer Hollow Farm, a working farm with pigs, goats, sheep, chickens, and other animals housed in turn-of-the-twentieth-century ranch buildings (open Tuesday through Sunday 8:00 a.m. to 4:00 p.m.; 650-903-6331).

Rancho San Antonio adjoins Hidden Villa Ranch, a nonprofit environmental education facility that has miles of lovely trails in 1,600 acres open to the public, and a hostel with a lodge and cabins (650-949-8650). The main entrance to Hidden Villa is located on Moody Road in Los Altos Hills. From Highway 35 (Skyline Boulevard), you have to hike through Monte Bello Open Space Preserve for 2.9 miles.

The preserve's main vehicle entrance is located in Rancho San Antonio County Park. Take Foothill Boulevard south from I-280, turn immediately right onto Cristo Rey Drive, and continue for about 1 mile. The northwest lot is the trailhead for the preserve. For more information contact Midpeninsula Regional Open Space District, 330 Distel Circle, Los Altos, CA 94022; (650) 691-1200; www.openspace.org.

N. Long Ridge Open Space Preserve

Ten miles of trails explore canyons of majestic oaks, grassy knolls with sculpture garden–like rock outcroppings, some of the best views in the area, and the rich, cool environment around Peters Creek in the Pescadero watershed. Within the preserve's 1,946 acres, you also find an old farm site and apple orchard, and trails through mixed evergreen forests of madrone and Douglas fir. Part of the Bay Area Ridge Trail, the pathways also connect to Skyline Ridge, making a continuous 13-mile trail from Russian Ridge Open Space Preserve in the north through Saratoga Gap Open Space Preserve to Sanborn-Skyline County Park in the south.

For Long Ridge Open Space Preserve, parking is available at the Upper Stevens Creek County Park–Grizzly Flat parking area on Skyline Boulevard, about 3 miles north of Saratoga Gap (the intersection of Highways 9 and 35). Parking for both preserves is at the intersection of Highway 9 and Skyline Boulevard. Saratoga Gap Open Space Preserve is located at the northern corner of this junction. For more information contact Midpeninsula Regional Open Space District, 330 Distel Circle, Los Altos, CA 94022; (650) 691-1200; www.openspace.org.

O. Pescadero Creek Park

In these four adjacent parks, you pass creeks blackened with natural tar, trek under giant evergreens dedicated to World War I soldiers, meander in peaceful old-growth redwood forests, and walk through land donated by Sam McDonald, the descendant of a slave.

This vast parcel of 8,020 acres is comprised of several smaller parks: Memorial, Heritage Grove, and Sam McDonald. Trails go through old- and new-growth redwood forests and mixed woodlands of Douglas fir, California wax myrtle, tan oak, madrone, California bay laurel, bigleaf maple, and oak. Pescadero and Alpine Creeks both contain steelhead trout and silver salmon.

You can choose from short family loops like the Mount Ellen Nature Trail or many longer loops. In Pescadero Creek Park, many of the trails follow old logging roads. The 5-mile Tarwater Trail Loop gives you a sense of the park's history as the site of natural gas and oil deposits. Heritage Grove, accessible through Sam McDonald County Park, is thirty-seven glorious acres of towering old-growth redwoods. You can reach it directly from the entrance on Alpine Road.

The entrance to Pescadero Creek Park is through Memorial Park or Sam McDonald Park. Several staging areas are off Highway 84 on Pescadero Road. For more information contact San Mateo County Parks and Recreation, 455 County Center, 4th Floor, Redwood City, CA 94063; (650) 363-4020; www.co.sanmateo .ca.us (follow links to the parks department).

Wild purple lupine flowers © Shutterstock

Mount Diablo and Las Trampas Foothills

View from Mount Diablo © Shutterstock

In the East Bay, Mount Diablo symbolizes home for people who live at its base in the San Ramon Valley, along the Antioch/Oakley line, and on hillsides and in valleys between.

Driving east toward the mountain on Highway 24 at sunset, Mount Diablo turns crimson. In the morning, it seems to rise with the sun. With the subtlety of California seasons, Diablo becomes a meter. In winter, the rolling green slopes reign majestically over the little city of Danville to the west and Clayton Valley to the north. Billowing clouds cover its peak. Revealed after a storm, the crest may be white for a day or two after the odd cold front sifts snow down on the 3,849-foot summit. In summertime, the golden mountain shows off its clumps of fine oaks. Fire is a danger in the fall to the dry savanna, and every few years, charred and smoldering hillsides start the process of reseeding and recovery. The Las Trampas hills, separating Contra Costa and Alameda Counties, present lush eastern slopes crowded with oak trees. The western faces feature hills of rock and nappy chaparral rolling into canyons.

Twelve million years ago, Mount Diablo and the Las Trampas ridge were under a vast ocean. As the Earth's tectonic plates moved past each other along the San Andreas Fault line, the land buckled, and a tough slab of volcanic rock rose up. The softer sediments around it washed away, forming the valleys around the peaks. Geologists suspect the mountain is still rising as landslides reshape it from time to time. Seashells are still readily visible among the serpentine and sandstone rocks on Las Trampas.

> Lizards do push-ups on sunny rocks as crickets chirp the rhythm.

For the hiker, these ridges offer miles of trails and mountains to climb. On the way up, you can see tumbling waterfalls, scamper up huge boulders with caves and contours, and visit historic sites, like the old coal and sand mines at Black Diamond. On Las Trampas, you can visit the home of playwright Eugene O'Neill and walk the hills as he did while writing *Long Day's Journey into Night*. You can picnic in Bollinger Canyon or camp in Rock City.

There are fields of orange poppies. Wild mustard turns whole hillsides yellow. Red Indian paintbrush and lavender lupine add bursts of color, and California sagebrush perfumes the air with herb and spice. Lizards do push-ups on sunny rocks as crickets chirp the rhythm. Despite the cattle grazing that still goes on in some of the parks, there's a lot of wildlife inhabiting these hills.

At the peak of Diablo, visit a nature center, stargaze at night, or just admire expansive 360-degree views. Drop a bicycle off at the top, and after hiking to the summit, enjoy a thrilling ride down the twisting main road. At the top of Las Trampas, follow the ridgeline for miles or, with a permit, drop down into watershed land and keep heading west.

Wild California poppy © Shutterstock

Las Trampas Regional Wilderness

A trek in 3,882-acre Las Trampas Wilderness promises you windswept ridges, rugged jigsaw rock outcroppings, dusty valleys, moist spring-fed ravines, and trails curving through sunny grasslands and under the shade of pungent bay trees. This hike also includes a couple of great calf-burning, heavy-breathing 1,000-foot climbs up Rocky Ridge and the Devil's Hole. But you are rewarded with breezy, expansive views of the San Francisco Bay, the city skylines, the distant Delta, and majestic Mount Diablo and its valleys. Look carefully around you and you'll see the abundant wildlife that lives in Las Trampas today and the remains of animals, plants, and geological features that tell a story that's about twenty-five million years old.

Start: At the Bollinger Canyon Staging Area

Distance: 6.5-mile loop

Approximate hiking time: 3.5 hours

Difficulty: Moderate to difficult due to two long uphill sections

Trail surface: Paved path to single- and double-track dirt trails

Other trail users: Equestrians on all but the Sycamore Trail; mountain bikers on the Upper Trail and Elderberry Trail

Canine compatibility: Leashed dogs permitted around the staging area and in the watershed

Land status: Regional wilderness

Fees and permits: There is no fee to hike in Las Trampas. An East Bay Municipal Utility District (EBMUD) hiking permit is $2 per day or $10 per year. Contact EBMUD at 866-40-EBMUD (866-403-2683)

Schedule: Open year-round daily from 5:00 a.m. to 10:00 p.m. unless otherwise posted

Maps: USGS Las Trampas Ridge. East Bay Regional Park District Headquarters, 2950 Peralta Oaks Court, P.O. Box 5381, Oakland, CA 94605; (888) EB-PARKS or (888) 327-2757; www.ebparks.org/parks/las_trampas

Trail contact: East Bay Regional Park District Headquarters, 2950 Peralta Oaks Court, P.O. Box 5381, Oakland, CA 94605; (888) EBPARKS or (888) 327-2757; www.ebparks .org/parks/las_trampas

Other: There is no drinking water available until you reach Corral Camp near the end of your hike. Bring plenty! If you are susceptible to poison oak, wear long pants and bring a strong soap; scrub and rinse well at Corral Camp.

Finding the trailhead

By Car: From Interstate 680, take the Crow Canyon Road exit west to Bollinger Canyon Road. Turn right (north) and go to the road's end.

By Public Transportation: For more information, contact AC Transit TravInfo
(510-817-1717; www.actransit.org) or call 511 (511.org).

THE HIKE

On the Upper Trail, near the 2,024-foot summit of Las Trampas, you follow the spine of Rocky Ridge and come upon the "Indian" wind caves. Sculptured by the wind and rain and colored by many lichen species, they are ideal for quiet, breezy contemplation and for fossil exploring. There are literally millions of seashells embedded in Rocky Ridge, dating back to the Pliocene era some twelve million years ago when Las Trampas was the Pacific Ocean floor.

Scattered and harder to find are the bones and teeth of fossil mammals representing mostly a fauna around nine million years old. Paleontologists say these remains are abundant in these hills. They have found "elephant teeth" from a four-tusked mastodon, primitive teeth belonging to four different species of camel, and most commonly the teeth of an extinct three-toed horse. Also here were primitive rabbits, honey badgers, archaic beavers, hyaenoid dogs, and wolverine-like carnivores. Believe it or not, there were also rhinoceroses, ground sloths, and mammoths in the Pliocene Las Trampas.

There may be no sloths here anymore (except the ones with you), but there are plenty of modern descendants living in the grassland, chaparral, woodland, and ravine habitats of Las Trampas. On the Sycamore Trail, you may glimpse garter snakes or king snakes slithering into the sagebrush (neither are dangerous to humans). You may spot jackrabbits bounding into manzanita scrub, squirrels clinging to the trunk of a bigleaf maple or buckeye tree, or California voles peaking out of burrows in the grassland. Overhead, you are bound to see hawks, and turkey vultures, and perhaps even the rare golden eagle. In the ravines, especially during wetter months, you may see salamanders and newts and hear the chirping of Pacific tree frogs, the croaking of endangered red-legged frogs, and the bellow of a western toad.

Keep your eyes open for the tracks and droppings of cougars, bobcats, badgers, ringtails, opossums, coyotes, and foxes. At dusk, dark-eyed juncos, finches, red-winged blackbirds, and hummingbirds call it a day and bats punch the clock, hunting for insects along the creeks and springs.

Wildflowers are prevalent in the springtime. One of the best displays is in rocky, steep-walled Sedum Ravine on Sycamore Trail. In mid-April the red delphinium is spectacular, and a couple of weeks later the yellow-flowered stonecrop forms bright floral mats in the upper part of the ravine.

View from Upper Trail on the way to Elderberry Trail

The bison, pronghorn antelope, grizzlies, and abundant elk that have been hunted to extinction in these lands indirectly contributed to the naming of Las Trampas. Meaning "the traps" in Spanish, the name honored the native Miwok Indians' method of driving elk and deer into the steep box canyons for easier hunting.

Three Spanish brothers acquired a grant in 1844 for 17,600 acres that included much of Las Trampas. But the brothers encountered bad fortune, losing the Rancho San Ramon El Sobrante in 1858. The government took over the land. In the 1970s, a group of kids organized a group called SANE (Save America's Natural Environment) and helped spearhead the preservation of Las Trampas wilderness as parkland. Families started slowly selling off hundreds of acres of ranchland to be protected.

A geologic feature worth noticing on Rocky Ridge and down Elderberry Trail is the Bollinger fault line. The largest of the many faults traversing Las Trampas Wilderness, it played a crucial role in the uplift of Rocky and Las Trampas ridges. It's probably not active today, say geologists, though some earthquakes have been recorded in its vicinity. You can observe it in the break in the slope near the crest of Rocky Ridge. Also, look for green areas and seeping mountain springs. They are a dead giveaway for the fault. In August and September, these areas are very apparent, appearing like oases among the baked golden grasslands, dying thistles, and fall weeds.

MILES AND DIRECTIONS

0.0   Start at the Bollinger Canyon Staging Area. Take the paved Rocky Ridge Road, walking through the gate at the northwest end of the parking lot. If you can't stand cement, the Rocky Ridge Trail, a single-track dirt path, starts to the right of the road and mostly parallels the road.

0.4   Rocky Ridge Trail meets Rocky Ridge Road at the junction with the Cuesta Trail. Continue up Rocky Ridge Road.

0.7   Reach the junction with Upper Trail. Rocky Ridge Trail meets the road again (with a closed gate ahead). The Upper Trail is on the left (south). Turn left (south) onto the single-track trail. It becomes double-track on the ridge.

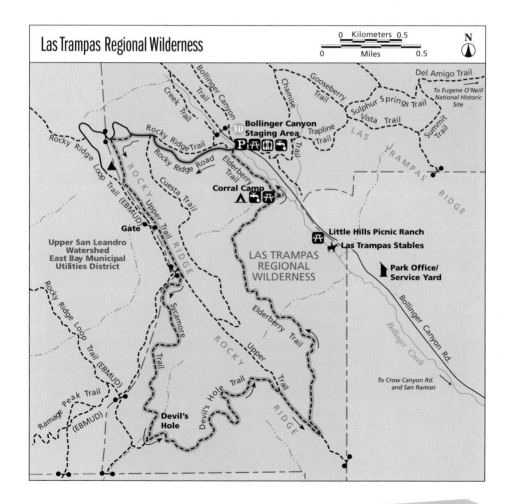

Las Trampas Regional Wilderness

30

1.0 Reach the gate to the East Bay Municipal Utility District watershed land. A permit is required to hike on watershed land. If you have the time and a permit, detour 0.2 mile through the gate to the ridge, where you can see the first series of wind caves. No permit? Don't want to risk it? There are more on upper Sycamore Trail.

1.5 Reach the junction with the Sycamore Trail. Turn right (southwest) onto the single-track dirt path. The Upper San Leandro Reservoir is visible in the distance, as is San Francisco and Sutro Tower.

1.8 The wind caves are up on the ridge to the right. (*Note:* Beware of poison oak.)

1.9 The Sycamore Trail leads up and over the rocky ridge. Reach a trail junction on the west side. Sycamore Trail heads to the right and continues with a series of hairpin turns.

2.7 Sycamore Trail crosses a creek. A cattle path crosses the grasslands; stay on the trail. Across the creek is a trail sign marking the Sycamore Trail.

2.8 Reach the junction with the Devil's Hole Trail. Turn left (east) onto the double-track dirt path and start climbing. The 1,000-foot ascent is moderate but continual. Views open to the San Ramon Valley at the top.

4.0 The Devil's Hole Trail ends at the junction with Upper Trail to Elderberry Trail. Turn right (southeast) onto the double-track dirt Upper Trail.

4.4 Upper Trail ends. Turn left (north) onto the double-track dirt Elderberry Trail.

6.1 Reach Corral Camp. Continue on the Elderberry Trail left (northwest) to the Bollinger Canyon Staging Area.

6.5 Arrive back at the Bollinger Canyon Staging Area and parking lot.

> **🌱 Green Tip:**
> *Don't take souvenirs home with you. This means natural materials such as plants, rocks, shells, and driftwood as well as historic artifacts such as fossils and arrowheads.*

The Tao House

Looking for a hike with a literary bend? Toward the northern end of Las Trampas is the Tao House, where playwright Eugene O'Neill lived from 1937 to 1944 and wrote some of his most famous plays. He and his wife, Carlotta, owned 158 acres, valuing these "corduroy hills" for both their beauty and isolation. He called his home Tao House, from Taoist philosophy meaning "the right way of life." For a fascinating tour of the interior, call (925) 838-0249 or visit www.eugeneoneill.org.

HIKE INFORMATION

Local Information: San Ramon Chamber of Commerce, 12667 Alcosta Boulevard, Suite 160, Bishop Ranch 15, San Ramon, CA 94583; (925) 242-0600; www.sanramon.org

Local Events/Attractions: Tao House, Las Trampas Regional Wilderness, (925) 838-0249; www.eugeneoneill.org

Hike Tours: East Bay Regional Park District Headquarters, 2950 Peralta Oaks Court, P.O. Box 5381, Oakland, CA 94605; (888) EBPARKS or (888) 327-2757; www.ebparks.org/parks/las_trampas

Mount Diablo State Park: Rock City to the Summit

Mount Diablo, the once sacred mountain of the Miwok Indians, continues to be sacred to today's Bay Area hikers, mountain bikers, equestrians, and nature lovers. On this hike, you can watch rock climbers, scramble up a few boulders yourself, or search for ancient ocean fossils at Rock City; bird and butterfly watch and enjoy a hearty oak-laurel and gray pine forest on the Juniper Trail; identify wildflowers on the Summit Trail; barbecue at any of a number of picnic areas on the way up; learn about local history, geology, and wildlife at the Summit Museum; and take in breathtaking views of the Pacific Ocean and the snow-crested Sierra from the observatory tower at the 3,806-foot peak.

Start: At the Rock City Trailhead north of the Rock City parking and picnic area

Distance: 8.5-mile double lollipop loop

Approximate hiking time: 4 hours

Difficulty: Strenuous, with a vertical climb of 2,885 feet to the top of Mount Diablo

Trail surface: Single- and double-track dirt trails; the trail crosses over a paved road several times and includes a short walk over a paved parking lot

Other trail users: Equestrians

Canine compatibility: Dogs on leash permitted

Land status: State park

Fees and permits: Parking fees are $6 per car; a $20 fee is levied for overnight camping.

Schedule: Open daily year-round from 8:00 a.m. to sunset

Maps: USGS Mount Diablo. Mount Diablo Interpretive Association, P.O. Box 346, Walnut Creek, CA 94597; (925) 927-7222; www.mdia .org/parkmap.htm

Trail contact: Mount Diablo State Park Headquarters, 96 Mitchell Canyon Road, Clayton, CA 94517; (925) 837-2525; ranger's office, (925) 837-6119; www.parks .ca.gov/?page_id=517

Other: Bring plenty of drinking water, layered clothing, a hat, sunscreen, and binoculars. It can be very hot in summer and muddy in winter, and the temperature varies up the mountain.

Finding the trailhead

By Car: From Interstate-680, exit at El Cerro Road and head west. It becomes Diablo Road. Past the Diablo Country Club, turn left (northwest) onto Mount Diablo Scenic Boulevard. Signs read TO ATHENIAN SCHOOL (a boarding school on the right-hand/east side of the street) and TO MT. DIABLO STATE PARK SOUTH GATE ENTRANCE. This becomes the South Gate Road once you are in the park and winds its way up the mountain. At Rock City, turn left (north) into the Rock City camping and picnic area parking lot. Follow signs TO BIG ROCK, SENTINEL ROCK AND WIND CAVES. Walk north to the end of the parking lot to start your hike on the Rock City Trail.

THE HIKE

According to Miwok Indian mythology, Mount Diablo was once an island surrounded by water. From this island, the creator Coyote and his assistant, Eagle-man, made the world. Coyote and his grandson, Wek-wek (Prairie Falcon-man), also created the Indian people, providing them with "everything, everywhere so they can live."

Though stories vary from tribe to tribe, all felt Mount Diablo was sacred. And you may feel this way, too, as you trek the 2,000 feet up to the summit over undulating grasslands, by rugged rock outcrops, and through the abundant blue oak, valley oak, and coast live oak from which the Bolbon, the Miwok tribe living closest to Mount Diablo, gathered their main staple food of acorns.

Geologically speaking, you go backwards in time as you climb toward the summit. The tan-colored Rock City marine sandstone and shale date back fifty million years. The soft rocks are easily eroded to create wind caves and interesting shapes. The Summit Trail takes you back seventy-five million years to the Cretaceous period. The upper part of Mount Diablo is made up of rocks as old as 190 million years. The dramatic colors of the earth around the summit are made from a combination of shale, basalt, chert, and occasional blocks of schist and green serpentinite. But it is a young mountain geologically, and an evolving one, slowly rising and pulling the San Ramon Valley beneath it with earthquakes (every 500 years or so) caused by a thrust fault below.

When Spanish explorers Pedro Fages and Father Juan Crespi climbed the mountain in 1782, they saw rich lands to claim for Spain. In 1851, during the gold rush, deputy surveyor-general Colonel Leander Ransom and his men ascended Diablo and erected a flagpole on the summit to mark the initial point of the Mount Diablo meridian; thus began the survey of public lands in California.

The California Geological Survey Group visited the mountain in 1861. William Brewer, part of that expedition, estimated that the view from the summit embraced 80,000 square miles. Within that vast vista you can see Lassen Peak to the north, the Farallon Islands to the west, and Loma Prieta in the Santa Cruz Mountains to the south. To the east, using binoculars, you may be able to pick out Half Dome in Yosemite National Park.

Sentinel Rock

On the Summit Trail, you'll pass the site of a first-rate hotel built in 1873 by Joseph Seavey Hall, a New Hampshire transplant who also built the two roads to the summit. Later that year, Hall opened the sixteen-room Mountain Hotel and Restaurant on the lofty ridge beside Pulpit Rock. At the summit, Hall erected a telescope through which visitors could spot Mount Whitney to the south, Mount Shasta to the north.

Local papers raved about the Diablo experience. Unfortunately, money troubles forced Hall to sell his hotel, and on July 4, 1891, fire swept up the slopes from Morgan Territory and destroyed the observatory erected to house the telescope.

Fewer people visited the top of the mountain from then on. But people were still drawn to the sacred mountain, including prestigious visitors like writer Bret Harte and conservationist John Muir.

In 1912 R. N. Burgess established the Mount Diablo Development Company, which built new toll roads all the way to Diablo's summit (North Gate and Mount Diablo Scenic Boulevard, completed in 1915). Burgess had even bigger plans for a tower hotel, Torre de Sol, on the summit, backed and publicized by William Randolph Hearst. But with World War I Hearst lost interest, and Burgess's company went bankrupt. This allowed for 630 acres on the top to become Mount Diablo State Park in 1921, six years before California established the state park system. In 1927 Frederick Law Olmsted, champion of U.S. parks, recommended acquisition of 6,000 acres at Mount Diablo to "amplify" the state park at the summit.

Standard Oil crews drove up the mountain in 1928 to construct a 75-foot aviation beacon as a guide for commercial and military planes, visible for 100 miles. Charles Lindbergh came up Diablo to light the beacon for the first time. Now in the Summit Building, it is lit only on Pearl Harbor Day, December 7.

In the 1930s and early 1940s, the Civilian Conservation Corps constructed campgrounds and picnic areas, marked hiking trails, and built park residences, dams, and the rustic stone Summit Building. Soldiers scaled Mount Diablo in the 1940s, establishing Camp Diablo to train for mountain warfare.

The only war affecting the mountain since then has been the conservation of the parkland in the face of widespread development. But thanks to the Save Mount Diablo organization, protected open space has expanded by tens of thousands of acres since the 1970s.

MILES AND DIRECTIONS

0.0 Start at the north end of the parking lot for Rock City. Start the hike on the single-track dirt trail to Sentinel Rock. The trail goes through the natural-rock Little Rock amphitheater. Take the trail behind the cave and stay left. (*Note:* For drinking water in the Little Rock picnic area, take the trail on the right, after Little Rock amphitheater, to the picnic tables beyond.)

0.1 Climb a rock to see Sentinel Rock to the west, and to get your bearings. Take an unmarked trail with a poison oak warning sign to head in the right direction. The trail will take you over rocks with stairs carved out in places. It is a moderately strenuous hike. There are numerous trails that lead to Sentinel Rock once you know which direction to go.

0.2 Reach Sentinel Rock; climb to the top with the help of railings and enjoy the view. Head back toward the parking lot for Rock City. The trail to the right leads around rocks, staying on soft ground. Beware of poison oak.

0.4 Take any trail through Rock City toward the main road.

0.5 On the bend in the road just past Rock City, across from an employee residence, there are two trailheads on the left (east). Pass the first (Wall Point Road to Macedo Ranch) and take the second, double-track, multiuse Summit Trail, which leads to the summit parking lot in 3.7 miles.

0.6 Pass another employee residence and the Horseshoe picnic area; road is on the right (east).

0.8 Make a sharp left turn and continue on Summit Trail, with the road still on the right-hand side. To the southwest is Rocky Ridge of the Las Trampas Wilderness.

1.2 Reach the junction of the Summit Trail Bypass. Stay right (northwest) on the Summit Trail, which becomes single-track.

1.8 Cross the paved Summit Road to stay on Summit Trail, which becomes double-track dirt trail again. The state park heliport is along the trail. Pass the junction to Barbecue Terrace Road, staying on the Summit Trail for a moderate climb. To the left (west) is North Gate Road.

2.1 The Sunset picnic area is on the left (west). The double-track trail becomes a paved road past the picnic area. It meets Summit Road at a crosswalk. Cross the road and continue on the Summit Trail, now paved road (that is also a driveway for an employee residence). Pass the house; the Summit Trail once again becomes a double-track dirt trail, mostly shady.

2.3 Reach the Mountain House junction. The ranger station is to the left (west) 0.2 mile. The fork to the right (north) is Summit Trail (now 1.9 miles from the top). The Mountain House site is just before the junction between the two trails (the path leading to the ranger station is part of the original stagecoach road). Continue on Summit Trail; Mountain House Creek, dry in summer, is on the right (east).

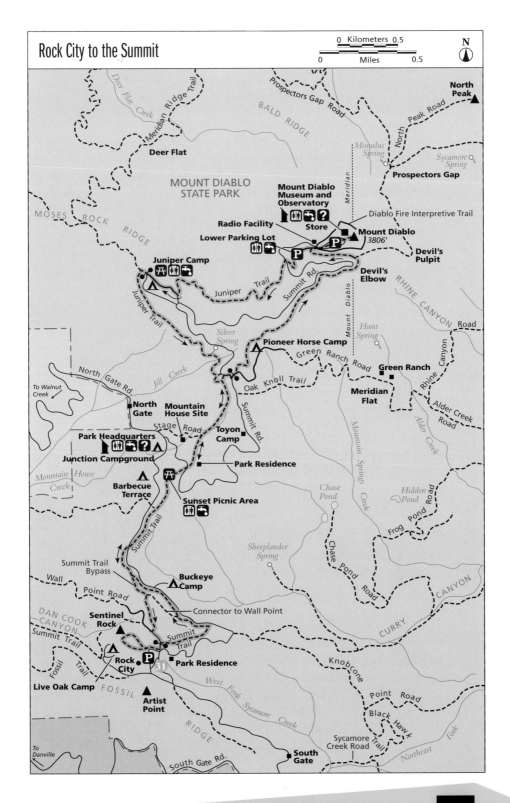

0 Kilometers 0.5

0 Miles 0.5

N

North Peak ▲

Prospectors Gap Road

BALD RIDGE

Deer Flat Creek

Meridian Ridge Trail

Deer Flat

MOUNT DIABLO STATE PARK

MOSES ROCK RIDGE

Mimulus Spring

Sycamore Spring

Prospectors Gap

Meridian

Mount Diablo Museum and Observatory

Radio Facility

Store

Diablo Fire Interpretive Trail

Lower Parking Lot

Mount Diablo 3806'

Devil's Pulpit

Juniper Camp

Devil's Elbow

RHINE CANYON

Juniper Trail

Summit Rd.

Mount Diablo

Road

Juniper Trail

Silver Spring

Hunt Spring

Pioneer Horse Camp

Green Ranch Road

Green Ranch

Rhine Canyon

North Gate Rd.

Jill Creek

Oak Knoll Trail

Meridian Flat

Alder Creek Road

To Walnut Creek

North Gate

Mountain House Site

Stage Road

Summit Rd.

Toyon Camp

Mountain Springs Creek

Alder Creek

Park Headquarters

Junction Campground

Park Residence

Mountain House Creek

Chase Pond

Hidden Pond

Barbecue Terrace

Sunset Picnic Area

Chase Pond Road

Frog Pond Road

Sheeplander Spring

Summit Trail Bypass

Wall

Buckeye Camp

CURRY CANYON

Point Road

Connector to Wall Point

DAN COOK CANYON

Sentinel Rock

Summit Trail

Knobcone

Fossil Trail

Rock City

31

Park Residence

Live Oak Camp

FOSSIL

West Fork Sycamore Creek

Point Road

Black Hawk

Artist Point

RIDGE

Sycamore Creek Road

Northeast Fork

To Danville

South Gate Rd.

South Gate

2.6   At the junction with the Juniper Trail; stay right (northeast) on the Summit Trail. Summit Trail crosses Summit Road again and continues onto a paved fire road (#59–8/Green Ranch Road to Frog Pond Road); the sign also says Summit Trail. In 0.1 mile, the Summit Trail heads left (northeast), where it becomes single-track for hikers only.

2.7   Pass a water tank, Pioneer Horse Camp, and an interpretive sign about the Alameda whipsnake. Summit Trail heads up left (northeast), becoming double-track dirt again. It ascends into single-track trail in less than 0.2 mile. The summit museum is visible above you.

3.5   The trail meets Summit Road. Follow the paved Summit Road about 20 feet, to where the Summit Trail continues to the right, starting as double-track gravel road then becoming a single-track dirt path again.

3.7   Reach the Devil's Elbow. The trail meets Summit Road again. There are two trailheads; stay left (west) on Summit Trail (the other is Prospectors Gap, which leads to Donner Canyon and Clayton).

4.0   The trail meets Summit Road again. The lower Summit parking lot is to the left (west). Turn right and stay on the paved road for less than 0.1 mile. The single-track Summit Trail leads left to the Summit parking lot and museum.

4.2   Arrive at the Mount Diablo summit and museum. Return as you came on Summit Trail to the lower parking lot.

4.4   Arrive at the lower parking lot. Walk straight across the lot to the trailhead for Juniper Trail to Juniper Camp.

4.6   Cross the road on the crosswalk, then proceed up the road to the right about 70 feet to continue on Juniper Trail. The trail heads downhill.

5.6   Arrive at Juniper Camp. Walk along the paved Juniper Campground Road, past campsites, to where the road curves. There, take the double-track dirt road; about 100 yards down the road is a gate and the trailhead for the Deer Flat Creek Road. Turn left (south) at the gate onto the single-track dirt, hikers-only Juniper Trail. About 100 yards later, the path splits; stay right.

5.8 Continue down the Juniper Trail. Below are the buildings of Diablo Ranch and the park headquarters at the junction between North Gate and South Gate Roads. Juniper and chaparral are very thick here, then the trail opens up into hillside grassland. Cross a small wooden bridge over Jill Creek (dry in summer).

6.5 Arrive at a junction. The trail meets a gravel parking lot; cross it and return to the Juniper Trail on other side. About 20 feet later, stay to the left on the trail.

6.7 Reach the junction with the Summit Trail. Turn right onto Summit Trail, going south/downhill on the double-track dirt trail.

7.0 Reach the Mountain House junction. Mountain House Creek is now on the left. Take the left (south) fork, the Summit Trail.

7.2 Pass the employee residence onto the paved road, cross the road, and pass the Sunset picnic area on the right (north). You are back on a double-track dirt trail.

7.3 Cross the road at the crosswalk and continue on Summit Trail. A sign reads TO SOUTHGATE ROAD.

7.9 Reach the junction with the Summit Trail Bypass. Take the bypass, turning right (south) onto the single-track trail. Enjoy great views of Rock City.

8.1 Reach the junction with the connector to Wall Point Road. Turn right onto the single-track connector trail.

8.3 The trail dead-ends at Wall Point Road. Turn left onto the double-track dirt Wall Point Road.

The Alameda Whipsnake

Mount Diablo's rocky, brush-covered slopes provide habitat preferred by both the Alameda whipsnake and its favorite prey, the western fence lizard. Not often seen, this wary snake hibernates in a rock crevice or rodent burrow during the winter months. It also escapes the summer's intense heat underground. Because most of its natural habitat in Alameda and Contra Costa Counties has been destroyed by housing, road construction, reservoirs, and other development, only three sizable populations of the Alameda whipsnake still exist. This harmless snake has been listed as a California endangered species and is now protected by law. Habitat preservation is the key to its survival.

8.4 The trail meets the road at the curve above Rock City where you started. Head up into Rock City Camp on any trail; turn right onto the paved road marked LITTLE ROCK PICNIC AREA. At the end of the gravel turnaround area, take the stone steps and pass through the Little Rock amphitheater. Follow the rock steps back to the parking lot.

8.5 Arrive back at the parking lot.

HIKE INFORMATION

Local Information: Danville Area Chamber of Commerce, 117-E Town and Country Drive, Danville, CA 94526; (925) 837-4400; www.danvillecachamber.com
Hike Tours: Mount Diablo State Park Headquarters, 96 Mitchell Canyon Road, Clayton CA 94517; (925) 837-2525; www.parks.ca.gov/?page_id=517
Mount Diablo Interpretive Association, P.O. Box 346, Walnut Creek, CA 94597; (925) 927-7222; www.mdia.org
Save Mount Diablo, 1901 Olympic Boulevard, Suite 220, Walnut Creek, CA 94596; (925) 947-3535; www.savemountdiablo.org

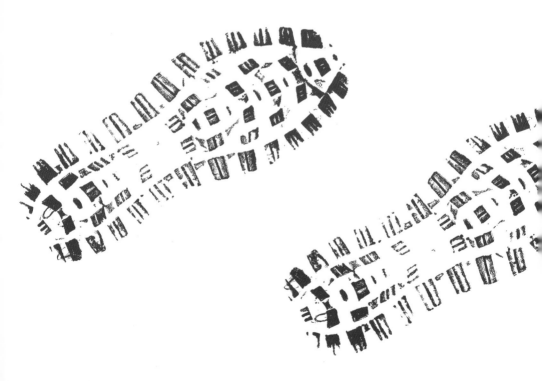

Mount Diablo State Park:
Donner Canyon to the Falls Trail

While creeks running down Mount Diablo may dry in summer, the reality is that there are always cool canyons, and even on hot days, cool breezes cross upper elevations on the less-traveled north side of the mountain. Because the trails here are protected from the sun most of the day, Donner, Back, and Mitchell Canyons have among California's best wildflower shows. The seasonal waterfalls in the upper reaches of Donner Canyon, especially in Wild Oat Canyon along the Falls Trail, are spectacular.

Start: Donner Canyon Road Trailhead at the end of Regency Drive
Distance: 5.9-mile double loop
Approximate hiking time: 4 hours
Difficulty: Moderate to strenuous
Trail surface: Double-track, dirt trail; narrow, single-track trail with some rocks to traverse
Other trail users: Equestrians and mountain bikers on Donner Canyon and Back Creek Trails
Canine compatibility: Dogs not permitted
Land status: State park
Fees and permits: No fees or permits required

Schedule: Open daily year-round from 8:00 a.m. to dusk
Maps: USGS Clayton; Diablo. Mount Diablo Interpretive Association; P.O. Box 346, Walnut Creek, CA 94597; (925) 927-7222; www.mdia.org/parkmap.htm
Trail contact: Mount Diablo State Park Headquarters, 96 Mitchell Canyon Road, Clayton, CA 94517; (925) 837-2525; ranger's office, (925) 837-6119; www.parks.ca.gov
Other: There are no facilities on this hike, so bring plenty of water and be prepared to make friends with a tree, if need be.

Finding the trailhead

By Car: From Highway 24 or Interstate 680 in Walnut Creek, exit at Ygnacio Valley Road and head east. Stay on Ygnacio Valley Road for 7.5 miles to the town of Clayton. Turn right (southeast) onto Clayton Road; go about 2.5 miles. Turn right (southeast) onto Marsh Creek Road. Turn right (south) onto Regency Drive and take it until it dead-ends. There is plenty of street parking. Walk south down the embankment to the Donner Canyon Road Trailhead.

> 🌿 **Green Tip:**
> *When hiking in a group, walk single file on established trails to avoid widening them.*

Unlike the dry and golden northeast ridges of the Diablo foothills, a glistening tree-lined creek starts this hike, along with fields of grass and wild mustard, the smell of wild sage, and glimpses of scurrying squirrels and lizards.

Both Donner Creek and Back Creek flow most of the year, though they are down to a trickle in golden summer. Not long ago, and for hundreds of years, they provided a peaceful hunting camp for Miwok Indians. In the 1860s and 1870s—the area's heyday—the surrounding valley became home to several thriving towns housing post–gold rush farmers, loggers, and coal miners. Joel Clayton, an English immigrant, discovered coal north of Clayton and founded his namesake town in 1857. Luckily, Donner and Back Canyons remained fairly quiet and peaceful. The mines were short-lived and were ghost towns by the 1880s.

The only remains of any structure on your hike are those of the Donner/Hetherington Cabin along Donner Creek. An eccentric landowner, Mrs. Donner (not related to the Donner Party) bought the land in the 1940s. The creek and canyon take her name. She raised sheep on the land and planted a small grove of fruit trees; apple, pear, and plum trees still thrive upslope right (west) of the trail. Mrs. Donner sold the building to the local sheriff's department as a hunting lodge; the hunters built the concrete slab you see, most likely as the base of a fire pit for roasting fresh venison.

The Hetheringtons purchased the land in 1952. Members of a horticulture society, the San Francisco couple spent time planting native species to restore the overgrazed land. In an effort to preserve the canyon, they sold it in 1972 to the Save Mount Diablo (SMD) organization, who turned Donner, Back, and Mitchell Canyons over to the state park. Even with the last forty years of vast development on all sides of the mountain, SMD has managed to increase the park from its original 6,788 acres to more than 89,000 acres today.

We have a candy maker to thank for the most memorable trails on this hike, the Falls Trail and Cardinet Oaks Road. In 1939 George Cardinet and his horse began hauling tools up into the canyons to construct new trails. Mr. Cardinet maintained the two trails he created for over sixty years, almost until his death in 2007 at the age of ninety-eight.

What makes his trails memorable? In wet months and after rains, you'll see a satisfying series of sparkling waterfalls, the largest dropping 25 feet. Also, wildflowers are abundant in upper Donner and Wild Oat Canyons. Besides the usual purple California lupine, orange poppies, and fiery Indian paintbrush, you'll see the yellow Mount Diablo daisy, pink mosquito-bills, delicate white milkmaids, powder blue grand hound's tongue, and hundreds of species of herbs, grasses, and shrubs. In the late winter, the pink blossoms of the manzanitas awaken to the approaching spring.

A waterfall along the Falls Trail in April during a dry spring

0.0   Start at the end of Regency Drive (it dead-ends at a waterway) and walk south. Be careful going down the embankment. The Donner Canyon Road trailhead is ahead. The trail runs perpendicular to Regency Drive, following Donner Creek.

0.1   Pass the trailhead to Bruce Lee and Back Creek Trails to Mitchell Canyon Road; stay left (southeast) on Donner Canyon Road. Above are the Mount Diablo foothills. (Note: Donner Canyon can be very muddy in winter, but that's a good sign for the waterfalls.) Pass the Bruce Lee Trail and split at Clayton Oaks Road. Stay right (south) on Donner Canyon Road. Check out the "Bowl Tree," carved out by fire.

0.8   Reach the single-track path to the Donner Cabin historic site; detour left (east) by the creek. Continue on Donner Canyon Road.

1.2   Pass the Tick Wood Trail. Donner Canyon Road starts a steady, moderate ascent.

1.4   Reach the top of the ridge; views open of Clayton, the Mount Diablo foothills, and the northernmost part of San Francisco Bay.

1.5   The trail dead-ends. Go left (east) onto Cardinet Oaks Road toward the Olympia Trail (you will take the Falls Trail before you reach Olympia). The trail crosses the creek. Head uphill again after the creek on a moderate climb.

1.9   Turn right (southeast) onto the Falls Trail. The steep, single-track Falls Trail is a strenuous climb with narrow ridge sections and some rocks to high-step. Watch for poison oak. As the trail crests, the waterfalls become visible. The first fall sometimes drops more than 25 feet. Depending on the season, you may cross three branches of the creek several times. The ridge drops off dramatically to right (west). Moderate hiking beyond heads deeper into the canyon.

3.1   At Middle Trail, go right (west); the sign reads TO MERIDIAN TRAIL 0.53 MILE.

3.7   Turn left (west/uphill) onto Meridian Ridge Fire Road.

4.2   Reach a trail junction; take the Meridian Point Trail left (southwest) toward the Back Creek Trail, crossing Back Creek.

4.7   The Meridian Point Trail dead-ends on the double-track Back Creek Trail; turn right, heading north.

5.1   Pass the Tick Wood Trail; stay on the Back Creek Trail, which follows Back Creek.

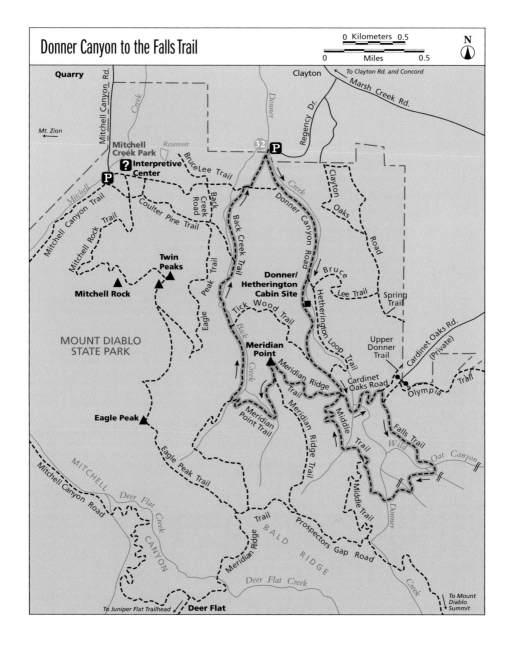

Donner Canyon to the Falls Trail

0 Kilometers 0.5

0 Miles 0.5

N

Quarry

Clayton

To Clayton Rd. and Concord

Marsh Creek Rd.

Mitchell Canyon Rd.

Creek

Donner

Regency Dr.

Mt. Zion ←

Mitchell Creek Park

Reservoir

32 P

P

? Interpretive Center

P

Bruce Lee Trail

Creek

Clayton

Oaks

Road

Mitchell

Mitchell Canyon Trail

Coulter Pine Trail

Back Creek Road

Back Creek Trail

Donner Canyon Road

Mitchell Rock Trail

Bruce Lee Trail

Twin Peaks

Eagle Peak Trail

Donner/ Hetherington Cabin Site

Hetherington Loop Trail

Spring Trail

Mitchell Rock

Tick Wood Trail

Back Creek

MOUNT DIABLO STATE PARK

Meridian Point

Meridian Ridge Trail

Cardinet Oaks Road

Upper Donner Trail

Cardinet Oaks Rd. (Private)

Trail

Olympia

Trail

Eagle Peak

Meridian Point Trail

Meridian Ridge Trail

Middle Trail

Falls Trail

Wild

Oat Canyon

Eagle Peak Trail

Middle Trail

Donner

MITCHELL

Deer Flat Creek

CANYON

Mitchell Canyon Road

Trail

B A L D   R I D G E

Prospectors Gap Road

Creek

To Mount Diablo Summit

Meridian Ridge

Deer Flat Creek

To Juniper Flat Trailhead

Deer Flat

5.4 Stay right (north) on Back Creek Trail, heading back to where it meets Donner Canyon Road (trail to the left (northwest) leads to the Mitchell Canyon Visitor Center and Ranger Station).

5.9 The Back Creek Trail meets Donner Canyon Road and the start of the hike on Regency Drive.

Option: For a shorter hike, double back on the Donner Canyon Road (cuts 1 mile off the distance). If you're hearty and have the time, climb another 2 miles up Prospectors Gap Road to the North Peak Trail to the Devil's Pulpit, the Devil's Elbow, and the Mount Diablo summit (3,849 feet).

HIKE INFORMATION

Local Information: Clayton Business and Community Association; (925) 673-7300; www.94517.com

Hike Tours: Mount Diablo State Park Headquarters; 96 Mitchell Canyon Road, Clayton, CA 94517; (925) 837-2525; www.parks.ca.gov/?page_id=517

Mount Diablo Interpretive Association, P.O. Box 346, Walnut Creek, CA 94597; (925) 927-7222; www.mdia.org

> **🍃 Green Tip:**
> *Be green and stylish too—wear clothing made of organic cotton and other recycled products.*

Black Diamond Mines Regional Preserve

You have your choice of 70 miles of trails in this nearly 7,000-acre preserve. This hike passes through two old mining town sites, Somersville and Nortonville, past many mine openings, and the Rose Hill Cemetery. You can explore air shafts for the old coal-mining tunnels and check out "Jim's Place," a mysterious underground dwelling. Hike through areas of grassland and mixed evergreen forest. Black Diamond is the northernmost location of Coulter pine, black sage, and desert olive. Springtime hosts abundant wildflowers. Leave time to tour the underground mining museum and the Hazel-Atlas Mine, which supplied sand for the Hazel-Atlas Glass Company of Oakland from the 1920s through the 1940s.

Start: Parking lot for Black Diamond Mines Regional Preserve
Distance: 5.2-mile loop
Approximate hiking time: 3 hours (allow 4 to 5 hours if you are taking the tour of the Hazel-Atlas Mine)
Difficulty: Moderate, with a few strenuous uphill sections
Trail surface: The footpath is dirt and sandstone, widening on the Black Diamond and Nortonville Trails to allow for bicyclists; the end of Black Diamond Trail is paved service road, which becomes dirt footpath again on Coal Canyon Trail
Other trail users: Equestrians and mountain bikers are allowed on some trails
Canine compatibility: Leashed dogs permitted (dogs may be unleashed in open areas)
Land status: Regional preserve
Fees and permits: Admission is free on weekdays or when the kiosk is unattended; you'll pay $4 per car on the weekend; $1 per dog; and $3 per person for the Hazel-Atlas Mine tour.
Schedule: Open daily year-round from 5:00 a.m. to 10:00 p.m. unless otherwise posted
Maps: USGS Antioch South; Clayton. East Bay Regional Park District Headquarters, 2950 Peralta Oaks Court, Oakland, CA 94605; (510) 633-0460; www.ebparks.org/parks
Trail contact: Black Diamond Regional Preserve, 5175 Somersville Road, Antioch, CA 94509-7807; (925) 757-2620; www.ebparks.org/parks/black_diamond
Other: Bring a flashlight to explore mining tunnels. A hundred species of birds have been spotted here, so you may want to bring binoculars, too. They'll come in handy for taking in ridgetop views of the Bay and the Central Valley as well.

THE HIKE

Hiking in the Black Diamond Mines Regional Preserve, you travel through a time machine. Your first stop is California circa 1772. The Miwok Indians had lived in this area for thousands of years; with the arrival of European settlers in 1772, the Miwok way of life was rapidly destroyed.

The next stop is circa 1855. This preserve was once the largest coal-mining district in the state. The Mount Diablo coal field, in operation from 1855 to 1902, gave birth to five prospering towns around twelve major mining sites: Nortonville, Somersville, Stewartville, Judsonville, and West Hartley. The Black Diamond Mine produced the weakest grade of coal: lignite (or subbituminous coal), crumbly, dull, and high in sulfur. Taken out of the Antioch Valley by train, the coal was used to run steamships and steam locomotives, and to heat post–gold rush homes in the San Francisco Bay Area, Sacramento, and Stockton. Better grade coal found in Washington State eventually put Black Diamond out of business, but not before the area prospered.

Below ground are some 100 miles of mining tunnels that produced 4 million tons of coal, amounting to $20 million during its heyday. And all this work was completed with simple equipment, by hand. Hard hats weren't yet invented. Men and boys (starting at eight years old) worked twelve-hour days together in the mines. And, of course, there were accidents. Next to what is now the parking lot, you find remains of the Independent Mine. In 1873 an attached boiler room exploded, killing two men and blowing parts of the boiler a quarter mile away.

Living was tough, too. Babies died in epidemics, women in childbirth, and men of disease from years in the mines. Some were buried in Rose Hill Cemetery, and their legends are documented in the museum.

The next stop is circa 1922. The ghost towns of Somersville and Nortonville are suddenly active again. Along with coal in the abandoned mines was high-grade silica sand. Marvin Greathouse, owner of the Somersville mine area, put it back

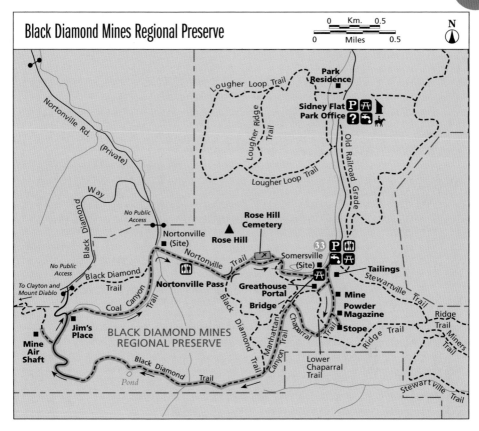

Black Diamond Mines Regional Preserve

0   Km.   0.5

0   Miles   0.5

N

Lougher Loop Trail

Park Residence

Sidney Flat Park Office

Lougher Ridge Trail

Nortonville Rd. (Private)

Lougher Loop Trail

Old Railroad Grade

Way

Black Diamond

No Public Access

Rose Hill Cemetery

Nortonville (Site)

Rose Hill

Nortonville Trail

Somersville (Site)

No Public Access

Black Diamond Trail

Nortonville Pass

Greathouse Portal

Bridge

Tailings

Stewartville Trail

To Clayton and Mount Diablo

Coal Canyon Trail

Black Diamond Trail

Mine Powder Magazine

Ridge Trail

Jim's Place

BLACK DIAMOND MINES REGIONAL PRESERVE

Manhattan Canyon Trail

Chaparral Trail

Ridge Trail

Stope

Miners Trail

Mine Air Shaft

Black Diamond Trail

Pond

Lower Chaparral Trail

Stewartville Trail

---

in operation in 1922 to supply sand used in glassmaking by the Hazel-Atlas Glass Company in Oakland. The Nortonville mine supplied the Columbia Steel Works in Pittsburg with foundry (casting) sand. Competition from Belgian glass and the closing of the steel foundry ended the sand mining in 1949. But by that time, more than 1.8 million tons of sand had been mined.

The Greathouse Portal and the Hazel-Atlas Mine tour are must-sees, with artifacts and great old photos of the towns and their people. Tour participants also take a 400-foot walk back into the mine and see the office of the shifter (mine boss), ore chutes, and ancient geological features. Tours start every hour from noon to 4:00 p.m. on Saturdays and Sundays. You can arrange a tour for an organization on weekdays by calling the park (925-757-2620).

The hike described here takes you past other mine openings, a powder magazine, mounds of tailings (residue of the mining process), and railroad beds, amidst a variety of native and exotic plant life. Coal miners introduced the black locust, pepper tree, almond, eucalyptus, and tree of heaven. Two rare animal species dwell here—the black-shouldered kite and the Alameda striped racer.

View from Black Diamond Trail

On the narrow Chaparral Trail, partially shaded by red-barked manzanita and thicket, oak and short pines, the trail's floor becomes soft sandstone. For walking, it grips well except when there's loose sand or leaves. The Manhattan Canyon Trail is shaded by oaks. Black Diamond Trail, a wider path, requires a steady climb into grassland, but rewards you with views of gently rolling hills and scattered oaks. At the top, vistas open north to the valley and west to Martinez, the Bay, and the Marin Headlands. On Coal Canyon Trail, "Jim's Place" may trigger your imagination. No one knows exactly who lived here. This narrow trail takes you into a wonderful pine-shaded canyon along a creekbed.

At the bottom of the canyon, the trail is sandwiched between two tall rock faces with a pit at the bottom, site of the Nortonville Mine. The town would have stood just ahead; the buildings are mostly gone, but a couple serve as the park offices.

With a half-mile climb, smelling wild anise in late summer and fall, pass over a ridge of Rose Hill to the Protestant burial ground. You also have a great view here of the Somersville site before heading down the hill.

MILES AND DIRECTIONS

0.0   Start by the park road at the parking lot for Black Diamond Mines Regional Preserve. Follow signs to the visitor center and the Hazel-Atlas Mine. Pass a mound of tailings on the left. At the Greathouse Portal, which houses the museum and visitor center, take the stairs just to the right (south) to begin the hike. Turn left (south) toward the Hazel-Atlas Mine and the Chaparral Loop Trail.

0.1   Reach the Hazel-Atlas Mine, where you meet for the tour (if you are taking one). The railway here used to haul coal to the main railroad that steamed into Antioch, one of three trains that served the mines.

0.2 Reach the powder magazine, used to store explosives.

0.3 Pass the stope, a chamber blasted out of sandstone by miners extracting rock for glassmaking.

0.4 Turn right (northwest) to continue on the Chaparral Loop Trail. The Ridge Trail to the left (east) leads to Stewartsville, an alternative loop.

0.8 Before the bridge, turn left (southwest) onto the Manhattan Canyon Trail, which dead-ends at the Black Diamond Trail.

1.0 Turn left (west) onto the Black Diamond Trail and proceed uphill.

2.1 Pass a pond on the left (south).

2.5 Black Diamond Trail becomes the paved Black Diamond Way.

2.9 Take a short detour to the left (west) on the Cumberland Trail. Go about 0.1 mile to an air shaft. Located on the left before the electric wires tower, the air shaft, once 150 feet deep and reached here by a short tunnel, was used to keep a coal mine ventilated and free from dangerous gases. The marks left by miners' picks are still evident on the excavation sides. Return to Black Diamond Way the same way you came and continue hiking north.

3.1 Look for the trailhead to Coal Canyon Trail. Turn right (east) onto the narrow dirt footpath.

3.2 Arrive at Jim's Place. Follow signs to the right (south) of the trail. After your visit, continue east on Coal Canyon Trail.

3.8 Pass the covered hole of the old vertical Nortonville Mine. Ahead is the Nortonville town site.

3.9 Turn right (southeast) onto the Nortonville Trail and climb the hill.

4.6 After passing over the ridge of Rose Hill, bear left to the cemetery gate. Go through the cemetery and head downhill toward the parking lot. Below is what used to be the town of Somersville.

5.2 Arrive back at the parking lot.

HIKE INFORMATION

Local Information: Antioch Chamber of Commerce, 324 G Street, Antioch, CA 94509; (925) 757-1800; www.antiochchamber.com

Hike Tours: Hazel-Atlas Mine tours are given every hour from noon to 4:00 p.m. on Saturday and Sunday March through November. Tours are strictly limited to ages seven and up. To make weekend reservations, call (888) EBPARKS (327-2757).

Briones Crest Trail heads into a grove of oaks.

Right above bustling cities and dense suburbs are three ridgetops, home to parks and open space preserves full of natural beauty and history, and punctuated with bodies of water. In the basins between the ridges, a hiker can find solitude exploring areas that are among the East Bay's best kept secrets.

Who would think that above the city "that puts the There in There,"—Oakland, California—you can find quiet, enchanting hills that were once covered with ancient, giant redwoods. After loggers downed the forest, much of the area gave way to development, but thousands of acres have survived to support native wildlife and remind us of our past.

You can find variety as well. Redwood Park and Joaquin Miller Park host gurgling creeks, second-generation redwoods, and cool, shady trails. Robert Sibley Volcanic Regional Preserve offers geological exploration with dikes, mudflows, and lava flows. Huckleberry Botanic Regional Preserve is an ecological jewel with a native plant population found nowhere else. The ridge also offers swimming in Roberts Park and bass fishing and boating at pretty Lake Chabot.

Nearby Briones Regional Park, above the affluent suburbs of Lafayette and Orinda, offers sweeping grasslands with ridgetop tarns and a view of San Pablo Bay and the Carquinez Straits, where retired warships sit in neat rows in the water.

Water is key to the drama on the Sunol Ridge. In early spring, Little Yosemite splashes down over gray boulders. The wildflower display is unmatched anywhere else in the East Bay. Backpackers can pass by all this into the Ohlone Regional Wilderness to spend the night under the stars and finish off with a cool dunk in Lake Del Valle.

> **A hiker can find solitude exploring areas that are among the East Bay's best kept secrets.**

On the San Pablo Ridge between Wild Cat Canyon and Claremont Canyon is a family favorite, Tilden Park. A study in combining recreation and preservation, Tilden offers wooded canyons, view trails, and a nature preserve, along with pony rides, a steam train, a working farm, and a beautiful old carousel. It also has Anza Lake, a favorite swimming hole. Just below is the University of California, Berkeley campus, where pedestrians always have the right of way and most things political are left of center. It's one of the best places in the world for people watching: Eccentrics, hippies, artists, international students, businesspeople, and the homeless intermingle in front of bookstores and music shops.

While most of these parks are part of the well-run East Bay Regional Park District, the East Bay Municipal Utility District (EBMUD) owns a lot of open space around these ridges, too. And here's the secret: To hike on EBMUD lands, you have to get a permit for a nominal fee. The process is simple, but because of it, few people walk the 55 miles of trails in the watershed, open to the public since 1973.

Sword fern with serrated edges

Briones Regional Park

Briones Regional Park offers long, ambling walks through grassy, rolling hills spotted with oak trees, some lovely views both of distant towns and landmarks and of neighboring parkland, with the pleasant surprises of lagoons and a contrasting dense, damp woodland. Hawks, eagles, and turkey vultures soar and circle above the canyons. Black-tailed deer love to munch on brush in the deeper canyons. There are several small creeks lined with ferns and shrubs, and patches of sun-loving wildflowers grow along most of the trails. The landscape changes seasonally from summer gold to winter green, and gives you a taste of California's Spanish ranch past.

Start: In the parking lot of Briones Regional Park

Distance: 7-mile loop

Approximate hiking time: 3.5 hours

Difficulty: Easy valley and ridge trails combined with strenuous uphill and steep downhill sections

Trail surface: Packed dirt double-track trail, single-track dirt trail, and one creek crossing

Other trail users: Equestrians and mountain bikers, except for Bear Creek Trail, which is hikers only

Canine compatibility: Leashed dogs permitted

Land status: Regional park

Fees and permits: Parking is $3 per vehicle when the kiosk is attended, which is mostly on weekends in summer months. Vehicles with trailers are $3. The dog fee is $2.

Schedule: Open daily year-round from 8:00 a.m. to 10:00 p.m. unless otherwise posted

Maps: USGS Oakland East; Briones Valley. Parks maps are available from East Bay Regional Park District Headquarters, 2950 Peralta Oaks Court, P.O. Box 5381, Oakland, CA 94605; (888) EB-PARKS or (888) 327-2757; www.ebparks.org/parks/briones.

Trail contact: East Bay Regional Park District Headquarters, 2950 Peralta Oaks Court, P.O. Box 5381, Oakland, CA 94605; (888) EB-PARKS or (888) 327-2757; www.ebparks .org/parks/briones

Other: Watch for poison oak trailside.

Finding the trailhead

By Car: From Highway 24, take the Orinda/Moraga exit and turn left (west) at the light onto Camino Pablo. After about a mile, turn right (east) onto Bear Creek Road. Look for the sign reading BRIONES REGIONAL PARK, BEAR CREEK STAGING AREA. Turn right (east) into the park. Just past the kiosk, turn left (north) into the parking lot. The Abrigo Valley Trailhead is on the right (east).

By Public Transportation: Currently, no public transportation is available directly to the Bear Creek Road Staging Area. County Connection bus 206 has limited service that will bring you within a short walk of the Lafayette Ridge Staging Area. Go to 511.org or www.cccta.org (County Connection), or phone (925) 676-7500 for more information.

THE HIKE

For nearly 200 years, the land that is now Briones Regional Park has provided grass for grazing cattle, which replaced the herds of elk and antelope reported by early settlers. Since the land grants of the Spanish in the early 1800s, livestock have shaped this landscape. The annual grasses are Spanish, carried accidentally as seeds by the cattle. The stepped hillsides are a result of cows creating paths to new grass. After the rains, the trails can be badly rutted from hooves, creating an uneven surface for hiking boots. And, of course, you should watch out for cow pies.

But if you look carefully, you can also see a Georgia O'Keeffe painting in the Briones scenery: long valleys between subtle and smooth rolling hills of grassland and scattered oaks. Those round, grassy hills dominate the park, pastoral green in winter and late spring, golden in summer and fall, radiating the heat of California sunshine and creating a scene of old western ranchland.

The park is named for Felipe Briones, the original Spanish grant holder of this land. In 1829, young Briones fell in love with a waterfall and built a home near what is now the Bear Creek entrance to the park. The retired Spanish soldier cultivated the land and kept a few hundred cattle and horses, supporting a family of eighteen.

Rejecting the Spanish missions, occasionally native Californians tried to reclaim their land. In 1839, a group stole nearly all the saddle horses belonging to Captain Ygnacio Martinez, Briones's neighbor to the north. The captain's son, Don Jose Martinez, and eight or ten other neighbors, including Briones, went in pursuit of them. They succeeded in recovering the animals, but Felipe Briones was struck by an arrow and killed. In 1842, his widow, Maria Manuela Valencia Briones, claimed the grant and continued to ranch here. And so it continued for fifty years.

In 1906 there was a water shortage in the growing East Bay. The People's Water Company began purchasing land in San Pablo and Bear Creek to create a watershed. The San Pablo Dam and reservoir (1919), Lake Chabot (1875), Upper San Leandro Reservoir (1926), and finally the Briones Reservoir (1964) were built for this purpose. It all became parkland in 1957.

Passing through green-painted cattle gates, the wide Abrigo Valley Trail brings you into an area lined with bays, oaks, and maples. The trail rises steeply in places.

Look for indications of landslides. These sparse hillsides of loose soil are prone to this natural phenomenon, as is the entire Lamorinda area.

The park leases to three ranchers. The rule with cows is to just walk on past them; the docile animals will likely move out of your way as you approach. But never stand directly behind a cow, which could kick if frightened.

On the Briones Crest, look north of the Benicia–Carquinez Bridge to see "The Mothball Fleet," more officially known as the MARAD Reserve Fleet at Suisun Bay, the largest single collection of ships on the Pacific Coast. The fleet includes retired cargo ships, tankers, Victory ships, missile cruisers, barges, and tugboats.

The Sindicich Lagoons, protected pond habitats, are fenced to keep out rogue cattle. They were probably created as cattle water holes and replenish themselves from a natural spring below. White egrets and blue herons stop here to rest. In the fall, dragonflies twirl over the water. In the spring, California newts lay their eggs here.

A well-endowed ram along the Valley Trail

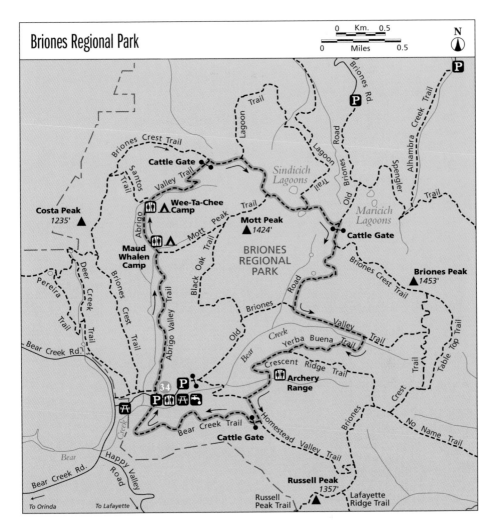

Briones Regional Park

0   Km.   0.5
0   Miles   0.5

N

Costa Peak
1235'

Cattle Gate

Briones Crest Trail

Santos Trail

Valley Trail

Wee-Ta-Chee Camp

Abrigo

Mott Peak Trail

Black Oak Trail

Mott Peak
1424'

Sindicich Lagoons

Lagoon Trail

Briones Rd.

Lagoon Road

Old Briones Road

Maricich Lagoons

Spengler Trail

Alhambra Creek Trail

Cattle Gate

BRIONES
REGIONAL
PARK

Briones Crest Trail

Briones Peak
1453'

Maud Whalen Camp

Pereira Trail

Deer Creek Trail

Briones Crest Trail

Abrigo Valley Trail

Old Briones Road

Briones Creek

Bear Creek

Yerba Buena Trail

Valley Trail

Crest Trail

Table Top Trail

Bear Creek Rd.

Crescent Ridge Trail

Archery Range

Bear Creek Trail

34

Cattle Gate

Homestead Valley Trail

Briones

No Name Trail

Bear

Happy Valley Road

Bear Creek Rd.

To Orinda

To Lafayette

Russell Peak Trail

Russell Peak
1357'

Lafayette Ridge Trail

On the Crescent Ridge Trail, you will pass the Briones Archery Club Range, where you will find pit toilets, picnic tables, and shelters with places for quivers and bows.

Bear Creek Trail, the only single-track, hikers-only trail in Briones, is a wonderful finale. It takes you up and down through thick woods and an underbrush of fern, moss, and flowering brush.

MILES AND DIRECTIONS

0.0   Start at the Abrigo Valley Trailhead. Take the trail past the Oak Grove picnic area to the cattle gate.

0.1   Go through cattle gate, staying on Abrigo Valley Trail.

1.0 Stay left (north) on the Abrigo Valley Trail past the Mott Peak Trail turnoff. Group Camp Maud Whalen is on the right (east).

1.4 Wee-Ta-Chee Camp is on the right (east) over the bridge. Continue on the Abrigo Valley Trail.

2.1 Go through the cattle gate and turn right (east) onto the Briones Crest Trail.

2.3 Stay right (east) on the Briones Crest Trail as you pass the first trailhead for Lagoon Trail.

3.0 Pass the smaller Sindicich Lagoon on the right (south). Just past the pond, take a left (north) turn onto Lagoon Trail to see the larger Sindicich Lagoon.

3.1 Arrive at the larger Sindicich Lagoon. Go back the way you came to Briones Crest Trail.

3.2 Turn left (east) onto Briones Crest Trail to continue along the ridge.

3.4 Turn right (south) onto Old Briones Road.

3.5 Pass through another cattle gate. It is downhill for a while.

4.1 Take a left (west) turn onto the Valley Trail.

4.7 Take a right (south) turn onto the Yerba Buena Trail. This leads back up and west into the wooded hillsides.

5.3 Go right (west) onto the Crescent Ridge Trail. A steep downhill section brings you to the archery club.

5.9 Turn left (south) onto the Homestead Valley Trail. You can see the next trailhead 0.1 mile ahead.

6.0 Turn right (west) onto the Bear Creek Trail. The single-track trail leads through a wildlife-populated woodland habitat. (*Note:* Beware of poison oak.)

7.0 Cross the creek. There's no bridge, but it's a short leap unless you are trekking after unusually heavy rains. Climb the stairs on the opposite bank, up a couple switchbacks, to the parking lot.

HIKE INFORMATION

Local Information: Orinda Chamber of Commerce, 24 Orinda Way, Orinda, CA 94563; (925) 254-3909; www.orindachamber.org
Hike Tours: Orinda Hiking Club, P.O. Box 934, Orinda, CA 94563; orindahiking.org

Redwood Regional Park: East to West Ridge Trails

This ridge and canyon hike offers dramatic changes in scenery, light, and even temperature. An easy first mile follows a wide dirt path among pines, oaks, and eucalyptus, exposed to the sky, with views of the foothills and Mount Diablo. Winding down Prince Road, the scenery changes, shaded by bay and madrone trees. Suddenly, you'll find yourself in the seclusion of a thriving redwood grove, walking beside Redwood Creek, with its banks full of ferns and water-loving plants. The trail heads back up to evergreens and views again.

Start: From the Skyline Gate Staging Area on Skyline Boulevard

Distance: 4-mile loop

Approximate hiking time: 2 hours

Difficulty: Moderate with a few short but steep ascents and downhill sections

Trail surface: A wide, dirt road narrows to a footpath that may be eroded and muddy in places, but passable

Other trail users: Mountain bikers and equestrians

Canine compatibility: Dogs permitted (must be leashed on the Stream Trail)

Land status: Regional park

Fees and permits: Free at Skyline Gate Staging Area. At the Redwood Road entrance, fees are $5 per vehicle, $4 per vehicle with trailer. Buses: $1 per person. Dog fee is $2.

Schedule: Open daily year-round from 5:00 a.m. to 10:00 p.m. unless otherwise posted

Maps: USGS Oakland East. Parks maps are available from East Bay Regional Park District Headquarters, 2950 Peralta Oaks Court, P.O. Box 5381, Oakland, CA 94605; (888) EB-PARKS or (888) 327-2757; www.ebparks.org/parks/redwood.

Trail contact: East Bay Regional Park District Headquarters, 2950 Peralta Oaks Court, P.O. Box 5381, Oakland, CA 94605; (888) EB-PARKS or (888) 327-2757; www.ebparks.org/parks/redwood

Other: Wear layered clothing to accommodate changes in temperature. At the Skyline Gate parking lot, you'll find pit toilets, a water fountain, a fountain for dogs, free biodegradable Pick-up Mitts to remove your dog's waste from the trails, trail maps, and a bulletin board that sometimes features an animal in need of a good home.

Finding the trailhead
By Car: From Highway 13 in Oakland, take the Redwood Road exit and go east (uphill). At the top of the hill, turn left (north) onto Skyline Boulevard.

You will pass the entrance to Roberts Regional Recreation Area and the Moon Gate Staging Area before reaching the larger Skyline Gate Staging Area and the trailhead for this hike. For locations and directions to other staging areas for the park, go to www.ebparks.org/parks/redwood.

By Public Transportation: Currently, no public transportation is available to Skyline Boulevard. However, routes change frequently. Go to 511.org or www.actransit.org, or phone (510) 817-1717 or 511 and say, "AC Transit," to speak with a person about route information including time points, destinations, and trip planning.

THE HIKE

You might never know, as you hike through serene Redwood Regional Park, that this was once the backdrop for mass destruction, fires, lynchings, manhunts, and vindictive justice laid down by rifle-toting lumberjacks. Before that, it was a magnificent land of giants. The 1,831-acre park also hosted farms, orchards, and ranches for ninety years. Today, a peaceful getaway amid suburban foothills and urban sprawl, the park proves the resilience of nature, sporting few indications of its dramatic past.

Just how big was the old growth? The 150-foot coastal redwoods you see in the park today are second generation. Their ancient mothers were so tall that sea captains sailing into the San Francisco Bay used them as navigational landmarks from 16 miles away, where the Pacific meets the Golden Gate. A report in 1893 measured stumps as wide as 33.5 feet in diameter. If this account is correct, the redwoods may have been the largest living things on earth.

Luis Maria Peralta, a Spanish settler who owned a nearby rancho, put a provision into his land grant allowing neighbors to cut lumber on the ranch for their personal use, but specifically prohibited commercial cutting. He recognized the grand beauty and uniqueness of this forest that was home to grizzly bears, mountain lions, rattlesnakes, and hundreds of California condors, now nearly extinct.

After the gold rush, settlers recognized the profit to be made in lumber. Ten sawmills set up shop in the redwoods. With each mill employing up to one hundred men, shantytowns sprang up. The loggers, mostly jump-ship sailors, were hard-drinking, oath-swearing, feared men. Several times they formed their own retributive posses, emerging from the forest to hang horse and cattle thieves. In 1854 they mounted a nighttime manhunt in the woods for twenty-five felons who had escaped from San Quentin Prison Camp. Most were shot on sight.

By 1860 commercial logging had clear-cut the entire forest. Less than fifteen years after the gold rush, the giant trees that once guided sailors through the Golden Gate were gone. Even the undergrowth was burned away, leaving a charred sea of stumps. Only one old tree still stands, protected in Oakland's Leona Park.

Redwood Park was one of the first purchases by the East Bay Regional Park District, becoming parkland in 1939. A second generation of the big trees took root and now thrives in an environment only a fraction of the forest's original size.

Starting your hike on the wide East Ridge Trail, you share the first mile with bicyclists, equestrians, runners, and undoubtedly dogs romping happily off-leash. With pet restrictions at many city parks, the East Bay Regional Park District offers the most lenient dog rules of almost any park system in the Bay Area.

Pines, coast live oaks, and aromatic bluegum eucalyptus border the trail on the ridge. Rabbits, red squirrels, and quail may appear out of the grasses. Starflowers, lupine, leatherwood, and cleavers grow alongside the path. A half mile in, stop at the bench to admire a great view of the rolling hills and dense woodland that make up Chabot Regional Park, the Las Trampas foothills, and Mount Diablo.

The Stream Trail is darker and damp in the redwood grove; picturesque fences protect riparian life by the creek.

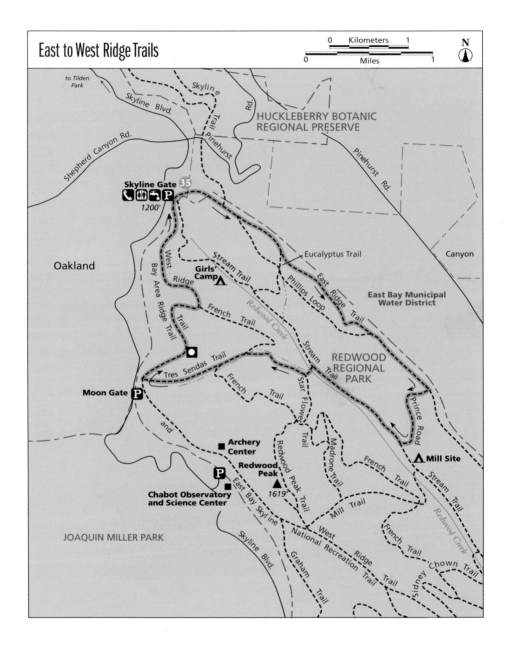

Kilometers

Miles

N

to Tilden
Park

Skyline

Skyline Blvd.

Rd

Pinehurst

HUCKLEBERRY BOTANIC
REGIONAL PRESERVE

Shepherd Canyon Rd.

Pinehurst Rd.

Skyline Gate 35

1200'

Eucalyptus Trail

Canyon

Oakland

West

Bay Area Ridge Trail

Ridge

Girls'
Camp

Stream Trail

Phillips Loop

East Ridge Trail

East Bay Municipal
Water District

French Trail

Redwood Creek

Moon Gate

Tres Sendas Trail

French Trail

Star Flower Trail

Stream Trail

REDWOOD
REGIONAL
PARK

Prince Road

and

Archery
Center

Redwood Peak Trail

Madrone Trail

French Trail

Mill Site

Stream Trail

Redwood
Peak

1619'

Chabot Observatory
and Science Center

East Bay Skyline

Mill Trail

Redwood Creek

JOAQUIN MILLER PARK

Skyline Blvd.

West Ridge Trail

National Recreation Trail

French Trail

Graham Trail

Chown Trail

Kaput

Prince Road was named for Thomas and William Prince, who established a steam-driven sawmill here in 1852. The landscape around the road darkens in the thicker forest, adding red-barked madrone and California bay trees to the mix. It feels a bit like falling into Alice's rabbit hole. Winding downhill, you'll see your first grove of coast redwoods. The temperature changes, the light dims, and you enter the damp, hidden redwood forest in the park's basin, the Redwood Bowl.

The wooden fence railing next to the Steam Trail protects the replenishing riparian habitat around Redwood Creek. Tres Sendas (Three Paths) Trail continues your journey through the woods. The West Ridge Trail, a portion of the 31-mile East Bay Skyline National Recreation Trail that runs along the Coast Range, opens once again to sky and expansive views.

MILES AND DIRECTIONS

0.0 Start at the Skyline Gate Staging Area. Take the East Ridge Trail, which begins on the left (east) side of the parking lot.

0.5 Enjoy the great view of Mount Diablo.

1.2 After passing the Eucalyptus Trail and Phillips Loop, turn right (south) onto Prince Road.

1.6 Bear right (northwest) where the path meets the Stream Trail. (*Note:* For restrooms, water, and picnic tables, turn left (southeast) onto Stream Trail and walk 1 mile. You must double back to pick up the route.)

2.1 Turn left (west) onto Tres Sendas Trail. (*Note:* If you want picnic tables, water, or restrooms, proceed up the Stream Trail another 0.5 mile to Girls' Camp.)

2.5 Tres Sendas Trail climbs a steep hill. Pass Star Flower Trail and French Trail.

2.8 Tres Sendas meets the West Ridge Trail. Turn right (northeast).

4.0 Arrive back at the Skyline Gate Staging Area and parking lot.

HIKE INFORMATION

Local Information: Montclair Business Association, 1980 Mountain Boulevard #205, Oakland, CA 94611; (510) 339-1000; www.montclairvillage.com
Oakland Convention and Visitors Bureau, 463 11th Street, Oakland, CA 94607; (510) 839-9000; www.oaklandcvb.com
Oakland.com; www.oakland.com
Local Events/Attractions: Chabot Space and Science Center, 10000 Skyline Boulevard, Oakland, CA 94619; (510) 336-7300; www.chabotspace.org
Hike Tours: Crab Cove Visitor Center, 1252 McKay Avenue, Alameda, CA 94501; (510) 521-6887; www.ebparks.org

Huckleberry Botanic Regional Preserve

The self-guided nature trail guide available at the trailhead encourages you to stop and notice the details on your walk through the 235-acre preserve. It makes for fun, learning, and discovery along this loop trail rich in rare vegetation. Or you can just walk through the thick brush and breathe. Descend a canyon under bays and oaks and hear the trickling of San Leandro Creek below. Follow the ridge on a narrow footpath through dense shrubs, mostly huckleberries. Short side trails take you up to bald vistas, home to rare manzanitas and hosting soothing pastoral views of the surrounding foothills.

Start: From the staging area on Skyline Boulevard

Distance: 2.4-mile loop

Approximate hiking time: 1.5 hours

Difficulty: Easy

Trail surface: Well-maintained, narrow dirt path with one short set of downslope stairs

Other trail users: Hikers only

Canine compatibility: Dogs not permitted except on the Skyline National Recreation Trail

Land status: Regional preserve

Fees and permits: No fees or permits required

Schedule: Open daily year-round from 5:00 a.m. to 10:00 p.m. unless otherwise posted

Maps: USGS Oakland East. Parks maps are available from East Bay Regional Park District Headquarters, 2950 Peralta Oaks Court, P.O. Box 5381, Oakland, CA 94605; (888) EB-PARKS or (888) 327-2757; www.ebparks.org/parks/huckleberry.

Trail contact: East Bay Regional Park District Headquarters, 2950 Peralta Oaks Court, P.O. Box 5381, Oakland, CA 94605; (888) EB-PARKS or (888) 327-2757; www.ebparks.org/parks/huckleberry

Finding the trailhead

By Car: From Highway 24 in Oakland, take the Fish Ranch Road exit, which is just east of the Caldecott Tunnel. Turn left (south) onto Grizzly Peak Boulevard to Skyline Boulevard. Turn left (southeast) onto Skyline and drive approximately 0.5 mile to the park entrance, which is on the left (east), past the Robert Sibley Volcanic Regional Preserve.

By Public Transportation: Currently, no public transportation is available to the preserve's Skyline Boulevard entrance. However, routes change frequently. Go to 511.org or www.actransit.org, or call AC Transit at (510) 817-1717. You can also call 511 and say, "AC Transit," to speak with a person about route information including time points, destinations, and trip planning.

Take the short detours up to the two manzanita barrens—a totally different landscape with sandy, shell rock, rare manzanitas, and views.

THE HIKE

A stroll along Huckleberry Botanic Regional Preserve's winding, narrow pathway, surrounded by dense, flowering shrubs, is like a walk through a medieval maze. It provides seclusion, triggers the imagination, and offers a botanical adventure on an almost entirely single-track trail.

The self-guided nature path guide, available at the bulletin board by the trailhead, describes the plant life you will see at the markers. The information is surprisingly fascinating (even for nongreen thumbs). Featured are the pliable western leatherwood, the pioneering brittleleaf manzanita, and the sticky-berried pallid manzanita. Extremely rare, you cannot find them anywhere else in the world but in these Bay Area foothills.

The park guide calls Huckleberry Preserve "an island of time . . . what's left of a time gone by." Not a part of the Spanish land grant system in the late 1700s, like surrounding areas, this canyon was saved from the grazing cattle that brought so many drastic changes to the landscape.

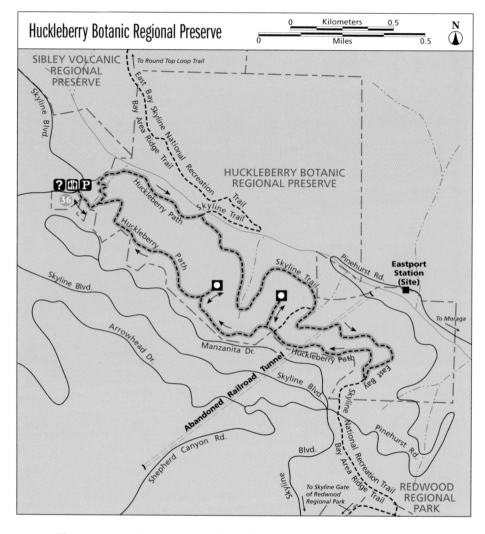

Huckleberry Botanic Regional Preserve

The ancient rock strata below the foliage once lay at the bottom of a deep ocean basin. It contains remains of microscopic diatoms and simple marine life. Subjected to uplift and folding, the bedrock now stands exposed as hard, brittle bands of chert and shale with soil low in nutritional value. Manzanitas like these conditions.

With the area's complex topography, Huckleberry has its own Mediterranean-type climate: warm, dry summers and cool, wet winters. Dense ocean fogs sometimes coat the place in summer, lasting for days. This creates moisture for the local plant life during a time when rainfall is rare.

Late summer and fall is berry season, and birds are abundant. The animals have their pick of juicy berries: Thimbleberries, osoberries, California coffeeberries, elderberries, and dwarf snowberries grow beside the fruitful huckleberries.

But it's not all peace and love among the plant life here. In the preserve you become witness to botanical warfare. The resilient huckleberry bushes are slowly taking over the manzanita, aided by the shade of live oaks and bay laurels that have moved into the area. You can see indications of this conflict throughout the park.

The Huckleberry area was among the first lands purchased in 1936 by the newly formed East Bay Regional Park District. Previously owned by the East Bay Municipal Utility District, the hills still serve as a watershed for San Leandro Creek. The park became a preserve in the 1970s.

Starting from the parking lot, an arrow on the trailhead sign will show you the way. You first descend into a canyon through a mature bay forest. Take a whiff of the pungent bays (they are five times more potent than the commercial spice). You can also hear running water from San Leandro Creek, where rainbow trout were first identified as a species. Walking along the ridge in the shade of the trees beside banks of ferns, the narrow path feels secluded and serene, except for the occasional jogger. On the Skyline Trail, oaks dominate and the trail is a bit dryer. The upper Huckleberry Path, going back toward the trailhead, hosts wonderfully thick plant life, occasionally creating a low canopy overhead. Beware of poison oak that grows right beside the trail.

In sharp contrast, there is one strip of land through the middle of Huckleberry owned by the Pacific Gas and Electric Company. You can't miss it, with the giant steel towers and electricity and telephone service lines. A meditation on industry, whether you want it or not; thankfully it is only brief in passing.

On the last part of the trail, you will find short diversions up to sandy manzanita barrens. The peaceful, open views include Flicker Ridge, Las Trampas Ridge, and the rise of Mount Diablo.

MILES AND DIRECTIONS

0.0   Start at the Huckleberry Botanic Regional Preserve trailhead on Skyline Boulevard in the staging area/parking lot. Where the path divides, turn left (north).

0.4   Huckleberry Path meets Skyline Trail. Stay right (southeast). **Option:** To the left (northeast) is the Skyline Trail heading to Sibley Volcanic Regional Preserve.

0.9   Go straight staying on the Skyline Trail. **Option:** Turning right (south) would bring you back to Huckleberry Path and shorten the hike to 1.69 miles.

1.3   Turn right (west) back onto the Huckleberry Path. **Option:** Turning left, the Skyline Trail continues to Redwood Regional Park.

1.6   Continue straight on Huckleberry Path (the trail from the right is the 1.69-mile Huckleberry Loop connector).

1.7 Go right (north) to take a 160-foot diversion up to a manzanita barren to see rare California coastal plant life and a good view of Mount Diablo.

1.9 Head right (northeast) on another 160-foot diversion with three markers for the Huckleberry self-guided nature path.

2.4 Stay left to arrive back at the parking lot.

HIKE INFORMATION

Local Information: Oakland Convention and Visitors Bureau, 463 11th Street, Oakland, CA 94607; (510) 839-9000; www.oaklandcvb.com
Oakland.com; www.oakland.com
Hike Tours: Crab Cove Visitor Center, 1252 McKay Avenue, Alameda, CA 94501; (510) 521-6887; www.ebparks.org

Regional Preserves

A regional preserve is an area of at least one hundred acres with a suitable staging area that must include either a significant historical or cultural resource or a natural feature of scientific importance. This last can be a rare or endangered plant or animal species and its supporting ecosystem, significant fossils or geological features, or unusual topographic features.

Sibley Volcanic Regional Preserve

What do the Sibley Volcanic Regional Preserve and Mount Saint Helens have in common? The subduction process that caused a volcanic explosion here ten million years ago eventually moved northward to cause the eruption of Washington's Mount Saint Helens. Hiking among Monterey pines and on open grassy hills, you will see walls of the caldera left by the ancient blast, old river gravels, basalt lava flows, and varicolored "redbeds," layers of oxidized iron explored worldwide for fossils. More recently, enthusiastic hikers have built a series of rock mazes in the preserve's old quarries, complete with altars.

Start: Sibley Volcanic Regional Preserve entrance on Skyline Boulevard

Distance: 3.2-mile loop, with some detours

Approximate hiking time: 2 hours

Difficulty: Easy to moderate

Trail surface: Mostly well-packed dirt trail that varies in width but with some loose gravel; finish on a paved path

Other trail users: Hikers and equestrians only except on the Volcanic Trail and the last section of the Round Top Loop Trail, where bicycles are also allowed

Canine compatibility: Leashed dogs permitted

Land status: Regional preserve

Fees and permits: No fees or permits required

Schedule: Open daily year-round from 5:00 a.m. to 10:00 p.m. unless otherwise posted

Maps: USGS Oakland East. Parks maps are available from East Bay Regional Park District Headquarters, 2950 Peralta Oaks Court, P.O. Box 5381, Oakland, CA 94605; (888) EB-PARKS; www.ebparks.org/parks/sibley.

Trail contact: Sibley Volcanic Regional Preserve, (510) 644-0436. East Bay Regional Park District Headquarters, 2950 Peralta Oaks Court, P.O. Box 5381, Oakland, CA 94605; (888) EB-PARKS or (888) 327-2757; www.ebparks.org/parks/sibley

Other: Pick up the park trail guide, available at the trailhead, for a self-guided tour of Round Top's fascinating geological journey. You'll find benches, flush toilets, and drinking water at the trailhead as well.

Finding the trailhead

By Car: From the San Francisco–Oakland Bay Bridge, take Interstate 580 to Highway 24. Take the Fish Ranch Road exit off Highway 24, which is just east of the Caldecott Tunnel. Continue 0.8 mile southeast to Grizzly Peak

Boulevard. Turn left (southeast) and go 0.24 mile on Grizzly Peak Boulevard to Skyline Boulevard. Turn left (south) onto Skyline and proceed to the well-marked park entrance on the left (east).

By Public Transportation: Currently, no public transportation is available to Skyline Boulevard and the preserve. However, routes change frequently. Go to 511.org or www.actransit.org, or phone (510) 817-1717 or 511 and say, "AC Transit," to speak with a person about route information including time points, destinations, and trip planning.

THE HIKE

The Sibley Volcanic Regional Preserve from its beginnings is a story of fire. This greatly loved 660-acre park includes a self-guided geologic tour and an assortment of terrain, views, and trails through Monterey pines, bluegum eucalyptus, and grasslands looping around Round Top Peak. A mere 1,742 feet, people still refer to Round Top as a mountain, perhaps in respect of its eruptive past.

Fire arose from water about ten million years ago. A freshwater lake extended from what is now Tilden Park north to San Leandro Reservoir and south and east to Lafayette. Within these waters, a volcano began to thrust itself upward. During its active period, the volcano released at least eleven lava flows with two explosive episodes of epic proportions. One violent eruption likely equaled that of Mount Saint Helens. This breath of fire helped shape the area's ridges and formed the mound known as Round Top. Today, you can see the alternating volcanic and sedimentary layers that were folded, tilted, crumpled, and tossed about by millions of years of earthquake activity. Welcome to California.

Sibley's complex rock formations are enough to make a grown geologist giggle. Rock quarries north of the peak have made features even more visible. Years of commercial gouging by the land's previous owner, the Kaiser Corporation, exposed old lava flows, mudflows, volcanic dikes, vents, cinder piles, and other geologic forms.

In 1910 millionaire Frank Havens founded the Mahogany Eucalyptus and Land Company and began to plant the crests of the Oakland and Berkeley Hills with great forests of Australian eucalyptus trees. Havens promised investors quick riches, persuading them that the wood was better for building than any other. His company planted eucalyptus by the millions. So vainly self-assured was Havens that he planted the trees without ever verifying his claim. In 1913 he learned the terrible truth: The bluegum eucalyptus he had planted was worthless. It turned out bluegum was never used for lumber in Australia, and the species of eucalyptus that the Australians did use could not be harvested until the trees were several hundred years old.

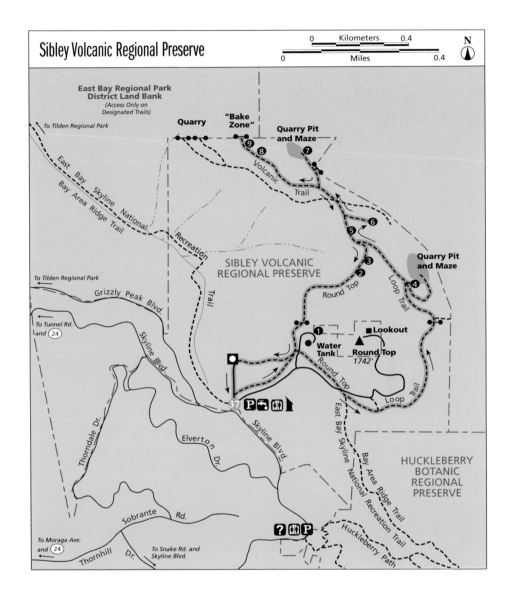

Sibley Volcanic Regional Preserve

East Bay Regional Park District Land Bank
(Access Only on Designated Trails)

To Tilden Regional Park

Quarry

"Bake Zone"

Quarry Pit and Maze

Volcanic Trail

Quarry Pit and Maze

SIBLEY VOLCANIC REGIONAL PRESERVE

To Tilden Regional Park

Grizzly Peak Blvd.

To Tunnel Rd. and 24

Skyline Blvd.

Round Top

Loop Trail

Water Tank

Lookout

Round Top 1742'

Recreation Trail

East Bay Skyline National Recreation Trail

Bay Area Ridge Trail

Loop Trail

Elverton Dr.

Thorndale Dr.

Skyline Blvd.

HUCKLEBERRY BOTANIC REGIONAL PRESERVE

Sobrante Rd.

To Moraga Ave. and 24

Thornhill Dr.

To Snake Rd. and Skyline Blvd.

Huckleberry Path

East Bay Skyline National Recreation Trail — To Tilden Regional Park — Bay Area Ridge Trail

Unfortunately, Haven's hot, oily, and quick-burning eucalyptus led to tragedy. The year 1923 saw a disastrous fire in Berkeley made worse by hot-burning eucalyptus. On Sunday, October 20, 1991, winds in excess of 65 miles per hour gusted and swirled through the dangerously dry Oakland hills, which had endured five years of drought. An unseen ember found a parched eucalyptus tree. It burst into flames, and fire raced down from the crest of the hills. The East Bay hills firestorm killed twenty-five people and destroyed 3,469 homes, with an estimated loss of $1.5 trillion.

The Mazzariello Maze is modeled after the mazes of ancient Crete and was created by the artist as a gift to fellow hikers.

Start your walk facing the visitor center, where you can read interpretive plaques describing the geologic history of the park. A single-track dirt path, the Bay Area Ridge Trail, beckons you into the hills. The peak of Round Top above you is an easement owned and controlled by the East Bay Municipal Utility District. On Round Top Loop Trail, you can see how the eucalyptus grew back after fires and freezes.

Hawks love to circle above these canyons. Keep an eye out for red-tailed hawks and even rare golden eagles. After you climb a short hill, the terrain ahead of you opens up to grassland, golden in summer and fall, green in winter and early spring. In the distance, you can see Mount Diablo and the ridges of Contra Costa County. The small body of water you see is the Lafayette Reservoir. In the foreground, you can see parts of hills cut away, a reminder that this area was heavily quarried prior to becoming parkland. During the rainy season, come prepared for mud. Runoff from Round Top can make shady sections of the Round Top Loop Trail a bit goopy.

Markers along the trail are linked to the self-guided geologic tour of the park. Huge amounts of massive basalt lava were removed from the quarry pit you'll see at marker #4. The result is a tremendous boon to geology, for the pit exposes the interior of the Round Top volcano.

At the base of the pit is one of the five mazes you'll find in the park. This one was created by Montclair artist Helena Mazzariello in 1989 as a gift to fellow hikers. She modeled it after ancient mazes on the island of Crete in the Mediterranean and uses it as a meditation device.

Another marker points to the Orinda Formation: river gravels, sands, and mudstones. The red streaks and layers in these riverbeds were caused by oxidation of iron in the sediments. Called "redbeds," they are explored worldwide for plant and animal fossils. "Bake zones," areas of intense red, are rocks that were baked by brushfires and sunlight.

Volcanic Trail takes you back to Round Top Loop Trail. Continue among the eucalyptus again, but note that the flora is changing. Precipitation is precious here. North-facing forests receive little sunlight. And with fog, the grove shields itself from parching Diablo winds. Winter rains penetrate the humus. Thus, moisture lingers, allowing decomposition to take place year-round. This safeguards a "new forest": bay laurel, madrone, and coast live oak, with an understory including coyote brush, blackberry, hazelnut, snowberries, toyon, and wild currant.

MILES AND DIRECTIONS

0.0 Start at the Sibley Volcanic Regional Preserve entrance on Skyline Boulevard. Pick up a trail guide. Facing the visitor center, walk to the right of it. To the right (east) of a paved path is the trailhead for the Bay Area Ridge Trail. Take this single-track, dirt path.

0.2 Stay on the Bay Area Ridge Trail as you cross the paved road that leads to the water tank.

0.4 Again, cross the paved road. Within about 30 feet, the path will split again. Take the fork to the left (southeast), the Round Top Loop Trail. This leads around the eastern side of Round Top. At the next split, stay right.

0.6 Burned and cut logs are a result of the August 1998 fire.

0.9 Go through a cattle gate.

1.0 Stop to admire the views. Then go to the railing and marker #4. (This corresponds to #4 of the self-guided tour guide.) View the largest of the quarry pits. Turn around and return to the double-track trail; take the trail to the left (east) for a diversion into the quarry.

1.1 Walk through the Mazzariello maze. Return to marker #4. Continue on the Round Top Loop Trail heading northwest.

1.2 Go straight (northwest) on the Volcanic Trail.

1.3 Reach marker #5 on the "Self-Guided Tour of Round Top Volcanoes"; "redbeds" are on the right (east).

1.4 Take a detour to the right (east) to see site #6, sandstone from the age of the dinosaurs.

1.5 The trail splits. Stay north on the Volcanic Trail.

1.6 Veer to the right (north) to see a smaller quarry and site #7. From the quarry, turn around and head back to where the trail veered.

1.8 To see sites #8 and #9, continue northwest on the Volcanic Trail.

2.1 Reach a cattle gate at the land bank area. Do not pass through the gate as the land beyond is closed to the public. Turn around here; pass sites #6 and #5 again.

2.6 Turn right (southwest) onto the Round Top Loop Trail. This heads around the western side of Round Top.

2.7 Pass marker #3 on the left (south). Site #2 comes up shortly after.

3.0 Walk about 10 feet or so on the paved road. To the left (east) are two dirt paths. Take the single-track path to the right.

3.1 Reach a viewing platform with interpretive plaques and benches. Views are of Grizzly, Chaparral, and Vollmer Peaks. Continue on the paved path.

3.2 Arrive back at the visitor center.

HIKE INFORMATION

Local Information: Oakland Convention and Visitors Bureau, 463 11th Street, Oakland, CA 94607; (510) 839-9000; www.oaklandcvb.com
Oakland.com; www.oakland.com

Local Events/Attractions: Oakland Museum of California, 1000 Oak Street, Oakland, CA 94607; (888) Oak-Muse or (510) 238-2200; www.museumca.org
Dining, shopping, and entertainment; 30 Jack London Square, Oakland; (510) 814-6000; www.jacklondonsquare.com

Hike Tours: Crab Cove Visitor Center, 1252 McKay Avenue, Alameda, CA 94501; (510) 521-6887; www.ebparks.org

Sunol Regional Wilderness

This loop in a 6,858-acre wilderness will take you along Alameda Creek, up through tranquil wooded canyons, past Indian Joe Cave Rocks, and onto grassy slopes covered with California poppies, lupine, and wild mustard in spring. Little Yosemite, with misting water cascading over boulders in the gorge, is especially heavy in early spring. If you compare it to the real Yosemite, you'll be disappointed, but the falls are still picturesque and a wonderful discovery. Traverse a ridge and head down a canyon with weathered green serpentine and sandstone outcrops, back through oak woodland, before finishing by the creek again.

Start: At the Indian Joe Nature Trail marker, by the bridge near the Sunol Regional Wilderness Visitor Center

Distance: 6-mile loop

Approximate hiking time: 3.5 hours

Difficulty: Moderate

Trail surface: Single-track dirt path and double-track trail

Other trail users: Hikers only on the Indian Joe Creek Trail and Canyon View Trail; equestrians and bicyclists on Cave Rocks and Camp Ohlone Roads

Canine compatibility: Leashed dogs permitted

Land status: Regional wilderness

Fees and permits: $5 per vehicle on weekends and holidays; $4 for trailered vehicles. Dog fee is $2 per day; guide dogs are free. Ohlone Regional Wilderness day permit is $2; for information on overnight backpacking, call (888) 327-2757; option 2, then option 1.

Schedule: Open daily year-round from 7:00 a.m. to dusk. Gates are locked at night; campers must arrive and sign in before dusk.

Maps: USGS Niles; LaCosta Valley. Parks maps are available from East Bay Regional Park District Headquarters, 2950 Peralta Oaks Court, P.O. Box 5381, Oakland, CA 94605; (888) EB-PARKS; www.ebparks.org/parks/sunol.

Trail contacts: Sunol Regional Wilderness Visitor Center, (925) 862-2244. East Bay Regional Park District Headquarters, 2950 Peralta Oaks Court, P.O. Box 5381, Oakland, CA 94605; (888) EB-PARKS or (888) 327-2757; www.ebparks.org/parks/sunol

Other: You can borrow or buy a self-guided nature trail booklet at the visitor center to identify markers on the Indian Joe Nature Trail. Wildflower identification kits and bird lists are also available.

38

Finding the trailhead

By Car: From the Fremont area, drive north on Interstate 680 and exit at Calaveras Road. Turn right (south) onto Calaveras Road and proceed to Geary Road. Turn left (east) onto Geary Road, which leads directly into the park.

From the Oakland/Berkeley area, drive east on Interstate 580 to the junction with I-680 in Pleasanton. At the junction, go south on I-680 and exit at Calaveras Road/Highway 84, just south of the town of Pleasanton. Turn left (south) onto Calaveras Road and proceed to Geary Road, which leads directly into the park.

From the Walnut Creek area, go south on I-680 and exit at Calaveras Road/Highway 84, just south of the town of Pleasanton. Turn left (south) onto Calaveras Road and proceed to Geary Road, which leads directly into the park.

By Public Transportation: Currently, no public transportation is available to Sunol Regional Park. However, routes change frequently. Go to 511.org or www.actransit.org, or phone (510) 817-1717 or 511 and say, "AC Transit," to speak with a person about route information including time points, destinations, and trip planning.

THE HIKE

The combination of landscapes here—riparian, woodland, and grassland—and the abundant plant and wildlife provide for an invigorating and charming experience in Sunol, especially during the springtime, when you are sure to see dozens of species of wildflowers, birds, butterflies, and other critters, and maybe a cow feeding its calf up on the hill.

The Costanoan Indians first enjoyed Sunol. Naturalists have found bedrock mortars used by the Native Americans for pounding acorns in the wilderness area. These early settlers found uses for most of the vegetation, rocks, and animals that thrived here, and this remote park retains a lot of native species that have not been overrun by the exotics that also found their way here.

Alien species were most likely brought by Spanish and later American ranchers and farmers. In 1839 this parkland, along with an additional 48,000 acres—most of the south-central portion of Alameda County—was granted as Rancho el Valle de San José to Antonio Mariá Suñol, the Bernal brothers, and Antonio Pico. They released cattle and sheep onto the land. The gold rush brought squatters in 1848. When California became a state in 1850, much of the land became government property, and large parcels of the ranch were sold off to settlers.

In 1865 Pat and Mary Ann Geary purchased 160 acres from the U.S. government for $2.50 an acre. The Gearys settled in a home site next to Indian Joe Creek, about a half mile upstream from where it joins Alameda Creek (you pass the area on the Indian Joe Creek Trail). All that remains of their cabin is a pile of flat stones. Needing help to build the ranch, the Gearys hired some Indians recently released from San Quentin Prison. Indian Joe was among this group, most of whom had been jailed for stealing horses. Indian Joe, however, had been sent there for stabbing a fellow Indian. Joe lived along the creek that would take his name until he died in the early 1950s.

The Gearys eventually acquired 1,500 acres and became prominent dairy farmers, providing milk and butter for the San Francisco market. They had eleven children. In 1895 the oldest son, Maurice, built the house and Old Green Barn now used by the park as the visitor center and nature center. Later on, Maurice and his family moved into a larger house along Alameda Creek, and Pat and Mary Ann Geary moved into what is now the visitor center (the house was rebuilt after a 1954 fire). They lived in that house until they moved back to Mission San Jose, leaving the ranch to their son John.

Cerro Este Road—heading downhill again with Del Valle Reservoir in the distance

Before the Calaveras dam was built (to provide water for San Francisco), Alameda Creek carried enough water to support large runs of steelhead trout, salmon, and Sacramento pike. Tule elk roamed this area (last one here killed in 1872), along with grizzly bears (last one killed in 1888), many deer, coyotes, mountain lions, and foxes. The deer and coyotes, made sparse by hunting, have been reestablished.

The last big private owner of these lands was Willis Brinker, a construction engineer from San Francisco. His company built the original San Francisco airport, the San Francisco Mint, and part of the Bay Bridge, among other structures. In 1959, amid controversy, the East Bay Regional Parks District purchased 3,863 acres from Brinker to establish the Sunol Valley Regional Park. Fights to protect the land from developers in the 1960s were successful, and in 1962, the Sunol Regional Wilderness took its current name.

MILES AND DIRECTIONS

0.0 Start at the Indian Joe Nature Trail marker. To reach the trailhead, facing the park buildings, walk behind them and left until you see a bridge crossing the creek. After the bridge, turn right (south) and follow the trail along the bank of Alameda Creek. Stay on the Indian Joe Nature Trail past Hayfield Road.

0.2 Reach the junction with the Indian Joe Creek Trail. After crossing the creek, turn left (northeast) onto the single-track trail, which leads uphill. Watch for poison oak.

0.4 Stay northeast on the Indian Joe Creek Trail past the junction with the Canyon View Trail. Indian Joe takes you through all three of the main botanical communities in the Sunol Valley: riparian (river side), oak woodland, and grassland. During the next 0.92 mile, you go through a cattle gate and cross the creek. (*Note:* If it's running, you will cross the creek a few times.) The trail gets steeper toward the top.

1.3 Pass the junction for Hayfield Road, staying on the Indian Joe Creek Trail. Come to an open area of sagebrush and grass, and a large rock outcropping. At the top of the Indian Joe Creek Trail, the terrain begins to change from oak woodland to grassland.

1.6 Indian Joe Creek Trail dead-ends onto Cave Rocks Road. Turn right (east) onto the double-track dirt trail. The route continues uphill, sharing the trail with equestrians and mountain bikers.

1.9 Reach the junction with Eagle View Road then Trail. Turn right (southeast), staying on Cave Rocks Road. The trail continues uphill gradually.

2.6 Arrive at the Cerro Este overlook; Del Valle Reservoir is in the distance. Soon after, you will reach the trail marker for Cerro Este Road toward McCorkle Trail and Little Yosemite (1.6 miles to Little Yosemite from here). Head downhill and south on the double-track dirt Cerro Este Road. (*Note:* This area is prone to fire and is subject to closure or restrictions during California's fire season in the late summer and fall.) Pass cattle ponds; ranchers still lease grazing rights here.

3.0 Reach the junction with the McCorkle Trail. Stay right (south) on Cerro Este Road toward Little Yosemite.

3.8 Reach the junction with the Canyon View Trail. Stay south on Cerro Este Road, continuing to Little Yosemite.

3.9 Cerro Este dead-ends at Camp Ohlone Road, a dirt and gravel service road. Turn right (west). The Little Yosemite area starts here and continues to the cattle gate. Continue just past Little Yosemite to the cattle gate.

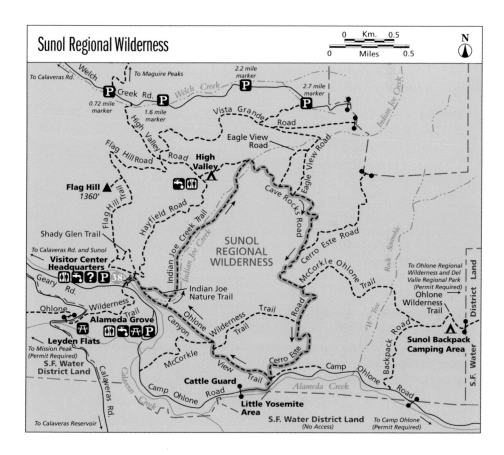

4.2 Turn around at the cattle gate and head back to Cerro Este Road.

4.5 Turn left (north) onto Cerro Este Road and walk about 0.2 mile to the Canyon View Trail.

4.7 Arrive at the trailhead for the Canyon View Trail. Turn left (west) onto the Canyon View Trail, which follows the cattle fence through a grassland corridor on a single-track path. The trail flattens out and goes along a ridge, where it drops off steeply to the left (west), with Camp Ohlone Road below. After the ridge, the trail heads over a hill (where you may run into cows and calves), then downhill through a wooded canyon.

5.3 Reach the junction with the McCorkle Trail. Stay straight (northwest) on the Canyon View Trail. The trail may be slightly eroded by hooves and rainwater, but is usually well maintained and dry.

5.7 Canyon View Trail becomes the Indian Joe Nature Trail. Continue straight (northwest) on the nature trail.

5.9 Reach the junction with the Indian Joe Creek Trail. Continue straight, following Alameda Creek (on the left/west) toward the bridge.

6.0 Arrive at the bridge and trailhead to park headquarters. Cross the bridge back to the nature center and parking lots.

Options: Going west, the McCorkle Trail connects to the Bay Area Ridge Trail and the Ohlone Wilderness Trail, which can take you all the way to Mission Peak. Going east, backpackers can take Backpack Road or make their way to the Ohlone Regional Wilderness through San Francisco Water District land to Del Valle Regional Park and beyond. This is your gateway to backpacking in the Ohlone Regional Wilderness.

HIKE INFORMATION

Local Information: Town of Sunol; www.sunol.net
Pleasanton Chamber of Commerce, 777 Peters Avenue, Pleasanton, CA 94566; (925) 846-5858; www.pleasanton.org
Local Events/Attractions: Mission San Jose, 43300 Mission Boulevard, Fremont, CA 95439; (510) 657-1797; www.missionsanjose.org
Niles Canyon Railway and Railroad Museum, Main Street and Kilkare Road, Sunol; (925) 862-9063; www.ncry.org
Hike Tours: East Bay Regional Parks District; 2950 Peralta Oaks Court, P.O. Box 5381, Oakland, CA 94605; (888) EB-PARKS or (925) 862-2601; www.ebparks.org/parks/sunol

Tilden Regional Park: Jewel Lake to Wildcat Peak

For seventy-five years, East Bay families have come to Tilden Regional Park to learn about nature, to play, and to create precious memories. You will likely see wildlife on your way up Wildcat Peak: a speckled egg on the trail dropped from a nest, squirrels hopping through the trees, a banana slug. The view from Wildcat Peak is breathtaking, including the San Francisco Bay and the Lamorinda areas. Pass through Rotary Peace Grove, then enjoy a self-guided nature hike on the Jewel Lake Trail on your way back to the Environmental Education Center, a well-equipped visitor center.

Start: Tilden Nature Area on Central Park Road, behind the Environmental Education Center at the Laurel Canyon Trailhead
Distance: 3.8-mile loop
Approximate hiking time: 2 hours
Difficulty: Moderate, with a couple short but strenuous uphill sections
Trail surface: Single-track dirt path to the double-track Wildcat Peak Trail
Other trail users: Hikers only on most of the loop; equestrians permitted on Wildcat Creek Trail
Canine compatibility: No dogs permitted in the nature study area
Land status: Regional park

Fees and permits: No fees or permits required
Schedule: Open daily year-round from 5:00 a.m. to 10:00 p.m. unless otherwise posted
Maps: USGS Oakland East; Briones Valley. You can also get parks maps through the East Bay Regional Park District Headquarters, 2950 Peralta Oaks Court, P.O. Box 5381, Oakland, CA 94605; (888) EB-PARKS; www.ebparks.org/parks/tilden.
Trail contact: East Bay Regional Park District Headquarters, 2950 Peralta Oaks Court, P.O. Box 5381, Oakland, CA 94605; (888) EB-PARKS (2757) or (510) 843-2137; www.ebparks.org/parks/tilden

Finding the trailhead
By Car: From Highway 24 on the east side of the Caldecott Tunnel, exit on Fish Ranch Road and go northwest. Follow Fish Ranch Road to Grizzly Peak Road and turn right (east); signs read TO TILDEN. This is a scenic drive that heads north, with great westward views, trailheads, and turnoffs to Tilden attractions like the Brazilian Room, the steam train, Lake Anza, and the carousel. Turn right (north) onto Golf Course Drive. Take a right (northeast) turn onto Shasta Road. Turn right (north) onto Wildcat Canyon Road. Turn right (east) onto Central Park Drive, the main entrance to Tilden Regional Park. Follow the signs to the nature area and Little Farm at road's end.

By Public Transportation: On weekends and holidays, AC Transit bus 67 provides service from the Berkeley BART station to the Brazilian Room. Go to 511.org or www.actransit.org, or phone (510) 817-1717 or 511 and say, "AC Transit," to speak with a person about route information.

THE HIKE

Tilden is the East Bay's wilderness playground, combining barnyard animals, trains, and a registered antique carousel with a protected nature area accessible to hikers only and home to readily seen wildlife and native and exotic plants. No park in the area better mirrors the intense public debate about balancing the preservation of parklands against the public use of these resources. It also illustrates changing eco-philosophies over the past seventy-five years. For example, a plan in the more development-oriented 1960s involving construction of an interpretive amphitheater, milk house and milk bar, smokehouse, and nine-hole golf course never came to fruition. With twenty-first-century sensibilities, people are now more grateful for open space than thirsty for fresh milk.

Tilden is truly the heart of the East Bay Regional Park District (EBRPD), part of the first land acquisition for wilderness preservation in the San Francisco Bay Area in 1934. The expansive park was named in honor of native Californian and park champion Charles Lee Tilden. Part of the first graduating class of the University of California, Berkeley and the first EBRPD president, Tilden helped found the park system.

On summer weekends, you will see a lot of people here. This is the most frequented park in the East Bay. But most visitors do not venture far past the man-made attractions and picnic areas. You can still find breathing space and a pleasing bit of wilderness in the canyons and hills.

Near the trailhead is the Little Farm, a community-created project designed to expose urban children to farm animals. The current Environmental Education Center (EEC) opened in 1974 and replaced the cluster of buildings used by the Civilian Conservation Corps (CCC) in the 1930s. The CCC cleared many of the trails here and built the stone signs, drinking fountains, and restrooms you see today.

The Tilden Nature Area's 740 acres are on the northern end of the park, adjacent to Wildcat Canyon Regional Park. Ten miles of hiking trails ramble through creekside woodlands, eucalyptus groves, grasslands, and coastal scrubland. The EEC (open from 10:00 a.m. to 5:00 p.m.) serves as the interpretive center for the nature area as well as the park headquarters. Buy or borrow the self-guiding trail booklet for the Jewel Lake Trail.

The Laurel Canyon Trail offers the shade of two large eucalyptus groves, several small groves of conifers, a dense oak and bay woodland, mature coastal brush, rich creek vegetation, grassland, and areas of coyote brush. The rare Oakland mariposa lily (*Calochortus umbellatus*) grows in the nature area. Trickling Laurel Creek is a major tributary of Wildcat Creek, home to native steelhead trout. The riparian woodland supports arroyo willow trees and white alder. Sword and wood ferns add to the lushness of the scene.

It's a steady, moderately strenuous trek uphill that brings you to the Wildcat Peak Trail, a ridge trail where you can admire westward views. A surprising and pleasant sight along this sunny trail is the garden of redwoods in the Rotary Peace Grove. The one hundred giant sequoias are each monuments to individuals who have made a notable contribution to the advancement of international understanding, peace, and goodwill.

The detour to Wildcat Peak (1,211 feet) is worth the short, steep trek, with 360-degree views that show off both the natural beauty and man-made splendor of the area.

Heading back down on the peak trail, you are likely to see native wildflowers: bright orange California poppies, lupine, wild hyacinth, buttercups, and mallow. Serenading you are songbirds like the bushtit, northern mockingbird, song sparrow, western meadowlark, and American goldfinch. If you don't see jackrabbits, black-tailed deer, bobcats, fox, or long-tailed weasel in person, look for their prints. Examples of their tracks are in the EEC.

The Rotary Peace Grove of giant sequoias on Wildcat Peak Trail

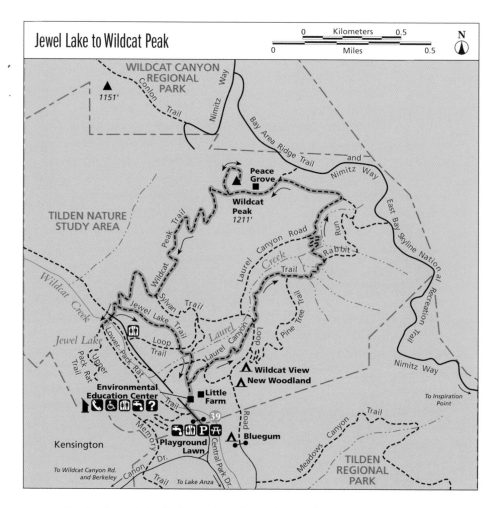

On the Jewel Lake Trail, numbered wooden markers correspond to the self-guided trail booklet. Learn about the spicy bay trees and all their uses. The bays were planted here in honor of Joshua Barkin, an eastern factory worker turned California naturalist who worked in Tilden for twenty years. Douglas fir, incense cedar, and Monterey pines also came to Tilden as memorial plantings. Standing on the bridge above Jewel Lake, see if you can spot western pond turtles among the cattails.

MILES AND DIRECTIONS

0.0 Start from the parking lot for the Tilden Nature Area. Walk across the bridge to the Environmental Education Center. If you are starting the hike between 10:00 a.m. and 5:00 p.m., visit the EEC. If the EEC is closed, go around the building to reach the trailhead.

0.1 Look for the Laurel Canyon Trail to the right (north).

0.2 Pass over the service road. Continue straight on the Laurel Canyon Trail.

0.5 Turn left (northeast) onto the double-track Loop Road. Go about 50 feet and turn right (northeast) to continue on the Laurel Canyon Trail. Watch for poison oak beside the trail.

0.8 Stay on the Laurel Canyon Trail as you pass the trailhead for the Pine Tree Trail. Several bridges pass over Laurel Creek.

0.9 Turn left (north) onto the crossover path to Laurel Canyon Road. (You can also go straight on the Laurel Canyon Trail and, in 0.5 mile, turn left (north) onto Laurel Canyon Road.)

1.0 Turn right (northeast) onto Laurel Canyon Road, a double-track trail heading up to Wildcat Peak Trail.

1.2 At the Y, go left (west) onto the Wildcat Peak Trail. It becomes single-track before becoming a wider dirt road. You hit a strenuous but short uphill section.

1.4 Keep to the left, continuing on the peak trail.

1.6 Reach the sequoias of Rotary Peace Grove.

1.7 Turn right (north) up to Wildcat Peak, another strenuous but short uphill section.

1.8 Arrive atop Wildcat Peak (1,211 feet). Enjoy great views from the observation area. To the west: the Bay Bridge, San Francisco, the Marin Headlands, and the Berkeley Marina; to the north: Point Richmond and the refineries of Martinez; to the east: San Pablo Dam Reservoir and Mount Diablo; to the south: Oakland and Alameda. Go back the way you came, returning to the Wildcat Peak Trail.

1.9 Turn right (west) onto the Wildcat Peak Trail. A sign reads TO NATURE AREA. It's downhill from here.

2.8 The trail splits. Go right (north) to the Jewel Lake Trail. The mark on the trail sign is a duck in flight.

3.1 Cross Central Park Drive to admire Jewel Lake. There are a few markers for the self-guided nature trail along the way.

3.2 Arrive at Jewel Lake. From here, head back the way you came.

3.3 Turn right (southeast) onto the Jewel Lake Trail, heading back to the EEC. Use the self-guided nature guide.

3.6 Pass over the Loop Trail, continuing on the Jewel Lake Trail. Pass service areas. (*Note:* Look for mushrooms along the trail. They are NOT edible, but fun to identify.)

3.8 Arrive back at the EEC and nature area parking lot.

HIKE INFORMATION

Local Information: Berkeley Convention and Visitors Bureau and Film Office, 2015 Center Street, Berkeley, CA 94704-1204; (510) 549-7040 or (800) 847-4823; www.berkeleycvb.com

Local Events/Attractions: Lawrence Hall of Science, University of California, Berkeley, Centennial Drive, Berkeley, CA 94720; (510) 642-5132; www.lhs.berkeley.edu

Regional Parks Botanic Garden in Tilden Regional Park, Anza View Road, Berkeley, CA 94708; (510) 841-8732; www.ebparks.org/parks/tilden

Hike Tours: East Bay Regional Park District Headquarters, 2950 Peralta Oaks Court, P.O. Box 5381, Oakland, CA 94605; (888) EB-PARKS; www.ebparks.org/parks/tilden

Attractions in Tilden

Tilden Park's carousel was built in 1911 by European artisans employed at the Hershell Spillman Company of Tonawanda, New York. It features fifty-nine hand-carved horses and other animals as well as a pipe organ. Purchased in 1953, it honored Charles Lee Tilden on his ninety-first birthday. It was added to the National Register of Historic Places in 1976.

The pony ride has been an attraction in Tilden since the late 1940s.

The Brazilian Room has a bronze statue of Tilden in front. The stone building was completed in 1941 to house an exhibit from the San Francisco World's Fair of 1939. Used to entertain World War II soldiers for parties and high teas, it is one of the most popular wedding sites in the Bay Area.

The botanical gardens cost $1 million to create back in 1953, but the twenty-acre site botanically represents the whole state of California.

Lake Anza opened to the public in 1939 with an aquatic sports carnival featuring synchronized swimmers. You can take a splash or fish for largemouth bass, rainbow trout, and catfish, among others.

The Tilden Golf Course, constructed by the CCC in 1937, is an eighteen-hole course operated by a private concessionaire.

The steam train is the Redwood Valley Railway (RVR), known as the "Little Train." Constructed in 1952, it is one of the most authentic miniature steam trains in the United States. It was built at a scale of 5 inches to 1 foot, and it burns oil. The 1.25-mile ride is on narrow slopes and gives brief views of San Pablo Bay.

Anthony Chabot Regional Park

The 5,067-acre Anthony Chabot Regional Park offers walks by burbling creeks, through groves of eucalyptus, redwood, and oak, over hills alive with swaying grasses, and along the rim of the well-loved Lake Chabot. The terrain ranges from gentle to rugged, with flat uplands, steep-sided ravines, and the deep, narrow Grass Canyon. Elevation ranges from 235 feet at Lake Chabot to about 1,200 feet at Vulture's View. The area reflects the small but mighty Chabot, who helped create and preserve the area as you see it today.

Start: Grass Valley Staging Area at Skyline Boulevard and Grass Valley Road
Distance: 8.7 miles out-and-back
Approximate hiking time: 4 hours
Difficulty: Moderate
Trail surface: Dirt trail, first double- then single-track
Other trail users: Equestrians and mountain bikers on Goldenrod Trail and Jackson Grade
Canine compatibility: Leashed dogs permitted
Land status: Regional park
Fees and permits: No fees or permits required at the Grass Valley Staging Area. At the Lake Chabot Marina, fees are $2.50 per car; there is also a $2.00 dog fee.
Schedule: Open year-round daily from 7:00 a.m. to 10:00 p.m. unless otherwise posted
Maps: USGS San Leandro; Hayward. You also can obtain parks maps at the East Bay Regional Park District Headquar-

ters, 2950 Peralta Oaks Court, P.O. Box 5381, Oakland, CA 94605; (888) EB-PARKS; www.ebparks.org/parks/anthony_chabot.
Trail contact: Anthony Chabot Regional Park, 9999 Redwood Road, Castro Valley, CA 94546; (510) 639-4751; www.ebparks.org/parks/anthony_chabot
Other: Besides the popular fishing and boating at Lake Chabot, recreational facilities in the park include Willow Park Public Golf Course, the Anthony Chabot Family Campground, the equestrian center, archery range, marksmanship range, motorcycle area, and several overnight group camps. If you need drinking water, there is a fountain just up the hill, to the right of the trailhead, on the Goldenrod Trail. There are no toilets at the staging area. The nearest bathrooms are at the equestrian center and once you get near the lake at a group camp. Mutt mitts to clean up after your dog are available.

THE HIKE

Before the first Europeans arrived in 1769, Chabot Park was home to the native Jalquin people. There was no lake then, no eucalyptus trees. Giant redwoods populated the northern end of the park. The growl of a grizzly bear sometimes rumbled through the canyon.

The vegetation of Chabot changed with the coming of the Spanish, who introduced grazing animals and hunted to extinction the tule elk and California grizzly. Victorian and twentieth-century Californians also influenced the land, removing grazing animals, suppressing wildfires, logging redwood trees, planting and logging eucalyptus trees, and creating Lake Chabot as a water supply for Oakland.

As you head down the Jackson Grade, brush and woodland become delightfully denser, especially on moist east-facing slopes. Above the monkeyflowers and eucalyptus, vultures circle the canyon. Wild blackberries, live oaks, buckeyes, a few Monterey pines, and young redwoods share the grove.

Just before the old Stone Bridge, probably built by the Civilian Conservation Corps (CCC) in the 1930s, the single-track Cascade Trail disappears into thick brush and healthy creekside trees. This trail does not disappoint. Lupine, Indian paintbrush, fairy bells, and geraniums grow along the dappled path. Clover and wild strawberries provide ground cover. Fifteen types of ferns and horsetails sprawl on the banks, including maidenhair, lady fern, bird's foot fern, and the common sword and wood ferns. Bigleaf maples, sweet cherry, madrone, black walnut, and black cottonwoods shade much of the path. Grass Valley Creek trickles beside you, bursting into cascades in early spring.

The southern part of the Columbine Trail hosts more sun-loving flowers. Diverse native wildflowers take bloom among the Spanish grasses, especially in spring. As you make your way south on the trail, you enter seamlessly what was once called Rancho San Lorenzo, owned by Don Guillermo Castro.

View of Lake Chabot (dam in background) from Columbine Trail

Castro received the grant to the southern half of the park in 1843, part of his 27,722-acre rancho. He put cattle on the land, and the hides of the cattle put money in his pocket. But it didn't stay there long. Don Castro was a gambler, and a pretty bad one. To pay losses from one unlucky game after the next, he started selling off portions of his land. Piece by piece, his ranch shrank.

By 1864, Castro had lost his land holdings to Faxen Dean Atherton. A businessman, not a farmer, Atherton sold off parcels of his new land to those who were interested in the agrarian life. Within what is now Chabot Regional Park, there were nine such farms. But just a few years later, the land was consolidated again, this time into watershed to provide a reliable source of water for the rapidly growing Oakland area. The largest of the ranches was the Grass Valley Ranch, where you begin the hike.

The search for water to quench the parched city of Oakland is eventually what saved this area from development. And leading the watery way was amateur engineer, businessman, and philanthropist Anthony Chabot. Bold yet wily, stubborn, quiet, solid, generous of nature, restless, and ever changing describes both the man and the land he helped to preserve.

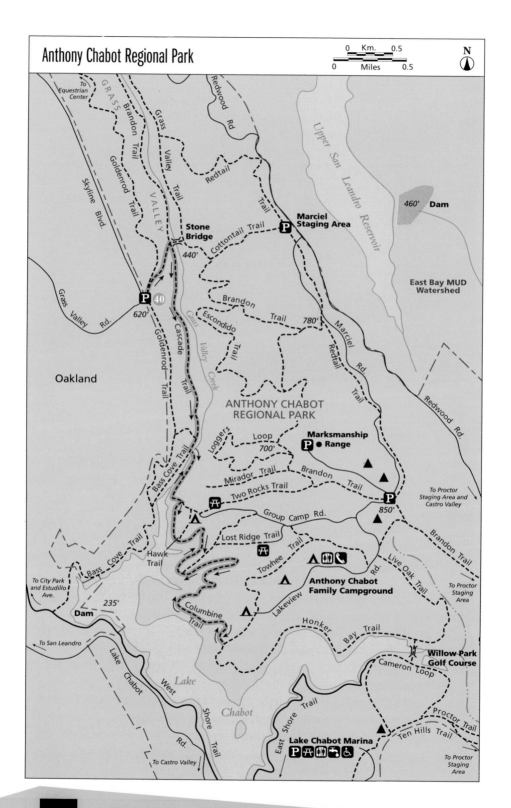

Anthony Chabot Regional Park

0 Km. 0.5
0 Miles 0.5

N

To Equestrian Center

GRASS VALLEY

Brandon Trail

Grass Valley Trail

Redwood Rd.

Upper San Leandro Reservoir

460' Dam

Skyline Blvd.

Goldenrod Trail

Redtail Trail

Cottontail Trail

Stone Bridge
440'

Marciel Staging Area

East Bay MUD Watershed

Grass Valley Rd.

P 40
620'

Cascade Trail

Goldenrod Trail

Grass Valley Creek

Brandon Trail

Escondido Trail

Trail 780'

Marciel Rd.

Redtail Trail

Oakland

ANTHONY CHABOT REGIONAL PARK

Loggers

Loop 700'

Mirador Trail

Brandon Trail

Marksmanship Range

P

To Proctor Staging Area and Castro Valley

P
850'

Bass Cove Trail

Two Rocks Trail

Group Camp Rd.

Lost Ridge Trail

Towhee Trail

Live Oak Trail

Brandon Trail

Hawk Trail

Bass Cove Trail

Anthony Chabot Family Campground

To Proctor Staging Area

To City Park and Estudillo Ave.

235'

Dam

Columbine Trail

Lakeview Trail

Honker Bay Trail

To San Leandro

Lake Chabot

West Shore

Lake Chabot

Cameron Loop

Willow Park Golf Course

To Castro Valley

East Shore Trail

Lake Chabot Marina
P

Ten Hills Trail

Proctor Trail

To Proctor Staging Area

Chabot and his associates had built Lake Temescal in 1868. The supply was not nearly enough during dry, drought years (a fairly frequent occurrence in the Golden State). To combat this, Chabot secured water rights to San Leandro Creek and began to acquire land in the narrow gorge around the creek. In 1875, he completed the San Leandro dam, creating Lake Chabot, the mainstay of the East Bay's water supply for forty years. You can see the dam from the beginning of the Columbine Trail; 115 feet high, made of earth fill, the structure is now a designated historic landmark.

In 1952, the park district managed to turn 3,100 acres of Chabot, then called Grass Valley Regional Recreation Area, into parkland. In 1965, Grass Valley was renamed the Anthony Chabot Regional Park, and in that same year, Lake Chabot went on "standby" status as a drinking water reservoir, allowing recreation on the lake that is the centerpiece of the park

MILES AND DIRECTIONS

0.0   Start at the Grass Valley Staging Area. The double-track Goldenrod Trail leaves the parking lot parallel to Skyline Boulevard. Go left on Goldenrod Trail. The trailhead for Jackson Grade is less than 0.1 mile ahead.

0.1   The trail splits. Take the Jackson Grade to the right (northeast) toward the Cascade Trail. It heads downhill into the canyon on a double-track path shared by horses and mountain bikes. The trail has lots of trees.

0.5   Around a bend is the Stone Bridge. The trailhead for the Cascade Trail is before the bridge on the right (south), clearly marked. (*Note:* Watch for poison oak.) The trail is mostly level. The creek is below on the left (east).

2.0   Cascade Trail becomes Columbine/Cascade Trail. Keep straight (south). The trail heads downhill, going deeper into the canyon and woods. The creek is on the left (east).

2.2   Cross the creek. (*Note:* In wetter seasons, in the late winter and early spring, the creek may flood the trail here. But it is very shallow, and branches and rocks make for easy crossing.)

2.4   Reach the trailhead for Bass Cove Trail. Go left (south), staying on Columbine Trail.

3.4   Keep straight on Columbine Trail for a view of the Lake Chabot Marina. (If you have had enough, this is a good turnaround and picnic stop. A short walk on Group Camp Road Trail to the left (east) takes you to group camps, restrooms, and drinking water.)

4.6   Columbine Trail meets the Honker Bay Trail. Turn around and head back the way you came.

5.8   Continue straight past the trailhead to the group camp.

6.7   Turn right (north) onto the Cascade/Columbine Trail (Bass Cove is to the left/west).

7.2   Continue straight on the Cascade Trail. You can also head left (west) up the Columbine Trail to the Goldenrod Trail, which is a double-track path along the golf course and neighborhood houses.

8.2   Cascade Trail runs into the Jackson Grade at the Stone Bridge. Turn left, heading west up Jackson Grade.

8.6   Jackson Grade meets the Goldenrod Trail. Bear left (south), back toward the parking lot.

8.7   Arrive at the parking lot of the Grass Valley Staging Area.

Options: At the 2.4-mile mark, the intersection of the Columbine and Bass Cove Trails, cross the creek and go right (southwest) on Bass Cove Trail, which leads to the Lake Chabot Marina (3.3 miles). This is a great option for a shuttle hike; leave a car on Lake Chabot Road by the main entrance to Lake Chabot.

For another great one-way shuttle hike, leave a pick-up car at the marina. From the end of the hike at the intersection of the Columbine Trail and the Honker Bay Trail (the 4.6-mile mark), continue south on Honker Bay around the lake to the marina.

HIKE INFORMATION

Local Information: San Leandro Chamber of Commerce; www.sanleandro.com
Local Events/Attractions: Anthony Chabot Equestrian Center; Anthony Chabot Regional Park, Oakland; (510) 569-4428
Lake Chabot Marina (boat rentals/fishing); Lake Chabot Road, Castro Valley; (510) 247-2526; www.ebparks.org/activities/boatingsailing#lakechabot
Hike Tours: East Bay Regional Park District Headquarters, 2950 Peralta Oaks Court, P.O. Box 5381, Oakland, CA 94605; (888) EB-PARKS; www.ebparks.org/parks/anthony_chabot
Hayward Hiking Club, P.O. Box 367, Hayward CA 94543-0367; www.geocities.com/haywardhikers

Honorable Mentions

P. Tilden Regional Park—Greater Tilden

Tilden Regional Park straddles the boundary between Alameda and Contra Costa Counties in the hills above Berkeley. If you're hiking with your dog, the nature area is off-limits, but in the rest of Tilden miles of trails will keep your feet and your pet happy. If you want a longer hike or would like to visit some of the unique Tilden attractions by foot, this is a great way to do it. A full loop around the park starting at the steam train swings by Lake Anza, the Brazilian Room, the golf course, the botanical garden, and two peaks offering expansive vistas: Vollmer Peak (1,905 feet) and Grizzly Peak (1,795 feet). Vollmer Peak can be reached via the Bay Area Ridge Trail, also part of the Skyline National Recreation Trail. You can enjoy 2 miles of views on the ridge; the dirt path is road-wide and allows bike and horse traffic.

A 7-mile loop includes treks on Curran, Selby, and Grizzly Peak Trails and takes four hours, not including stops at the sites, so bring lunch and plan for a whole day. For a shorter hike, you can start and end at a number of trailheads in the park. There are many delightful loops, some through eucalyptus, pine, or redwood groves, some with views from open grassland. Many, like Big Springs Trail, combine the two. For more information contact East Bay Regional Park District Headquarters, 2950 Peralta Oaks Court, P.O. Box 5381, Oakland, CA 94605; (888) EB-PARKS or (888) 327-2757; www.ebparks.org/parks/tilden.

Q. Briones Reservoir

Briones Reservoir is one of several hiking areas on East Bay Municipal Utility District (EBMUD) land requiring a permit. To obtain a pass or find out about more trails, go to www.ebmud.com or call 1-866-40-EBMUD (1-866-403-2683). Permits are $2.50 for a day pass, $10.00 for one year, $20.00 for three years, and $30.00 for five years.

Start either at the Bear Creek Staging Area (on the left side of Bear Creek Road between Happy Valley Road and the Briones Regional Park entrance) or at the Briones Overlook Staging Area (on Bear Creek Road about a mile before the regional park, coming from Camino Pablo). Trails in this watershed interconnect with paths into the regional park, around San Pablo Reservoir, and all the way to Inspiration Point in Tilden Regional Park. Maps are available through the EBMUD office.

The Bear Creek Trail (4.5 miles) traverses the south slopes above Briones Reservoir, moderately steep in places, mostly forested. You are treated to mostly serene single-track trail, home to rabbits, foxes, and deer. The only drawback is the faint sound of occasional traffic from Bear Creek Road and some horse droppings on the narrow trail. At the Overlook Staging Area (a good place to drop a shuttle car for a group hike), you'll find a restroom. The trail here follows the lake's edge to the dam and down the grassy slope alongside the spillway to the junction with Oursan Trail.

Oursan Trail (10.2 miles) is a long, fairly easy trail through high, often windy meadows that descends lakeside again, skirting the northern shores of Briones Reservoir. It returns to the Bear Creek Staging Area. For more information contact EBMUD at 1-866-40-EBMUD (866-403-2683); www.ebmud.com.

R. Mission Peak Regional Preserve

When people think of mountains to climb in the Bay Area, they don't always think of Mission Peak, but perhaps they should. Shaped by the shifting of the earth, by quakes along the Hayward fault and landslides down its steep faces, nature is still sculpting this 2,517-foot mountain.

There are four ways to climb to the summit. The shortest but steepest starts at the end of Stanford Avenue in Fremont. The Hidden Valley Trail is a calf-burning climb, better in winter because it has few trees. Slightly longer, but a more gradual ascent through wildflowers and some woodland, a second trail begins at Ohlone College on Mission Boulevard. The trailhead is behind the swimming pool at the college's southeast corner. A third, seldom-used path starts at Sunol Regional Wilderness and requires a wilderness permit (available at the park headquarters). This 11-mile round-trip follows a gentle route west to the peak. The fourth route is from the Ed Levin County Park in Milpitas and follows the Bay Area Ridge Trail for about 12 miles, from Santa Clara County into Contra Costa County.

For all the hikes, carry lots of water and wear layers. The mountain is either bathed in sun or white-capped on occasion in winter. Your reward, besides a great workout, are views of Mount Hamilton, Mount Diablo, Mount Tamalpais, the Santa Cruz Mountains, Silicon Valley, San Francisco, and, if it's really clear, the Sierra Nevada to the northeast (clearest views are after rains).

To get to the Stanford Avenue trailhead, take the first Mission Boulevard exit from Interstate 680 northbound and go east. Turn right onto Stanford Avenue (look for the MISSION PEAK REGIONAL PRESERVE sign) and drive to the end. Parking is free. For the Ohlone College trailhead, take the second Mission Boulevard exit (Highway 238) from I-680. Drive past Mission San Jose and turn left (east) into the Ohlone College parking lot. Parking fees apply when classes are in session.

For the Sunol Regional Wilderness trailhead, take the Calaveras Road exit from I-680. Turn east onto Calaveras, then go left (southeast) onto Geary Road, which goes into the park. Parking costs $3; trail permits are $2 per person. Sign in and out at trailheads. Take note of when the park gate closes (it varies by season) so you don't get locked in. For more information call the preserve at (925) 862-2244 or the East Bay Regional Park District at (888) EB-PARKS; www.ebparks.org/parks/mission.

S. Coyote Hills Regional Park

On the bay by the Dumbarton Bridge, the Coyote Hills Regional Park is a sanctuary for all kinds of wetland birds, wild pheasants, and raptors, and for hikers and bicyclists as well. You can experience windswept grassland with wildflowers in spring, and the sounds and views of the San Francisco Bay year-round. The paved Bayview Trail skirts around Red Hill by the marshes and bay levees, which are fun to explore. The Red Hill Trail takes you on packed dirt to the breezy top of Red Hill for a great workout and views of the Santa Cruz Mountains to the west and the East Bay hills inland. The Tuibin Trail, Chochenyo Trail, and the trails over the boardwalks show off the marshes, where white egrets and great blue herons feed at the water's edge. Check out the Ohlone Shellmound, accompanied by a reconstructed tule house, shade shelter, dance circle, and sweat lodge. The waters to the west and south of Coyote Hills are part of the Don Edwards San Francisco Bay National Wildlife Refuge, operated by the U.S. Fish and Wildlife Service. The Shoreline, No Name, Apay Way, and Alameda Creek Trails provide access to the refuge. Apay Way leads to the refuge visitor center via a bridge over Highway 84. The Alameda Creek Trail stretches 12 miles south to Niles Canyon.

The San Francisco Bay National Wildlife Refuge Visitor Center is worth a visit. Sitting pleasantly up on a rocky ridge, it provides information about the animals in the area as well as the surrounding salt flats, which went into operation in the 1850s. The white hills south of the refuge are actually salt piles. The family might enjoy a visit to nearby Ardenwood Historic Farm as well, especially in the fall to pick out a pumpkin.

Coyote Hills is at the west end of Patterson Ranch Road/Commerce Drive in Fremont. From Interstate 880, take Highway 84 west, exit at Paseo Padre Parkway and drive north. Turn left onto Patterson Ranch Road (parking fee). For more information call the park at (510) 795-9385 or the East Bay Regional Park District at (888) EB-PARKS; www.ebparks.org/parks/coyote_hills.

T. Joaquin Miller Park

Since 1928, hikers have meandered on trails beneath second-growth redwood trees in this 500-acre Oakland city park. You can find great heart-pumping steep trails and, for a warm day, a mostly shady, fairly flat hike that's great for a trail run, too. You can bring your leashed dog and connect to neighboring Redwood and Roberts regional parks. The park is named for pony-express rider, lawyer, judge, teacher, gold prospector, author, and local hero Joaquin Miller (1841–1913). After a life of travel, "The Poet of the Sierras" made his home and artist's retreat in the Oakland Hills in 1886.

The Sequoia-Bayview Trail starts right off Skyline Boulevard. It offers a wide trail through the woods opening to two vistas with bay views. The Big Trees Trail adds an enjoyable loop. For more information go to www.oaklandnet.com/JoaquinMiller-Park or call (510) 238-PARK. The park is also home to Woodminster Amphitheater, presenting outdoor musicals seasonally (www.woodminster.com).

Acknowledgments

Thanks to my parents, Bob and Nancy Parker, for instilling my love of hiking and supporting me in achieving my dream to become a professional writer.

I appreciate all my hiking buddies over the years: Dave, Shari, Jessalyn and Ali, Michelle and Trevor, Denise, Ann and Bryan, the SLZ book club, Hilary, Rob and Toby, our godsons Josh and Sam, Laurie and Jodie, Brian, Thea and August, the Oakland Rotarians, and all the rest who've walked the trails with me.

Thanks to all the rangers, naturalists, docents, and historians in Bay Area parks for your advice and assistance. And to all those who provide park services, open space preserves, and land preservation programs and who work so diligently to make sure my children and their children will be able to touch a redwood and see a black-tailed deer in its natural habitat, I sing your praises!

Our state and national parks are so underfunded. Please write to your congressperson or councilperson to ask them to extend financial support for upkeep of these treasures.

I am grateful to all the wonderful innkeepers, especially in Point Reyes and Bolinas, who provided a roof over my head and a hot shower after hiking in the rain. There are so many comfortable and friendly places to stay in the Bay Area close to hiking trails.

Thanks to Scott Adams and Bill Schneider at The Globe Pequot Press. I'm honored to be a FalconGuides author. Thanks to Ashley Vind for help with fact checking and Elisabeth Leitch for helping me carve it down to the essential.

A special thanks to Bob and Dona for your love and support. I'm so happy to have you down the street and in my life!

Doug, my husband, I can't thank you enough for your support through both of my hiking books. Want to go for a hike?! Ben and Max, I'm so excited to share with you the natural beauty of your Bay Area home as you grow up. I love you guys.

Appendix: Hiking Clubs

Antioch Trail Masters
Sponsors local day hikes, backpacks, bike rides, trail building and maintenance, and activism in all trail-related issues. (925) 778-0490; www.geocities.com/yosemite/trails/4849/atm/atmnewshead.html

Bay Area Hiking (e-mail list group)
A forum for discussing hiking and backpacking in and near the San Francisco Bay Area. Also a forum for finding hiking partners and setting up group hikes. www.pair.com/hiking/bayareahiking

Bay Area Orienteering Club
"In orienteering, the thinking sport, you use a map and compass to navigate a course through unfamiliar terrain. It can be enjoyed as a walk in the woods or as a cross-country competition." http://baoc.org

Berkeley Hiking Club
"Purpose: To draw together, in mutual consideration, persons interested in hiking to develop an appreciation of the out-of-doors; to foster the preservation and extension of them, and to furnish such recreation as may seem desirable." P.O. Box 147, Berkeley, CA 94701; (510) 663-0263; www.berkeley hikingclub.pair.com

Berkeley Path Wanderers
"Dedicated to the preservation and restoration of public paths, steps, and walkways in Berkeley for the use and enjoyment of all." 1442A Walnut Street, Box 269, Berkeley, CA 94709; www.berkeleypaths.org

Cal Hiking and Outdoor Society (CHAOS)
"CHAOS is a group of University of California-Berkeley students, staff, Berkeley area residents, and assorted other friendly souls who meet regularly to experience the outdoors, have fun and eat chocolate." www.uc-hiking-club.berkeley.ca.us

California Adventure Club
"We are an overly ambitious group of athletes, trail runners, hikers, backpackers, snowshoers and mountaineering fools who are looking for others to join us in our madness. The parent organization to the popular Mount Diablo Family Trekkers

of Eastern Contra Costa County, we organize extended overnight, exotic trips, to unique venues in and out of state." (925) 439-0434; e-mail: hiking@signature Esolutions.com (contact: Allen Tatomer); www.geocities.com/mtdiablohiking/caladventureclub.html

California Alpine Club

"The purpose of this club is to explore, enjoy and protect the natural resources of our land, including wildlife, forests and plants, water and scenic values; to support and promote educational programs on these and related topics; and at all times to protect and, as far as we are able, to improve the environment in which we live." P.O. Box 2180, Mill Valley, CA 94942-2180; www.calalpine.org

Commonwealth of Nature Fanatics Unofficial SF/South Bay Excursion Division (CONFUSED)

"We're an informal group of outdoor enthusiasts based in the greater San Francisco Bay Area who get together to organize and enjoy outdoor activities of all kinds." www.confused.org

Contra Costa Hills Club

"Plant a seed. Grow a tree. Conservation—Companionship—Hiking." P.O. Box 97, El Cerrito, CA 94612-3355; www.geocities.com/contracostahills

East Bay Barefoot Hikers

"Enjoy walking barefoot? So do we!! The East Bay Barefoot Hikers take to the trails every 2 to 3 weeks, year-round. It's fun, it's healthy and it's FREE." www.unshod.org/ebbfhike

EnviroSports

"EnviroSports is a club specializing in unique environmental outings and environmental education, and supports trail maintenance and habitat restoration in the various parks in which we run to preserve wilderness and parklands." P.O. Box 1040, Stinson Beach, CA 94970; (415) 868-1829; e-mail: info@envirosports.com; www.envirosports.com

Gourmet Hikers Club

" . . . After walking for a couple of hours, the most amazing gourmet feast appears from backpacks and we enjoy once again . . . food, nature and friends." E-mail: Wwmabenson@aol.com

Hayward Hiking Club

"The Hayward Hiking Club invites you to try a hike with us. Have fun, get plenty of exercise, make friends, and experience nature all in one activity. Our hikes are scheduled every Saturday and range from easy to strenuous." P.O. Box 367, Hayward, CA 94543-0367; www.geocities.com/haywardhikers/

HikanByke

"We are a nonprofit group of single friends, dedicated to sharing the enjoyment of activities, such as biking, hiking, skiing, jogging, dining and camping, in a supportive, non-threatening atmosphere." 125 Lees Place, Martinez, CA 94553; e-mail: hiknbyke@netscape.net; www.hikanbyke.org

Intrepid Northern California Hikers (INCH)

"Some people hike to enjoy the beauty of nature . . . some people hike to achieve inner serenity . . . some people hike for the physical and mental challenge . . . we hike because we love to eat!" E-mail: peter.saviz@intel.com; www.rawbw .com/~svw/inch/index.html

Lafayette Hiking Club

The Lafayette Parks and Recreation Commission schedules an average of two hikes a month as a service to the community. Generally, no fee or advance registration is required. (925) 284-2232; www.ci.lafayette.ca.us

Livermore Hiking Club

The Livermore Hiking Club is an informal group with no published schedule. Hikers meet every Friday at 8:30 a.m. sharp in front of the Old Carnegie Library in Livermore, on South K Street between Third and Fourth Streets. (925) 447-4280; www.geocities.com/evbuck/lhc/lhcblurb.html

Montclair Hiking Club

"City of Oakland, Life Enrichment Agency Office of Parks and Recreation. Hikes are open to everyone. There are no fees. To attend, be at the Montclair Rec Center on Tuesday at 9:00 a.m. sharp (unless noted) to make up carpools." Montclair Recreation Center, 6300 Moraga Avenue, Oakland, CA 94611; (510) 482-7812; e-mail: Montclairhikers@topica.com; www.geocities.com/montclairhikers/schedule.html

Orinda Hiking Club

The Orinda Hiking Club sponsors weekend hikes, Wednesday hikes, and evening strolls. P.O. Box 934, Orinda, CA 94563; www.orindahiking.org

Pacific Trail Society

The Pacific Trail Society is an informal group that hikes in Marin, Point Reyes, and the East Bay two to four times a month. Most of the hikes are 5 to 10 miles long and moderate in difficulty. www.geocities.com/pacifictrailsociety

San Francisco Hiking Club

The San Francisco Hiking Club organizes hikes and similar outings for gays, lesbians, and friends. An event is generally planned on either Saturday or Sunday each weekend. P.O. Box 14065, San Francisco, CA 94114; www.sfhiking.com

Stanford Outing Club

"Our most common activity is hiking (day trips) at one of the Bay Area's many parks, such as Point Reyes, Big Basin, Mount Tamalpais, or Pinnacles, to name a few. Our activities are open for everyone (i.e., also for people not affiliated with Stanford University)." www.stanford.edu/group/outing/

Yahoo Clubs—Bay Area Hiking (e-mail list group)

"This is a place to find people who want to go hiking in Northern California's Bay Area. All levels are welcome." groups.yahoo.com/clubs/bayareahiking2

Organizations That Offer Hikes in the Bay Area

Bay Area Ridge Trail

The Bay Area Ridge Trail Council offers a variety of activities, open to the public, along the Bay Area Ridge Trail. Activities include hikes, trail bike rides, and horse rides. 1007 General Kennedy Avenue, Suite 3, San Francisco, CA 94129; (415) 561-2595; e-mail: info@ridgetrail.org; www.ridgetrail.org

California Coastwalk

"Our purpose is to explore and promote the opening of remote and heretofore inaccessible sections of our coastline, and to shift perception of the coastline from one of a few isolated beaches and accesses to one of a continuous 55 (now 1,156) miles of unbroken beauty." 825 Gravenstein Highway, Sebastopol, CA 95472; (800) 550-6854; e-mail: coastwalk@coastwalk.org; www.coastwalk.org

East Bay Regional Park District

The East Bay Regional Park District has hundreds of events scheduled all year long. 2950 Peralta Oaks Court, P.O. Box 5381, Oakland, CA 94605 (888) EB-PARKS (327-2757); www.ebparks.org

Fifty-Plus Fitness Association (FPFA)

The Fifty-Plus Fitness Association is a twenty-year-old nonprofit organization whose mission is to promote an active lifestyle for older people. Lifelong Fitness Alliance, 658 Bair Island Road, Suite 200, Redwood City, CA 94063; (650) 361-8282; www.50plus.org

Greenbelt Alliance

"Our mission is to make the nine-county San Francisco Bay Area a better place to live by protecting the region's Greenbelt and improving the livability of its cities and towns. FREE hikes, bikes rides and more." 631 Howard Street, Suite 510, San Francisco, CA 94105; (415) 543-6771; fax: (415) 543-6771; e-mail: info@greenbelt .org; www.greenbelt.org

Midpeninsula Regional Open Space District

The twenty-four Midpeninsula Regional Open Space District preserves include over 45,000 acres of permanently protected open space, from redwood forests to bay shoreline. 330 Distel Circle, Los Altos, CA 94022; (650) 691-1200; www .openspace.org

Mount Diablo Interpretive Association (MDIA)

The MDIA sponsors walks and hikes, which are led by Mount Diablo State Park volunteers. P.O. Box 346, Walnut Creek, CA 94597-0346; (925) 927-7222; www.mdia.org

Mount Tamalpais Interpretive Association

The Mount Tamalpais Interpretive Association is a volunteer organization whose purpose is to promote the conservation, education, and interpretation of California state parks, primarily at Mount Tamalpais State Park. Sponsors interpretive hikes open to the public. P.O. Box 3318, San Rafael, CA 94912; (415) 258-2410; www.mttam.net

Santa Cruz Mountains Trail Association (SCMTA)

"Founded in 1969, the Trail Association was formed under the guidance of the California State Parks and Sempervirens Fund (a nonprofit land conservancy) to build and maintain trails in the Santa Cruz Mountains. The building of the Skyline-to-the-Sea Trail that year inaugurated Trail Days in the Santa Cruz Mountains. Since then our activities have broadened to include weekly hikes." P.O. Box 1141, Los Altos, CA 94023; e-mail: MHD@slac.stanford.edu; www .scmta-trails.org

Sierra Club

Most regional chapters offer regular outings. The regional headquarters is at 85 Second Street, 2nd Floor, San Francisco, CA 94105; (415) 977-5500; www .sierraclub.org. Regional groups are listed below.

San Francisco Bay Chapter

The Hiking Section of the San Francisco Bay chapter of the Sierra Club sponsors a variety of day hikes in Marin, Alameda, and Contra Costa Counties, and city hikes in San Francisco. Fifty to sixty hikes are scheduled each month on Saturdays, Sundays, Wednesdays, and most holidays.

Loma Prieta Sierra Singles

"Sierra Singles is a group of more than 800 singles of all ages, who enjoy a wide range of activities, from outdoor to social. Most of our events are centered in Santa Clara, San Benito, and San Mateo Counties, near the beautiful San Francisco Bay." Sierra Singles, 3921 East Bayshore Road, Suite 204, Palo Alto, CA 94303; (408) 795-3237; www.lomaprieta.sierraclub.org/lpss

Black Mountain Group

"Many of our activities are hikes. Unless you are familiar with the hike or hike regularly, please consider contacting the leader. While we maintain a moderate pace, we do occasionally encounter a steep hill. We use the common number and letter code to denote a hike's difficulty." www.lomaprieta.sierraclub. org/bmg/schedule.html

Hike Index

Angel Island State Park 100

Año Nuevo State Park and Reserve 142

Anthony Chabot Regional Park 257

Barnabe Peak 39

Berry Creek Falls Trail Loop 164

Big Basin Redwoods State Park 164

Black Diamond Mines Regional Preserve 217

Bootjack Trail to Dipsea Trail Loop 48

Briones Regional Park 224

Briones Reservoir 263

Butano State Park 136

Camp Tamarancho 96

Castle Rock State Park 171

Cataract Trail 96

Chimney Rock Trail 24

Cliff House Walk at Lands End 106

Coyote Hills Regional Park 264

Donner Canyon to the Falls Trail 211

East Peak Loop 65

East to West Ridge Trails 229

Golden Gate Park 126

Greater Tilden 263

Hearts Desire Beach to Shell Beach 34

Huckleberry Botanic Regional Preserve 234

Huddart Park and Phleger Estate 188

Inverness Ridge 44

James V. Fitzgerald Marine Reserve 152

Jewel Lake to Wildcat Peak 251

Joaquin Miller Park 265

Kent Trail along Alpine Lake 80

Las Trampas Regional Wilderness 196

Long Ridge Open Space Preserve 192

Lovers' Lane and the Ecology Trail 115

Marin Headlands 72

Marin Municipal Water District 80

McNee Ranch State Park and Montara State Beach 147

Mission Peak Regional Preserve 264

Miwok Trail to Point Bonita 72

Monte Bello Open Space Preserve 190

Mount Burdell Open Space Preserve 86

Mount Diablo State Park 202, 211

Mount Wittenberg and Bear Valley Loop 14

Muir Woods 48

Palomarin Trailhead to Alamere Falls 29

Pescadero Creek Park 192

Pescadero Marsh Trails 130

Phoenix Reservoir 55

Point Reyes National Seashore 12–33, 44

Point Reyes on Rainy Days 44

Portolá Discovery Site 111

Portola Redwoods State Park 177

Presidio, The 115

Purisima Creek Redwoods Open Space Preserve 182

Rancho San Antonio Open Space Preserve and County Park 191

Redwood Regional Park 229

Ring Mountain 91

Rock City to the Summit 202

Russian Ridge Open Space Preserve 189

Samuel P. Taylor State Park 39

San Bruno State Park 121

San Pedro Valley Park 158

Sibley Volcanic Regional Preserve 239

Skyline Ridge Open Space Preserve 190

Steep Ravine Loop to Stinson
    Beach 60
Summit Loop Trail 121
Sunol Regional Wilderness 245
Sweeney Ridge 111
Tide Pool Loop 152
Tilden Regional Park 251, 263

Tomales Bay State Park 34
Tomales Point 19
Tucker and Bill Williams Trails 55
Upper Stevens Creek County Park 191
Windy Hill Open Space Preserve 189
Wunderlich Park 188

About the Author

A native to the Bay Area, Linda Hamilton was elated to rediscover the incredible beauty of her home region, beyond the crowded highways. Her first (of so many) solo hiking adventures occurred at age four, when she happily wandered off alone to explore nature, scaring the daylights out of her family. After nine years of teaching high school English, drama, and college composition, and with an MA in English under her belt, she set out to achieve the daunting goal of writing for a living. Her work has appeared in the *San Francisco Chronicle, American Heritage of Invention and Technology* magazine, MyFamily Travel newsletters, Americaslibrary.gov, and many online business sites. When not on foot or hugging her laptop, Linda is singing, drawing, traveling, kayaking, or laughing with her husband, Doug, in their Oakland, California, home.